The Liar's Companion

A Field Guide for Fiction Writers

LAWRENCE BLOCK

ARE DYING • A DROP OF THE HARD STUFF • THE NIGHT AND THE MUSIC

THE BERNIE RHODENBARR MYSTERIES

BURGLARS CAN'T BE CHOOSERS • THE BURGLAR IN THE CLOSET • THE BURGLAR WHO LIKED TO QUOTE KIPLING • THE BURGLAR WHO STUDIED SPINOZA • THE BURGLAR WHO PAINTED LIKE MONDRIAN • THE BURGLAR WHO TRADED TED WILLIAMS • THE BURGLAR WHO THOUGHT HE WAS BOGART • THE BURGLAR IN THE LIBRARY • THE BURGLAR IN THE RYE • THE BURGLAR ON THE PROWL • THE BURGLAR WHO COUNTED THE SPOONS

KELLER'S GREATEST HITS

HIT MAN • HIT LIST • HIT PARADE • HIT & RUN • HIT ME • KELLER'S FEDORA

THE ADVENTURES OF EVAN TANNER

THE THIEF WHO COULDN'T SLEEP • THE CANCELED CZECH • TANNER'S TWELVE SWINGERS • TWO FOR TANNER • TANNER'S TIGER • TANNER'S VIRGIN • ME TANNER, YOU JANE • TANNER ON ICE

THE AFFAIRS OF CHIP HARRISON

NO SCORE • CHIP HARRISON SCORES AGAIN • MAKE OUT WITH MURDER • THE TOPLESS TULIP CAPER

NOVELS

BORDERLINE • GETTING OFF • RANDOM WALK • RESUME SPEED • RONALD RABBIT IS A DIRTY OLD MAN • SINNER MAN • SMALL TOWN • THE GIRL WITH THE DEEP BLUE EYES

COLLECTED SHORT STORIES

SOMETIMES THEY BITE • LIKE A LAMB TO SLAUGHTER • SOME DAYS YOU GET THE BEAR • ONE NIGHT STANDS AND LOST WEEKENDS • ENOUGH ROPE • CATCH AND RELEASE • DEFENDER OF THE INNOCENT

NON-FICTION

STEP BY STEP • GENERALLY SPEAKING • THE CRIME OF OUR LIVES • AFTERTHOUGHTS

WRITTEN FOR PERFORMANCE

TILT! (EPISODIC TELEVISION) • HOW FAR? (ONE-ACT PLAY) • MY BLUEBERRY NIGHTS (FILM)

Grateful acknowledgement is made to *Writer's Digest*, in which the articles contained in this book were originally published.

The Liar's Companion

A Field Guide for Fiction Writers

LAWRENCE BLOCK

Introduction

For fourteen years, from 1976 to 1990, I wrote a column on the writing of fiction for *Writer's Digest*. At the very beginning it was an every-other-month affair, alternating with a column on cartooning, but in short order the magazine dropped the cartoonist, and my column went monthly.

I have to say it did me a world of good.

I make my living writing books, and it's an unstructured and uncertain occupation. So it did me good to have one specific thing to do every month, and to be assured of receiving a monthly check for it. The numbers on those checks were never enormous; I got $150 a column at the beginning, and coaxed enough raises out of them over the years to get that number up to $500 at the end. Now that was nothing to sneeze at, but neither was it anything to drool over.

But the money was the least of it.

Over the years, four books emerged. The first was *Writing the Novel from Plot to Print*, specifically commissioned by Writer's Digest Books after I'd been writing the column for a year or so. It's never been out of print, and now, I'm pleased to report, it's available as an Open Road ebook.

Next was *Telling Lies for Fun and Profit*. It was published in 1981, and composed of past columns, and I offered it to WD Books but the editor wasn't enthusiastic; my agent sent it to Don Fine at Arbor House, who published it in hardcover and trade paperback and placed it with the Book-of-the-Month Club.

WD Books looked at how *Telling Lies* was doing and felt they'd missed the boat, so when I had enough columns for a second volume, they got on board right away. I called the book *Spider, Spin Me a Web*.

Both books have been in print pretty much continually since their original publication, and both are available now from HarperCollins in either trade paperback or ebook form.

That's been gratifying, believe me. When I write something, I really like to see it remain available for people to read. My great friend, the late Donald E. Westlake, was asked by a mutual friend why he'd agreed to the republication of some of his very early work. The money couldn't amount to that much, the friend said, so why bother with the deal?

"The difference between being in print and out of print," Don told him, "is the difference between being alive and being dead."

Right.

And yet the books aren't the most important benefit I got from that column, either.

I could string this out, and talk about other fringe benefits—that the column gave me sufficient credibility as a writer about writing so that I could successfully develop an interactional writing seminar and present it all over the country for a couple of years, that this in turn led to my writing and self- publishing a book version of the seminar. (*Write for Your Life,* and it too is available as a HarperCollins ebook.) That the column brought me speaking invitations. That it very likely led some people to have a look at my novels.

All true, and all good. But secondary, really, to the most important thing that column did for me, and I'll quit stalling now and tell you what that was.

It made me a better writer.

Once a month I had to come up with an idea for a column, some aspect of writing to address in around 1,800 words. Now after I'd been doing the column for a year or so, then-editor John Brady discovered flow charts, and decided that was what was needed for the optimal functioning of his editorial operation. So he wrote me a letter requesting that I supply him with the subjects I intended to cover in the next six months.

Now how the hell did I know? I didn't, obviously, and told him as much, and he told me this was really important, and after we'd gone back and forth a time or two more, I sat down and wrote out a list. Then, a month at a time, I wrote and submitted my columns, and not a one of them could be found on that list. So much for the flow chart.

I wasn't being deliberately contrary. (Well, maybe a little.) But there was no way I could know in advance what I'd be able to write about in a given month. There were more than a few months when I didn't know what I was going to write until the day when I sat down and wrote it.

But an idea always came along. I don't think I was ever once late with a column.

So it would seem that the need to produce a column was always very much in my mind, if not consciously on it. And one way or another this column-to-be-written informed both my reading and my writing.

It's a rare writer indeed who is not also a world-class reader. I had always been an omnivorous reader, and one blessed with a hearty appetite. When I became a writer, I immediately became a better reader; I found myself noticing what worked or didn't work in the story I was reading, and in turn became a better writer when I found myself applying what I'd noticed to my own work.

Writing about writing added another level to the whole enterprise. I continued to read for pleasure—I don't think I've ever been able to read in its absence—but now I would come across elements in what I read that got me thinking, and that now and then provided me with the subject matter for a future column.

Similarly, writing about writing made me more aware of elements in my own work.

I don't want to belabor this, it hardly seems worth it, so I'll just state it again and let it go at that: writing that column for fourteen years made me a better writer.

What on earth qualified me to tell people how to write?

I'd get that question occasionally, and it struck me as a reasonable one. I'd generally respond by explaining that I didn't tell people how to write, that I would never presume to do such a thing. While my column was instructional by definition, I didn't provide a lot of specific instruction. For the most part I talked about something I'd noticed in my work or another's, and how I'd solved (or at least coped with) something that had come up in the course of a book or story. I was endeavoring to share some of what I'd experienced and observed. If that constitutes teaching, then I was a teacher. If not, not.

Because I never thought of myself as teaching in the traditional sense, I never wanted to present the same lesson twice. WD's various editors over the years would have liked to see me return to the same basic topics rather more often than I did. But I really wasn't interested in repeating myself.

Now in some magazines repetition is inevitable. If you've got a home gardening magazine, you can't decide not to write about tomatoes simply because you ran a comprehensive tomato article five years ago. There are folks out there who weren't reading the magazine back then, and the others, who've been with you all along, won't remember that old article. Or, even if they do, they won't mind reading it again.

But once I'd written something, I wouldn't go back to it unless I had something reasonably interesting to add. And that had its advantages, especially when it came time to collect the columns into a book. It wasn't just the same thing over and over again.

I stopped writing the column in 1990. It wasn't a very happy parting of the ways, and I left with a sour taste in my mouth. And I figured that all in all it was more than time for me to be done writing about writing. I seemed somehow to have written close to half a million words on the subject, and that was plenty.

And I had four books to show for it. That, too, was more than enough. Wasn't it?

Well, now there are six. A couple of months ago, Open Road brought out *The Liar's Bible: A Handbook for Fiction Writers*. And here we have *The Liar's Companion: A Field Guide for Fiction Writers*.

In a moment I'll tell you how they came to be, but first I want to say something about titles. My two books drawn from *WD* columns were *Telling Lies for Fun and Profit* and *Spider, Spin Me a Web*. I don't know that one is any better or stronger or more user-friendly than its fellow, but if I had to pick one over the other, I'd go with *Spider*. The columns are more recent, and I was very likely a little more knowledgeable when I wrote them.

Year in and year out, *Telling Lies* sells more copies than *Spider*. Like, *lots* more copies.

What's the difference? Well, obviously, the chief difference between the books lies in their titles. A great title, it's been often said, is a title on a bestselling book. *Telling Lies for Fun and Profit* is a great title.

Well, I'm no dummy. And that's why the two new books aren't called *The Spider's Bible* and *The Spider's Companion*.

But where did they come from?

Well, it's not really all that hard to explain. *Telling Lies* gathered columns from my first four years at *WD*, *Spider* from the four or so years after that. That left a lot of columns uncollected, and in the ordinary course of things I would very likely have sorted through them and looked around for a publisher.

But when I rather abruptly stopped writing the column, I quit thinking about the subject.

And then, a couple of years ago, I heard from a fellow I know named Terry Zobeck. He's a fan and a collector, and his particular collecting interest is centered on the initial magazine appearance of works by those writers he most esteems. Toward this end he had compiled a great number of issues of *WD,* and by purchasing bulk lots he'd wound up with duplicate copies of many of those issues.

He'd checked them against his copies of my books, and established that he had a host of columns and articles of mine that had not appeared in either *Telling Lies* or *Spider.* That was more than enough uncollected material for a new book, and would I like him to send me his duplicate issues?

I could hardly say no. In addition to the duplicates, he went to the trouble of photocopying those columns of mine for which he had only a single copy. In all, I now had in hand 77 pieces that had never previously been published in book form, an ample amount for not one but two books.

So I thanked him profusely and put the box in the corner of my office and forgot about it for a couple of years. Making use of the material promised to be a whole lot of work, and I wasn't sure a print publisher would be that enthusiastic anyway.

Then Open Road came along, and set about publishing forty-plus backlist books of mine as ebooks. I'd long since come to believe that ebooks are the future of publishing, and it's beginning to look as though the future has arrived, and not a moment too soon. I asked the Open Road folks if they'd be interested in a pair of books on the gentle art of prevarication, and they responded with great enthusiasm, and we were on our way.

So now I'm the author of six instructional books for writers. And no, I don't think writing can be taught, but I know it can be learned. Most of us learn in two ways, by reading and by writing. (I found a third way to add to the mix: by writing *about* writing.) What we read and what we write, and the extent to which we'll find it helpful, is very much an individual matter. Some people say they've found what I've written about writing to be useful reading matter. I hope that turns out to be true for you.

Sometimes I'm asked what's the one piece of writing advice I consider most important.

Write to please yourself, I reply.

That's not all there is to it, not by any means. But there's nothing without it.

—Lawrence Block
Greenwich Village

1

Writing, Always Writing

October 1987

THE JOB OF BEING A WRITER NEVER ENDS. NEVER.

Man must work from sun to sun.
Woman's work is never done.

That, at least, is how they put it in the bad old days of sexism and long hours. Now, what with union contracts and feminism, not to mention the around-the-clock shifts facilitated by electrification, the old rhyme simply won't stand up. How can we update it, to produce a suitable bromide for our times?

Mere mortals work from 9 to 5.
A writer works when he's alive.

Well, it rhymes and it scans, but I can't say I'm crazy about it. There ought to be a better way to convey in verse the idea that the writer's work never ceases. Perhaps we'll take another stab at it in a little while. Meanwhile, let's examine not the rhyme but the reason.

Is it true? Do writers really work all the time? Is the creative process a metronome that drives us endlessly, keeping us tapping to the beat?

Or is this, as many of our spouses and children and friends and relatives have long suspected, a lot of hooey? Is this just our way of weaseling out of car-pool duties and piano recitals, a rationale for long walks, afternoons in a hammock, hours of uninterrupted reading time, and the approximate social skills of a wolverine? Is "I'm actually working all the time" something young writers learn to say at writing school, much as cleaning women learn to say "It broke"?

Relax. Don't panic. Not to worry.

It's really true.

Writers work all the time.

Take the other day, for example. What did I do with myself? How did the busy little bee improve each hour? Just what action did I take to put words on the page and bring money into the house?

Well, let's see. I read a couple of books and a magazine or two. I watched a ball game on television. I got wet in the Gulf and dried off in the sun.

What's that? You say it doesn't sound like work?

A lot you know.

Take the reading, for example. Now, a lot of reading is research. Sometimes it's specific research, when I want to learn something that I need to know in order to write something I'm working on, or planning to work on. Sometimes it's general research, like reading a book on precious and semiprecious gemstones because I frequently write books about people who steal such things. And sometimes it's not exactly research, but it's a matter of keeping up with what other people in my field are doing.

And is this what you were reading the other day, sir?

Well, no, Rachel. As a matter of fact, I was reading for enjoyment.

Then it wasn't work, sir, was it?

Ah, but it was, Rachel. I'm afraid it's impossible for a writer to read without working.

Consider. One of the books I read was *The Good Mother*, a bestselling mainstream novel by Sue Miller lately out in paperback. I got interested in the characters and caught up in the plot, and then on page 156 I returned to the business of being a writer.

A few pages earlier, the narrator entered a coin-operated laundry and commenced doing a load of wash. There she meets a young man with whom she had words on a previous laundry visit. They have a conversation in which he apologizes for his surly behavior earlier, and then he tries to pick her up, and then

> *He turned and looked out the window. The dog came and stood in the doorway briefly, and he and Leo seemed to exchange a long look before he left.*

Wait a minute. *What* dog?

So I find myself looking over what I've read. Half a page earlier a dog had figured metaphorically; when Leo tosses a verbal overture at the narrator, she thinks: *Here it comes, as inevitable as a dog at a hydrant.* But that's not a real dog, it can't be actually walking in the door and cocking an eye at Leo and a leg at one of the washers, can it?

Three pages earlier, there's this at the end of a long paragraph of description:

> *Every now and then the same rangy black dog would come in and check the wastebaskets and changing personnel.*

Well, that's the dog. I must have read the sentence that introduced him, but he hadn't stayed in my mind for the thousand or so words that followed. Now, having rediscovered him, I couldn't let go of him. Would other readers react as I had reacted? Had the dog been insufficiently established by that single reference to let readers recognize him when he reappeared? How much do you have to implant that sort of stage dressing, and how long will the reader retain it?

There may not be any answers to these questions, but the fact that the questions themselves come up confirms that reading is always work for a writer. Even when you read for sheer enjoyment, at least a part of your mind is busy deciding what works and what doesn't, and how the writer gets certain effects and what alternatives might have been employed. It's a nuisance when I find myself rewriting perfectly adequate sentences in my mind, or wasting time figuring out where the black dog came from. But it's part of my job.

Take Two

> *Though he appears a lazy slob*
> *A writer's always on the job.*

I don't know if I like that any better. It seems defensive, doesn't it?

What else did I read lately, and how was I practicing my profession when I did so? Well, I read part of a trashy novel about a prestigious law firm. The author was a lawyer with impressive qualifications, so I expected the inside story, whether or not the fiction was well-crafted.

Very early on, a young lawyer under consideration for a position with the firm has a business lunch with one of the partners. The author makes a real point of having him not order a drink first because he'll need his wits about him; it never occurs to either the young man or the writer to have something non-alcoholic. The older attorney, while ordering a martini of his own, smiles approvingly at the young man's decision not to have anything, and then the two of them have a full business discussion, with a job offered and accepted and the young man volunteering to start work that very afternoon, all before they even order their lunch.

Well, I'll tell you. A scene like that makes you wonder if the author ever went out to lunch, let alone with a partner in a top Manhattan law firm. Any lunch of this sort would involve a whole lot of small talk, with precious little serious business broached before the coffee and dessert. One wouldn't have to be a writer to get angry with this particular author. But, as a writer, I found myself musing on how I might have written the same scene. I wouldn't report all the small talk, of course. Writing is always a matter of selection. Start with an opening exchange, then cut to the dessert course? Stay with the small talk and summarize the rest?

I thought, too, about the importance of accuracy. Conversations in fiction are not exactly as they are in the real world, and events can happen more rapidly. The older man might legitimately reach a decision at the dinner table in fiction that he would sleep on in the real world.

But the reader's suspension of disbelief has a breaking point. When the reader says, "Wait a minute, that's not the way it is," you're in trouble.

Take Three

Better keep the coffee perking—
Day or night, the writer's working!

What else have I read lately? Well, the August issue of *Ellery Queen's Mystery Magazine* showed up the other day. I could say I have to read it in order to keep up with work in my field, and that's true enough, but I read it because I felt like it. And one of the stories was "Long Shot on a Stone Angel," by Donald Olson.

It was a good story, nicely told. In it a retired gentleman begins visiting prisoners in order to have something to do, and he winds up doing some investigative work to clear a man who has been convicted of killing his wife. Part of his investigation consists of a visit to the convicted man's apartment where the murder took place.

Wait a minute, I said to myself. How is this possible? The guy has been arrested, stood trial, got convicted, and is serving a stretch in prison. The sentence is unspecified, but it's either life or a lot of years, and what's his apartment doing with his pictures and furniture still in it? Even if he owned the apartment, it would be sold for legal fees. If it's a rental, it would have long since been rented. No way on earth it's just going to sit there waiting for him to get lucky and make parole seven years down the line.

And that's a real plot problem, because something the old man finds in the apartment turns out to be essential to the development of the story. There's no way to do it without a visit to the apartment. You either do it as he did it or you forget the story altogether.

Of course, if it had been a house, one that had been in the family a couple of generations and was thus owned free of any mortgage, he might have elected to hold onto it. Or maybe if it was a condo he could have had it set up to rent furnished, and thus his things would still be there. Still . . .

Well, it doesn't matter, obviously. The story worked fine as Mr. Olson wrote it, and if I hadn't been in a nitpicking mood, I probably wouldn't have noticed the plot problem in the first place. But, as a writer who doesn't stop working, I couldn't notice it and cluck my tongue and let it go at that. I had to look for a way to replot the story and solve the problem.

Take Four

> Even when the fish are biting
> The hapless writer's always writing.

I think I liked the last one better. But the point is—yes, Rachel?
Sir, I think we get the point that reading is work. But what about baseball?

It's the highest form of spiritual activity.

But how does it get to be work, sir?

You think it's easy for those guys? Standing around in the hot sun? Chewing and spitting, they lay waste their power. It may look like a game, Rachel, but . . .

I mean for you, sir. How is it work for you?

Oh.

Well, take the other day. I was watching the Mets and Darryl Strawberry was batting. Now Darryl Strawberry can hit a baseball about as far as any human being alive, but he can only do this when he swings the bat, which is an action he sometimes fails to perform. I sat on the couch while Mr. Strawberry looked at a called third strike to end the inning. His eyes widened in abject astonishment at the umpire's verdict.

"What a surprise," I said.

Then my wife, Lynne, said something, and I suppose the announcer did, too, but don't ask me what it was. Because I was busy trying to decide how *What a surprise* would work upon the page. I had meant it sarcastically, as you have probably already surmised, but would a reader know as much if I just set the words down without explanation? In actual speech we convey a lot by inflection and tone of voice, and that doesn't always come across in print.

"What a surprise," he said sarcastically.

Well, sure, that works, but I'd generally prefer not to use an adverb to do the dialogue's job. I'd rather let it fall upon your ear as sarcasm than wave my arms and shout out that it's sarcasm.

He arched a brow. "What a surprise," he said.

That works, too. Or the other character would react to the line in such a way that we get the inflection:

"Then what happened?"

"Strawberry took a called third strike."

"What a surprise."

"Come on, he hasn't been doing it that *much this year . . ."*

Down to Work

I could go on. Writing is a full-time job, it really is, and you never really take a vacation from it. I could go through a whole day and show you how every conscious moment—and the unconscious ones as well—were part of the business of being a writer.

I could, but I won't. We're out of space.

Besides, the Reds are at Wrigley for an afternoon game with the Cubs. I've got work to do.

2

The Hearts of the Matter

November 1987

ON WRITING FROM THE HEART, TO THE HEART.

I just read a book that ought to be unequivocally unpublishable. But it is going to be published, and its publisher thinks it's going to be a bestseller, and I think the publisher's probably right.

The book is *Poppy,* by Barbara Larriva. Ballantine Books is publishing it as a hardcover title in October, and has taken the unusual step of launching the book with a special reader's edition in trade paperback format for free distribution at the American Booksellers Association convention. They sent me a copy, which is how I am able to rush into print with a column inspired by *Poppy* even as the book is finding its way onto bookstore shelves.

Poppy is the story of Allegra Alexander, once the brightest of stars in the Hollywood firmament, now a bitter old woman with terminal cancer who has elected to refuse radiation and chemotherapy and is waiting to die. While she lies grumbling in her hospital bed, she is visited by a relentlessly cheerful and cheering young girl named Poppy. Ultimately, inevitably, Poppy's sunshine pierces Allegra's dark despair.

That's enough by way of plot summary. The book is brief and the plot none too complex, and I don't want to give away its few surprises.

But why did I begin by categorizing it as "unequivocally unpublishable"?

For starters, consider its length. *Poppy* runs to something like 30,000 words. If you were to set out to write something unpublishable, and you wanted to make it unpublishable in every respect, you couldn't pick a better word length than 30,000. A short novel runs 60,000 words, and a very short novel runs 50,000. Thirty thousand words is far too long for a magazine and far too short for a book.

What does this mean when a manuscript is making the rounds? It means that a lot of markets would reject it without really looking at it. If I were an editor with a desk piled high with submissions, and if I saw at a glance that a particular manuscript was half as long as the shortest novel we'd published in the past 20 years, I might very well send it back to its author without even scanning the first page. Not every editor would do so—some are as compulsive as the rest of us, and can't dash a few drops of A.1. Sauce on a hamburger without reading the label on the bottle. But some would.

More to the point, virtually every editor who did read the manuscript would do so knowing full well he was reading a manuscript that was unmarketably short. Given the realities of publishing, given the glut of submissions, given the fact that one is never called to account for the bestsellers that got away but must justify the flops he said yes to, every editor who's been on the job for more than a few months has a built-in predisposition toward rejection. A first novel by an unknown writer and it's only 30,000 words long? Come *on!*

Enough about length; if I don't watch myself I'll devote more words to the subject than Barbara Larriva did to her whole book. Obviously *Poppy* got published in spite of its length, not because of it. The book has something that made it impossible for an editor to say that automatic No to it.

What is it?

It is not the brilliance of its style, the poetry of its composition. I do not want to imply that *Poppy* is poorly written. It is not. Barbara Larriva is a good writer, and *Poppy* is well-organized, lucid and accessible. But it is not so superbly written that the writing announces itself as a master-piece. The individual sentences are not so flawlessly composed that they resonate within us as prose poetry. The prose and dialogue are adequate. They carry the story quite effectively, but they never transcend the story. We do not read *Poppy* in spite of the way it was written, but neither do we read it because of the way it was written.

Is it the characterization that grabs us? I don't think so. The only characters of much importance are Allegra and Poppy. While they are both drawn with some finesse, and while they are etched strongly enough to linger in the mind, I didn't find either all that compelling. It's no chore to spend an hour or two in their company, but I wouldn't ink in either on my list of fiction's most unforgettable characters.

The plot, then? Some books overcome a multitude of flaws because the plot just draws us in and won't let go. We can't wait to find out what happens next, and our eagerness to do so allows us to overlook any other deficiencies the book may have.

Is that the case with *Poppy*? Again, I think not. If anything, it seems to me that the plot errs on the side of simplicity. I was able to anticipate most of its twists and turns.

So what's the answer? Why did the book get published? Why does the publisher think he's got a bestseller here, and why do I suspect he's right?

I don't think intellectual analysis will supply the answer, because I don't believe the magic success factor here is one that has anything much to do with the intellect. *Poppy* works on an extra-intellectual level. It hasn't got all that much to say to the mind, certainly nothing the mind hasn't heard before. But it somehow manages the feat of speaking directly to the heart.

Fiction's emotional impact is achieved through the transfer of feeling from the writer to the reader. The writer feels something, encodes that feeling in words upon the page, and transfers that feeling through those words to the reader at the other end of the line. And all of this takes place irrespective of what's going on in the conscious minds of writer or reader.

While I read *Poppy*, there was not a moment when I was unaware that I was reading a story someone had written. My mind was busy throughout, analyzing, evaluating, criticizing. Because I am not only someone who writes fiction but also someone who writes about writing fiction, I have become a very tough audience for fiction. I am constantly weighing alternative ways of phrasing the sentence I've just read, paying an untoward amount of attention to the technical choices the author has made and the extent to which they have or haven't worked. As a result, I inevitably keep a certain amount of distance from virtually everything I read, even the books I'm drawn into.

I wasn't all that much drawn into *Poppy*, and I had no trouble keeping a detached eye on the narrative. *This is a little obvious,* my mind would say. *This doesn't really work. I see what she's doing here. I know what she's getting at.* And so on.

And, while I was busy being aware of everything that was less than perfect about *Poppy,* I kept finding myself moved to the point of tears.

I have to tell you that this was disconcerting. It is one thing to be all caught up in a book or movie and be moved to tears. That happens to me now and then and I welcome it. But in this instance I was *not* all caught up in the book, I was detached and remote and analytical throughout, and I was moved to tears *anyway.*

That sort of thing doesn't happen often. Oh, if I've been up for 36 hours on airplanes, or if I'm under a ton of stress of one sort or another, I may be emotionally vulnerable to an unusual extent. When I'm like that, I may get misty-eyed over a supermarket opening. But the day I read *Poppy* I was as close to stability as I ever get, and the little book worked its magic upon me nonetheless.

Magic. I think that's a fair word for it. I was not deeply drawn into the story, I didn't care a whole lot about the characters, and yet my heart was touched. According to Pascal, the heart has its reasons that reason knows nothing of. If I want to know why my heart was touched, I can't look to the world of reason for the answer.

Feeling comes from feeling, the reader's feeling from the writer's feeling. *Poppy* is not the first book to succeed emotionally beyond its artistic and intellectual success. After I laid *Poppy* aside, the book that came first to mind was *Love Story,* by Erich Segal. That too was a short book that tugged (shamelessly, I always thought) at the reader's heartstrings. It was also a book one could very easily ridicule, as I don't doubt *Poppy* will be ridiculed in some quarters if it is the commercial success I expect it to be. (No one bothers to ridicule flops.)

Whatever was right or wrong with *Love Story,* I can recall that Mr. Segal always claimed to have been overcome emotionally when he wrote it; he said he had trouble typing the final section because he kept breaking down and weeping. The same people who criticized the book as mindless pap had a fair amount of fun with the image of the author blinking back tears through those last pages and all the way to the bank, but I have never doubted that Mr. Segal was speaking the literal truth. I think he was indeed moved to tears writing the book, and I think he instilled that feeling in the book, and that it worked as it did for readers because of the feeling that communicated itself from him to them. Other factors may help explain why *Love Story* was the specific book it was, but that alone explains to me why it worked the way it did.

With *Poppy,* I think the feeling is love. The rather simple message of this rather simple book would seem to be (rather simply) that love heals all. Poppy's selfless and unconditional love transforms Allegra. The love Allegra is then able to express transforms her life and her world. This is by no means the first time this message has been told, in fiction or elsewhere; it works so powerfully here because of the love which em-powered Barbara Larriva when she put it on paper. That love, which she seems to have been able to receive and embody and transmit, is what makes her little book work.

Isn't it a hell of a note? We try to study writing as a craft, seeking to learn what to put in and what to leave out and how to best arrange our selected ingredients, and then it turns out that, as E. E. Cummings put it,

> *since feeling is first*
> *who pays any attention*
> *to the syntax of things*
> *will never wholly kiss you*

Is that all there is to it? Should we forget about the syntax of things altogether?

No, of course not. The better we are at our craft, the tighter a ship we provide for our feelings to set sail in. But there must be more to it than craft; we must learn too how to put our own hearts into what we write. Otherwise we're sending empty vessels out to sea, and the world will not much care whether or not they reach port safely.

3

The Scene of the Crime

December 1987

THOUGHTS ON RESEARCH: HOW MUCH IS ENOUGH, HOW MUCH IS TOO MUCH?

Toward the end of July, Lynne and I were in Detroit, where we spent a couple of hours visiting Joan and Elmore Leonard. Mr. Leonard is the bestselling author of *Glitz* and *Bandits* and *Touch,* and if we'd arrived a few days later we would have missed him, because he was planning a visit to Cape Girardeau, Missouri.

Cape Girardeau, as you may know, is a city of 35,000 situated on the Mississippi in the southeast corner of the state, a little more than a hundred miles south of St. Louis. It might seem an unlikely spot for a visit from a top suspense novelist, especially one who has been cited by *Playgirl* magazine as one of the ten sexiest men in America. What, I wondered, was drawing Dutch Leonard to Cape Girardeau?

The name, he explained. "I liked the sound of it," he said, "and I had it in mind for some time that I might set a book there. And then I had the idea of starting a book with an airplane crash, and someone's killed in it, and there's an insurance investigation of a relative of the victim. And I thought maybe the crash could take place in Cape Girardeau, and then the story would move on somewhere else from there."

Mr. Leonard makes occasional use of a researcher, and in this instance his researcher had other business that would bring him close to Cape Girardeau. He went there and returned with the answers to some questions, along with an array of material from the local chamber of commerce. All of this had enabled Mr. Leonard to conclude that Cape Girardeau would do nicely for the book he had in mind, and now he was going there himself to see the place with his own eyes and get the feel of it.

I found this very interesting, not least because I had just recently completed a novel that sprawls across 18 states. While I had, at one time or another, been in all of those states, I had by no means visited every city and town where I'd set a scene. In my book, a group of people walk from Oregon to Minnesota, and some of the roads they use are ones I've never seen, let alone covered on foot.

Was my research slipshod? Was Dutch Leonard's excessive?

Scouting Locations

When filmmakers select the settings for the various scenes of their film, they call the process "scouting locations." The writer of prose fiction goes through a similar process. He may do his scouting in person, winging off to Cape Girardeau or hopping on a crosstown bus, or he may accomplish much the same thing in the library, or over the telephone.

On the other hand, he can produce a lifetime of fiction without ever having the need to scout a location. He can set all his works in locations that he knows intimately to begin with. Or, like a filmmaker fabricating a set on a Hollywood studio sound stage, he can invent a location out of the whole cloth, just as he invents his characters and his storyline.

This is the rule, of course, when one is dealing with mythical worlds or writing books set on other planets or in vanished or as-yet-unborn civilizations, but it is just as valid an option when one is writing realistic contemporary fiction. William Faulkner, using rural Mississippi as the setting for his fiction, called it Yoknapatawpha County and invented its history and geography accordingly. John O'Hara changed his hometown's name from Pottsville to Gibbsville and changed Harrisburg to Fort Penn, partly perhaps as a barrier to libel suits, but at least as much to be free to create his own fictional reality. Ed McBain's 87th Precinct novels are set in Isola, a city that is clearly meant to be New York, but with its geography purposely skewed. Mr. McBain knows New York, and has written about it in other books under its own name (and under *his* own name of Evan Hunter) but in his police procedural novels he chose to reinvent New York so as to avoid having to revise police procedure with every structural change in the actual New York Police Department, and to escape the need to keep pace with the constantly changing landscape of the city.

It seems to me that Mr. McBain, in choosing Isola over New York as his setting, was also making a fundamental decision as to what his books were going to be *about*. They are about the particular stories they tell, the commissions and solutions of specific crimes. They are about the lives of their characters, the police officers and criminals and others who people them. Each book, too, is about its own particular theme, whatever that may be, and all of the books are about crime and detection and punishment and life and death.

Finally, because the characters and their lives are of the sort indigenous to New York City, the books *are* about New York—but to a much lesser extent than if Mr. McBain called the city by its rightful name. One need only refer to his recent novel, *Another Part of the City*, a book specifically about a New York policeman, to see the difference.

In my own six novels about ex-cop Matthew Scudder, New York is unquestionably one of the things I'm writing about, and accordingly the city looms as a strong presence and the neighborhoods in which scenes are set received more than cursory research. The books range rather widely through Manhattan, Brooklyn and Queens—I don't recall having set scenes in the Bronx or Staten Island—so I took a fair number of long subway rides and meandering walks while researching and writing them.

Sometimes this research provided me with details that helped highlight a scene. Sometimes, serendipitously, I would turn up something at a location that would suggest a turn in a plot. And on some occasions I probably didn't encounter anything noteworthy, and could have written the scene about as effectively without leaving my apartment—but having been on the scene enabled me to visualize what I was writing about and to write about it with, I suspect, more authority than I would have otherwise.

The Writer's Pilgrimage

While writing *Random Walk*, I sat in a small studio at the Virginia Center for the Creative Arts and wrote scenes set in innumerable locations strewn across those 18 states. While I would have loved to trace the route in advance, in a car if not on foot, I never seriously considered doing so. For one thing, I didn't have the time; for another, I didn't *know* the route in advance, any more than I knew exactly how the plot would take form. All of this revealed itself to me while I sat in my studio in Virginia.

The simplest alternative to research, it seemed to me, would be to make up names for the towns my pilgrims passed through and numbers for the roads they traversed. There wouldn't have been anything wrong with such an approach, and it would have freed me to invent towns and terrain to suit my story. I don't know that it would have made much difference to the average reader; what reader in Texas, say, would care if an incident took place in Clay County, Montana, which doesn't exist, or in Musselshell County, which does?

Somehow, though, I felt I wanted to anchor my story with real towns and real roads, not because it would make a difference to readers but because it would make a considerable difference to *me*. I wanted to know where those people were. The more specific I was about locations, the more real the story became in my own mind. I wanted to be able to look at a map and know how far they'd come, and how far along the next town was and what highway they'd come to next. My vision did not have to coincide with reality—I was perfectly willing to put a gas station at a particular intersection, without knowing whether some entrepreneur had seen fit to put one there in actuality—but it had to be specific enough so that it felt real to me.

I had three atlases with me, and perhaps a dozen guide books of one sort or another. I put in ten-hour days on *Random Walk,* and when I wasn't actually writing I was generally paging through guide books or poring over maps. The maps in particular were a way of tapping into fictive reality. I would look at a road on the map and see what that road was like, and what sort of country lay on either side of it. I don't mean to suggest that what I saw had anything to do with what's actually out there, but it helped make the whole thing real enough for me so that I could write the scenes.

I had several goals. I wanted to feel confident enough about what I was doing so that my confidence would make itself felt in my writing. I wanted to appear sufficiently informed so that a native of, say, Burns, Oregon, would not come away from a scene set in that town with the suspicion that the writer had never been there. And, at the same time, I wanted to bear in mind throughout that I was not writing a travel book. I was trying to produce a novel, to tell a story, and all the locations were there to anchor the story and enhance its effect upon the reader.

On the Scene

Let's return for a moment to Dutch Leonard's trip to Cape Girardeau. He was putting in more research time to add verisimilitude to an opening scene than I'd invested in my whole novel. Was I being slipshod? Or was he wasting time?

He had other options, certainly. He could have learned enough about Cape Girardeau without leaving his desk to set a scene there that anyone would find convincing, whether or not they'd ever spent time in the area. He has, after all, written excellent novels of the American West in addition to his contemporary crime fiction, and he hasn't had to travel in time to manage it.

Or, if he wanted to stick to what he knows firsthand, he could have had his airplane crash occur in some town with which he's familiar. There was no predetermined plotting requirement that the book open in Cape Girardeau; he'd picked it in the first place because he sort of liked the sound of it.

I would certainly argue that Mr. Leonard's instinctive impulse to set the book's opening in Cape Girardeau was worth following, and that the intuitive decision to see the place with his own eyes is wholly justifiable. He is, let it be said, a writer who has done extremely well critically and commercially over a fair number of years by writing his books as he thinks and feels they ought to be written. His plots generally evolve as he writes the books; he has found that if he comes up with some compelling characters and puts them in a dramatic situation he will be able to think up things for them to do. Who knows what bits of plot business, what incidents, what added dimensions of character, might come into being as a result of an actual visit to Cape Girardeau? And who knows what sort of intuitive guidance might have led him to select that city in the first place?

Writing, as I've observed before, is not an exact science. There's no right or wrong way to do it. When you find a method that works, you change it at your peril.

Should everyone make a comparable pilgrimage to Cape Girardeau? More to the point, is every intuitive prompting toward on-the-spot research one that ought to be heeded?

I think not. A few years ago a student in one of my classes was writing a short story set in Jerusalem, and she had stopped work on it in order to obtain maps of the city so that she could get the names of the streets right. The type of story she was writing did not require that the streets be named, or that she have any of the data she was planning to research, and in the course of discussion it became clear that she was using research as a way to avoid getting to work on a story she was scared to write. I could sympathize; ages ago, before I had ever written a novel, I decided to write a political thriller set during the Irish Rising of 1916. I knew nothing about the period, began reading books on Irish history, decided that an understanding of Irish history would require as a foundation an understanding of English history, and that one might as well begin at the beginning; accordingly I started reading Oman's six-volume history of Britain before the Norman Conquest. I did not finish Oman—nor, of course, did I ever begin work on that Irish novel, a book that I was in every respect quite unequipped to write. By piling on the research, I was making sure that I would never be ready to write the book, and would thus never have to face the fact that I was unequal to the task.

4

The Courage to Change

January 1988

THE MORE THINGS REMAIN THE SAME, THE MORE YOU SHOULD CONSIDER A CHANGE.

Long ago and far away, when I was trying to become a professional writer of fiction, I braced myself with the thought that this was something I was going to have to do only once. After all, once you become a professional, all that remained was for you to practice your newfound profession. Once you had written a book successfully, you had only to produce variations on that theme forever.

In the mystery and suspense field, which I chose (or which chose me) early on, doing the same thing over and over made eminent sense, and the simplest way to do that seemed to lie in the development of a series character. While plots and settings and subordinate characters would vary from one book to the next, the same lead character would appear in each book, providing a measure of continuity and allowing the books to develop an increasing following among the reading public. Find a character, write about him forever, and you've got it made.

You've got it made. Non-writers frequently think in those terms. "I guess you've got the formula now," people will tell me, "and all you've got to do is crank 'em out." Well, that's nonsense. You've never got it made, and there's no such thing as a formula, and you've got to do a lot more than crank 'em out.

This idea—that you can have a formula, that you can become

successful by repeating yourself endlessly—seems to me to grow out of a desire to demystify the writing process and to turn it into a left brain rational mechanistic affair. Non-writers want to do this in order to have the sense that they understand what writers do, and we writers tend to buy into the same notion because we would like our work to make sense, to be logical, and to become easier with time.

If you stop to think about it, the idea of a formula becomes pretty silly. If I have a formula for my books, it can't be much of a secret; it's hidden in plain sight in the books themselves. If you want to see how I did it, all you have to do is look at what I did. There's no hidden agenda in a novel. It's all out in the open.

In *Writing the Novel: From Plot to Print* (WD Books), I discuss a method of outlining another writer's novel, boiling it down to a bare-bones plot synopsis, in order to learn how novels are put together. You can indeed learn a good deal this way, but you can't learn enough to make the business of writing your own novel a simple matter of painting by numbers. Everything you write is written for the first time, and that's true even if you do have a series character you follow from book to book, and even if you tend to mine the same vein over and over in your fiction.

Consider Gerald Browne, if you will. Mr. Browne has written any number of bestsellers, and several of his most successful works have dealt with the world of precious stones. He knows this background thoroughly and renders it wonderfully accessible to the reader. Two of his books, *11 Harrowhouse* and *Green Ice,* are startlingly similar in plot and construction. The first concerns diamonds, the second emeralds, and they are so much alike that they should not be read within several months of one another. I should not be surprised to learn that, having succeeded to such an extent with *11 Harrowhouse,* Mr. Browne made a conscious decision to do the same thing in green. Even so, they are not identical, and the second book was not necessarily a cinch to write. Mr.

Browne's latest book, *Stone 588*, is again the story of the jewelry trade, and it bears some similarity in plot structure and characterization to its fellows, but it is also very different from them, and shows the way a writer can grow and change while presumably repeating himself.

The Growth Process

All right, so it never gets easy. You never really write by numbers. Even in series fiction, when you write the same kind of book over and over about the same character, you are in certain respects doing it each time for the first time. No formula provides an *Open, sesame!* to literary success, and you've never got it made.

That said, the fact remains that some writers grow and change more than others. There are pressures—self-imposed and external—to write the same book over and over, however impossible it may be to do precisely that. And there are pressures, too, to write a completely different book each time—however impossible it may be to do precisely that, either.

The most seductive thing about doing the same thing over and over (in fiction as in life itself) is that it looks safe. I have at this point written five books about Bernie Rhodenbarr, a nice-guy burglar who solves murders, and each has sold a significant number of copies more than its predecessor. At the same time, each has drawn a little more critical attention, and the reviews throughout have been overwhelmingly favorable. While there are no sure things in this highly chancy universe we inhabit, it is more than probable that a sixth Bernie Rhodenbarr would find a welcome in the marketplace, that the critics would receive it warmly, and that it would outperform the earlier volumes in the series. It might not be a bestseller (although you never know; series fiction sometimes reaches critical mass in audience appeal and leaps spontaneously onto the list) but it would almost certainly sell well.

Writing another book about Bernie looks safe in other respects as well. First off, I know I can do it. I've done it five times, and it does not seem wildly presumptuous to believe that I could do it again. The writing of any novel requires a leap of faith as great as that shown by those divers in Acapulco, the kids who plunge off the cliffs confident that the wave will be there when they hit. It's easier to take that kind of leap if you've taken it before, and lived to tell the tale.

If the writer's self-imposed pressures to repeat himself are considerable, they're nothing compared to the external pressures. With the occasional exception of the creative artist himself, virtually everyone engaged in the marketing and consumption of art wants to see the same thing again and again. The last thing the average publisher wants is for a proven writer to strike out in a new direction. Even if the new work is good, even if it's appealing, even if it's demonstrably better than what the writer has done before, this innovation makes life infinitely more difficult for those people whose job it is to sell what the writer has written.

A friend of mine, a graphic artist, was telling me a few weeks ago how exciting the past five years have been for her. "My work has gone through four major changes," she said, "and I'm painting completely different now. I love what I'm doing, it represents enormous growth, and it's all terribly exciting for me." She sighed. "Of course," she said, "I can't keep a gallery. Each time I go through a metamorphosis, the owner doesn't know what to make of it or how to sell it, and I have to go find somebody else."

This does not mean that publishers or gallery owners or anyone else in the creativity biz are mossback sticks-in-the-mud. What it does mean is that, having established an artist in a certain way and for a certain audience, and having once figured out how to merchandise that artist's work effectively, it's a rare merchandiser indeed who welcomes the opportunity to tear up the game plan and come up with a whole new approach.

If publishers are conservative in this respect, it's because readers are even more conservative; once they like a writer, they want him to do more of what made them like him in the first place. Each book doesn't have to be identical with its predecessors—we'd like them to be sufficiently different so that we can tell them apart—but we don't want any major departures. We'd prefer the writer to stay within what we imagine his parameters to be.

Consider John Le Carré. After breaking through to bestsellerdom with *The Spy Who Came In from the Cold,* his third novel of Cold War espionage, Mr. Le Carré wrote a couple more books in the same vein. Then he wrote something completely different, a romance entitled *The Naive and Sentimental Lover.* The book disappointed almost everyone who read it. Those of Mr. Le Carré's fans who bought the book were disappointed because it was not what they expected from the author. Readers who might conceivably have liked the book never picked it up in the first place because they knew of the author as a suspense and espionage writer and were accordingly not interested. I didn't like the book and never felt it worked on its own terms or anyone else's, but it might have had a better chance in the marketplace had it been issued under a pen name. While the Le Carré name did guarantee a certain sales level, it also prevented the book from having a chance of reaching the real audience that may have existed for it.

Similarly, when Robert Ludlum departed from his usual mode to write a comic novel about a plot to kidnap the Pope, he was advised to publish it under a pen name. The book, *The Road to Gandolfo,* has since been reissued in paperback under the author's own name, but at that time it was agreed that readers would be confused and alienated if it were to appear under the author's real name. After some time had passed, and with Mr. Ludlum's position in the book world unassailable, a change in byline could help sales of *Gandolfo* without hurting the other books.

As a reader, I'm as guilty of this conservatism as anyone. Once I've found someone I like to read, I want him to keep on writing what I know I'll like. Why change anything? If it's not broke, why fix it?

The Sheer Joy of It

Except you have to fix it. If you don't, it'll rust.

We become writers for any number of reasons, some of them out in the open, others covert. To validate ourselves, surely. To show our inner selves to the world while maintaining a discreet distance. To win respect. To touch people's lives.

Underlying all of this is a purely artistic motive that generally impels us. We seek the sheer joy that comes of doing that which has not been done before. And once we've done it, and done it to our satisfaction, it's time to do something else new.

Similarly, we write fiction as a way of holding a sort of Fun House mirror to our own inner selves. When that self grows and changes, the reflection had better change as well if the image is to possess its fictive truth.

There are some writers who do not change much over a career or a lifetime. Evidently they reached a particular level of maturity before they started writing and remained frozen at it, in their work if not in their life. There are other writers who have managed to grow considerably within the context of a cohesive body of work. For an example, you might look at the Lew Archer novels of Ross Macdonald. Written over a 30-year span, the books are all about the same character and are all similar in structure and style—and yet the later books are to the early ones as Beethoven's late string quartets are to his early work.

And there are others of us who have to ring out the old in order to ring in the new, and who have to take commercial and artistic risks in the process. All the arguments for writing a sixth book about Bernie Rhodenbarr or a seventh about Matthew Scudder pale against the realization that I cannot just now write about either of those characters, that I have said what I have to say about them, that if I force myself into another repeat performance I will either lapse into immobility after 50 pages or, even worse, produce a book devoid of the life force that made the earlier volumes successful.

And so my own next book is *Random Walk,* and it is not about any of the characters I have written about in the past. It is not a mystery. Although there is considerable violence in it, it cannot properly be called a novel of suspense. I have never had a more exciting time writing anything, or a greater feeling of satisfaction afterward; at the same time, I can just about take it for granted that many readers who have come to like my work over the years will not like what I've done.

Why, Stephen King was asked, do you write the books you write? And why, he replied, do you assume I have any choice?

I do assume choices. I could have chosen not to write *Random Walk*; I probably could have chosen to write a burglar book in its stead. But one makes such a choice at one's peril; doing so, one lowers the flame of one's talent, and risks blowing it out altogether. And for what?

The writing of *Random Walk* was, as I've intimated, an extraordinary experience. I suspect it's an instructive one as well, with something to say regarding the nature of inspiration and the creative process. Tune in next month and I'll tell you all about it.

5

The Writing of *Random Walk*

February 1988

AN UNUSUAL NOVEL REQUIRES UNUSUAL GESTATION, UNUSUAL CONCEPTION.

Make of this what you will:

In January of '87, I booked myself into the Virginia Center for the Creative Arts for the month of June. I figured it was high time I wrote a novel, which I hadn't done since completing *When the Sacred Ginmill Closes* in March of '85. I had not been altogether idle in the interval; I had traveled around the country conducting writing seminars, had written and self-published *Write for Your Life* as a seminar in book form, had written the ultimately unpublished novelization of a film, and had collaborated with a friend on his life story. But I had not written a novel of my own in two years, and that is what I do, and it was about time for me to do it.

It had become clear to me that there was a reason why I was taking an uncharacteristically long time between novels, and that reason was that I didn't know what I was going to write next. It seemed to me, though, that it ought to be something rather different from what I had been doing. In recent years my writing had centered almost exclusively on two series characters, Matt Scudder and Bernie Rhodenbarr, and I felt I had said what I had to say about those characters. I was ready for something new, but it hadn't yet taken shape for me.

In February my wife, Lynne, and I traveled to West Africa with a group studying spiritual healing and traditional African medicine. In Togo we met several times with the shaman Durchback Akuete, and several of us not only participated in tribal rites but underwent private ceremonies with him. In my ceremony, Akuete installed a spirit in me designed to assist me in moving to new levels with my writing.

A month or so later back in the States I had a tarot reading with a woman in Florida who told me I was going through a great shift in consciousness which would result, among other things, in a quantum leap in my work. Some of the things she said resonated in such a way as to move me to consult a trance medium friend on my next trip to New York, where I received a similar message.

This was exciting news, but it was also a little unsettling, because I had not the slightest idea what I was supposed to write. I did have ideas for two Bernie Rhodenbarr–Burglar mysteries. While I knew neither could possibly represent the sea change in my writing that seemed to loom on the horizon, I figured one or the other of them might serve me in my month in Virginia. It was, after all, the middle of May when I returned from New York. In less than two weeks I would be holed up at VCCA, typing away, and I couldn't expect to be struck by inspiration in time. I would go with what I had, and the Major New Work would have to wait until it revealed itself to me.

Enter the Idea

Well, go figure these things.

Perhaps ten days before the end of May, I was sitting in my living room reading something. (*Poppy,* by Barbara Larriva, as it happens; I wrote a column about it a few months ago.) A couple of chapters in, I set the book down for a moment, and the idea came to me of a group of people walking across the country. I let myself think about this, and, the more I thought about it, the more I *thought* about it.

Ideas began flooding in. Characters, situations, the overall shape of a plot. And, in the next several days, I kept thinking about the book. I didn't *decide* to think about it. I would be watching a ballgame, or reading something, or driving around, and thoughts would come unbidden. The book, it was clear, was going to be a long one, peopled with a large cast of characters and sprawling across a vast amount of real estate. The plot would be complex, and full of incident, and while I was thinking about it a great deal and getting any number of bits and pieces, I did not by any means know where the book was going or which imagined incidents and characters would actually appear in it.

So it was clear that I wouldn't be able to start writing it in a matter of days. There was much sifting of thoughts that would have to be done first, and much research. But I had enough of a hold on it so that I knew I wouldn't lose it. I would go off to VCCA, write a Burglar mystery, and perhaps sometime in the fall I would get started on *Random Walk*. (I had by this point thought of the title.)

As the days dribbled away, I came to see that I wasn't going to be able to go off and write a Burglar book. *Random Walk* was all that was on my mind. If I were to write anything, that was what it would have to be.

So I went to the barber and got my head shaved.

Why? I don't know why. So that the thoughts could get in more easily? Seems unlikely. As a way of letting go of the past and opening up to what was coming up next? That seems a little more reasonable, albeit barely so. On a conscious level, all I can report is that I experienced a strong urge to take this uncharacteristic action, and that it somehow felt appropriate to act on urges of this nature. But that's just what was operating consciously, and the whole point of this report is that there is more involved in the process of literary creation than meets the conscious mind.

Four days before the end of the month, I loaded the car and set out for Virginia. It's a two-day drive, but I wanted to give myself extra time.

The pre-book isolation would start as soon as I departed, and I wanted several days of it before I arrived there and went to work.

Enter the Colony

I had a 30-day fellowship at VCCA, and I hoped I'd be able to average five pages a day of *Random Walk,* which would give me a fourth to a third of the book by the time I left. I got there early in the afternoon of the appointed day, unpacked my clothes in my sleeping room in the residence hall, set up my typewriter and supplies and research material in my studio a quarter-mile up the hill.

In the morning I rose early, went to my studio, and had 20 pages written by the day's end. And I did that every day, seven days a week, until the book was finished several days before my month was up.

Random Talk

It was the most extraordinary writing experience I have ever had. In one sense it was magically easy, in that whatever I needed for the book was always at hand. My mind was ever able to supply the character or incident or bit of plot business that I needed when I needed it. At the same time, I don't think I have ever been so completely taken over by a piece of writing. The book was very demanding. It was on my mind all the time. Typically, I rose somewhere between 5 and 6 and went to the studio. I would proofread the previous day's pages and start writing, breaking around 8 for breakfast. Somewhere around noon I would collect my lunch pail from in front of the studio door, wolf a sandwich at my desk, and keep going; somewhere between 3 and 5 I would be done for the day. For all of that time I was either at the typewriter or staring at maps, figuring out where my characters were going next and what they'd see and do there.

Before I left Florida, I had sensed that the book would have two chief story lines. One would consist of this curious pilgrimage of people walking east from Oregon. The other would follow a man around the Central Plains states as he stalked and killed women. One thing that struck me, from the moment of inspiration all through the writing of the book, was the evident incompatibility of the two stories. It was not only that they seemed quite unrelated, but that they didn't belong in the same book, that they were of two different kinds of books. Here we had this group of seekers, caught up in some New Age energy, walking out of their lives and into unknown territory and undergoing some miraculous transformational experiences in the process. And over here we had this middle-class monster, snuffing out attractive young women one after the other, without an apparent qualm of conscience and, worse the luck, taking enormous satisfaction from it all. The first story looked to be part of some spiritual manifesto; the second skirted perilously close to the pornography of violence.

Throughout the writing, I kept wondering at the appropriateness of my dual story line. I did not know how the two plots were going to mesh, or if they could coexist in the same book. It struck me that a lot of people would very likely be put off by what I was doing, and that it was possible no one would much like it. I went ahead anyway, deciding to trust whatever seemed to be directing me in the writing of the book.

Because it is abundantly clear to me that I was being guided. While it has been the norm for me to write rapidly, especially under conditions of isolation such as VCCA supplied, this was something altogether different from my past experiences. Two weeks before I started work, I had not had a single thought related to the book. All of the characters and incidents had emerged as I needed them. I was being somehow inspired, and I was willing to trust the source of that inspiration.

And what might that source have been?

I don't think it was something outside myself. There have been a number of channeled manuscripts in the past few years, the most prominent of which is probably *A Course in Miracles*, which was dictated to a woman over a period of months by a disembodied voice. I never had the sense that I was taking down celestial dictation, or that some external entity or personality was expressing itself on my Smith-Corona. On the contrary, it's easy for me to see myself as *Random Walk*'s source; the book's ideas are ones that have concerned me in recent years, and the characters and plot elements all derived in discernible ways from my own life experience.

Nor did I just have to write down sentences that spoke themselves within my mind. I thought of scenes, worked them out in my mind, then constructed them on the page. The book was no less an exercise of craft than anything else I've written.

And yet it came to me, it was given to me. It was as if all the book's elements were arranged on a shelf somewhere outside of my field of vision, and all I had to do was reach back and my hand would fill with whatever it was I needed.

What seems most probable to me is that *Random Walk* was a channeled work, but that I channeled my own subconscious mind. Somehow or other the book had taken form there; when I was ready to write it, I tapped into that subterranean pool and struck oil.

My whole stay at VCCA was spent in a sort of altered state. The book, as I've said, was on my mind all the time. After each day's work I would return to the room, shower, meditate, and sit around in a stupor until dinnertime. After dinner I would become catatonic until it was time to go to bed, and after five or six hours of sleep I would wake up before the alarm and go do it all over again.

And, when the book was done, so was I. I hadn't meditated regularly for ages before beginning the book, and I got so much out of it I vowed to continue after the book's completion. The day after I finished the book I had difficulty getting into my meditation, and the following day I gave it up altogether. It was evidently something I needed to do while I was working on the book, and something to let go of afterward.

The same was true of a breathing exercise I performed each morning upon arising. Once the book was done, I was done with it.

Ah, I see some of you are waving your hands in the air, while others are frowning and scratching their unshaven heads. Yes, Rachel?

Sir, does this mean you think we all ought to go to Africa and get infested with spirits? And go to mediums and card readers? And shave our heads?

Only if that's the particular path where your own inner voices lead you, Rachel. Perhaps you'll be guided to watch *The New Newlywed Game* and listen to all your old Beach Boys albums. Yes, Mimi?

Do you think the things you did before and during the writing of the book were an actual help to you?

First of all, I think it helped that I did them. By following my inner promptings, I was demonstrating my willingness to do anything that would help the book to grow. I was telling myself and the universe that I really wanted to write on a more significant level, and that I would make sacrifices toward that end. Was I in fact guided by the tarot reader and the trance medium, or empowered by the African ceremony? My belief is that I was, but that guidance and empowerment was probably secondary to what my own willingness gave me. That same willingness allowed me to trust the story line of *Random Walk* as it took shape, and without that trust I'm sure I would have choked off the flow of inspiration and stifled the book.

And is that the chief lesson here, sir?

I'm not sure, Rachel. One lesson, surely, is that much of the writer's work is done on a level far removed from the conscious one, that books take shape in inner chambers of the mind, and that the process of literary creation is always mysterious and perhaps ultimately unfathomable. It's quite clear to me, for instance, that the two years prior to the writing of *Random Walk* constituted a gestation period for the book. The fact that I had no conscious notion what I was working on during those years, or that I was working on anything, does nothing to lessen their importance.

Another lesson, for me, is that I always come out ahead when I heed the still small voice within. This is no less true when other outside voices disagree. My publishers at Arbor House wanted changes in *Random Walk* that struck me as violations of the book's spirit. I instructed my agent to retrieve the manuscript and try it elsewhere, and I'm delighted to report that Tor Books will bring out the book in October, with every hope of making a bestseller of it.

Yes, Arnold?

Sir, I see that your hair has grown back.

That's very perceptive of you, Arnold.

I think I speak for the entire class when I say that we like you better this way, sir.

Why, thank you, Arnold. So does my mother.

6

Keeping Up Appearances

March 1988

YES, THE WORDS ARE MORE IMPORTANT THAN HOW
THEY'RE TYPED, BUT ON THE OTHER HAND . . .

All right now, class. Before I dismiss you today, I want to make sure you all understand the assignment. You're to go home now and begin work on a novel, and next Wednesday at this time I'll expect you each to deliver a finished manuscript of 60,000–75,000 words. At least one of the characters must be a woman who fights forest fires in the Pacific Northwest, and a key element of the plot is to be the revelation that she is a collateral descendant of John Bunyan, author of *Pilgrim's Progress*. And, if you should have any free time during the week, you might want to—yes, Rachel?

Sir, will you accept dot-matrix submissions for this assignment?

Will I accept dot-matrix submissions, which is to say manuscripts produced on a dot-matrix printer? I'll accept manuscripts written in crayon on an uncut scroll of yellow teletype paper. I'll accept manuscripts chiseled into stone tablets. I'll accept manuscripts scratched into the dirt with a stick, then photographed from a hovering helicopter. It doesn't really matter to me what your manuscript looks like, Rachel, since I have no intention of reading it.

You don't?

Of course not. How could I be expected to read all the novels this class is going to produce, and what good would it do if I did? The point of your assignment is for you to do it, not for me to tell you how you did.

There are, however, reasons more important than my own personal prejudices that might make you avoid crayon, or stone tablets, or dot-matrix printers. The appearance of your work can influence its reception.

Before I go on, however, I want to say loud and clear that the subject under discussion is *not* the pros and cons of dot-matrix printers. I know that there are some dot-matrix printers that are virtually indistinguishable from letter-quality printers without the aid of a magnifying glass, and I know that there are other dot-matrix printers that produce a text that looks as though it could best be decoded by running one's fingertips across the dots, and I know that there are all grades of printers between the two. In my experience, everybody's personal dot-matrix printer is one level less readable than its owner thinks it is. But that's not the subject. The subject is appearance.

Judging a Book by Its Insides

Logic tells us that appearances shouldn't matter. Our work, after all, consists of shaking a whole slew of words loose from the dictionary and arranging them in a presumably pleasing order. It is this arrangement of our words rather than their appearance upon the page that communicates itself to the reader, for better or for worse. Furthermore, what we produce is by definition unfinished; unless we are desktop publishers of our own work, someone else will determine such matters as typeface and page size and other elements of book design, asking of us only that we provide the words themselves. If this is all the world requires of us, what does it matter if those words are composed of dots? Or, for that matter, if they're in crayon?

The answer, of course, is that certain persons will have to read the manuscript before it reaches its final form, and that their reactions to it may affect its ultimate fate for better or worse. On a most obvious level, if you submit a manuscript that is hopelessly amateurish in appearance, one that is typed in brown italic on beige paper, let us say, the likelihood of its being read at all is extremely small. People whose job it is to read manuscripts, and for who reading is more a chore than a pleasure, would resent you from the first glance for making their job more burdensome. But this resentment would barely enter into it. They would know on the basis of experience that manuscripts so amateurish in appearance are invariably just as hopeless in execution. They would know not to waste their time struggling.

It is for this reason that one learns early on to follow the formats for manuscripts that have evolved over the years. Understand, please, that no one specifically decides to reject a manuscript because it deviates from standard format. No editor says: "Hmmm, this joker puts his page numbers on the left instead of the right" or the other way around "so I'll have to send this back. Too bad—it was pretty good otherwise."

That doesn't happen. What does happen is that a manuscript that departs significantly stands out. It proclaims itself the work of someone who does not know better, and this predisposes the reader to be aware of everything else that is awkward and uninformed about the work.

Does this mean manuscripts have to be perfect? Flawlessly typed on high-rag bond? No, I think not. No editor I've ever known objects to a certain number of hand corrections, or the occasional xxxxxx'd out section. As long as everything's clear and easy to read, readily comprehensible to everyone called upon to deal with it, it's acceptable for a manuscript to look as though someone had to work a little to get it right.

As a matter of fact, it may be a mistake to submit a manuscript that looks *too* good. Years ago there was a writer of westerns whose other occupation was operating a Linotype machine; he would compose his fiction at the Linotype, pull page proofs, and submit those to his publisher. He got away with this because he was a pro and had established a good relationship with the publisher, otherwise, though, I think his typeset submissions would have been ill-advised. People who are professionally accustomed to reading and editing work in manuscript form are going to have a harder time coping with it in any radically different form.

Similarly, a fellow I know was one of the first to move from a typewriter to a computer, and he was delighted by the tricks the machine would perform. One thing it would do on command was justify margins. (This is computerese. It doesn't mean the machine would provide a philosophic rationale for the existence of margins. It means that it would automatically space the words and letters so as to create straight margins on both sides of the page. But you already knew that, didn't you?)

At first, my friend submitted manuscripts with justified margins. They looked very good, better than anyone's manuscripts generally look, but there was something wrong with them. They didn't look like manuscripts, and people accustomed to reading manuscripts with a ragged margin on the right found this justification, well, unjustifiable. My friend, no fool, stopped doing that. He still justifies margins in his personal correspondence, and that looks a little weird, too, but it hasn't moved me to return one of his letters with a rejection slip.

The Man Behind the Curtain

Recently I gave a copy of the manuscript of my most recent novel, *Random Walk,* to my son-in-law. He liked it well enough, but said he kept being distracted by wondering how it would work for the general reader. "I think I'll have to read it again sometime," he said, "so that I can just let myself get involved in the story."

A partial explanation, I suggested, lay in his having read a manuscript rather than a bound book. When I read a manuscript, I read more as an editor and less as a pure reader—irrespective of whether I have any editorial or critical function to perform. A manuscript is something in the process of becoming a book, still unfinished, subject to change and revision, open to editorial input, and very much the product of a human mind. A book, on the other hand, is finished. It's set in type, it's printed, it's copyrighted, it's done. My critical muscles relax somewhat, and I'm more likely to get caught up in the story.

Kenny said he could see this must have been operating. "When I would hit a deleted section, I'd try to figure out what you had written and then cut out. And that would take me out of the flow of the story."

Before I submit a manuscript, I go over any xxxxxxx'd out sections with a marker, rendering them neatly illegible. So no one can get distracted into puzzling out just what I changed my mind about. Still, with the predominant number of word-processed (and thus typographically perfect) manuscripts in circulation, it may be that a manuscript with hand corrections and deletions calls unwelcome attention to itself these days. I myself may be too much of a Neanderthal to change, but it's a point to ponder.

Skin Deep

The influence of appearance on reality doesn't end with the manuscript. Further down the line in the publishing process, the same elements apply.

There are several intermediate stages between manuscript and book, and people are apt to read a novel in any of these stages, and the form in which they read it may affect their reaction to it. Book club editors, reprint editors, trade reviewers, various subsidiary rights buyers, foreign publishers, all may have a look at the book before it is indeed a book, and their response may have a good deal to do with its success or failure. Some will be sent a photocopy of the manuscript. Some may look at loose galley proofs. More will see bound galleys, or proof copies, which consist of unedited galleys chopped up into page-sized chunks and bound together in the approximate form of a book.

When the publisher's lead time and promotional budget are sufficient, bound galleys may take the form of a reader's edition, which is essentially a copy of the trade edition, its interior pages all in final form, but with a soft cover rather than a hard one. The best reader's editions these days look like legitimate trade paperbacks, with cover art and all.

A reader's edition has several virtues. First of all, it lets people in the book trade (and the author, and the author's agent) know that the publisher thinks enough of the book to go to the trouble of issuing it. At the same time, it provides all these influential readers with a nice finished book, something attractive enough to keep, and something sufficiently clean and polished in appearance to be a shade more readable, more inviting, more engrossing, than a bound galley.

(Finally, let it be said, it can be cost-effective. Bound galleys are OK when you just need a few dozen copies, but they're quite expensive on a per-copy basis and the cost doesn't drop much with quantity. If you're going to bring out a reader's edition of a thousand or more, it's *cheaper* than issuing bound galleys, although it looks as though it costs a lot more.)

Does the form really make a difference? I think so. Some months ago a publisher sent me, in hope of a blurb, a bound copy of a manuscript, with the text printed on both sides of the 8½ x 11 page. While I didn't find it impossible to read, I'm sure the format was partly responsible for my disinclination to finish the book. If it had been absolutely wonderful I probably would have read it anyway, and if it had been terrible I wouldn't have read it no matter how beautifully it was printed, but this book was somewhere in the middle, and I'm positive the presentation had a negative effect on my response. More recently, another publisher sent me a photocopy of a dot-matrix manuscript; I read a few pages, realized I liked the book enough to want to enjoy the experience of reading it, and discarded the manuscript so that I could wait and read it in book form later.

The Need for Fundamentals

And what does all of this mean to you? If you're starting out, of course, it means that you would do well to learn how a manuscript ought to look. There are books that cover such fundamentals, and the desire to be more than a beginner should not prevent one from learning what beginners ought to learn.

Most of you already know how to prepare a manuscript. But perhaps a consideration of appearances and how they alter circumstances might be appropriate nevertheless. The words we write ought to be our sole message, but it doesn't seem to work that way. The medium is indeed the message, or part of it, anyway. And if this column gives you something to think about along those lines, well, that's part of *its* message.

7

Writing at an Artists' Colony
April 1988

PEACE, AND TIME, AND A SPECIAL PLACE TO WRITE. NICE
WORK IF YOU CAN GET IT.

Picture an idyllic landscape. Acres of rolling countryside. Mountains in
the distance. A vast expanse of lawn. Towering specimen trees. Holstein
heifers grazing placidly in a field.

Sketch in a residence hall. A large living room. A television library.
A spacious library, its floor-to-ceiling shelves overflowing with books.
Add a kitchen, a communal dining room. Fit in a couple dozen spartan
but serviceable bedrooms.

And, perhaps a quarter-mile away at the top of a rise, put in a
sprawling complex of studios. A dozen or so rooms for writers. Almost
as many spaces for visual artists, larger because they need more space,
and with the floor bare because they'd just drip paint on the carpet otherwise. Tuck in three studios for composers, equipped with pianos and
soundproofed for the protection of everyone else.

Then fill the place with artists. Feed them three times a day. Change
their bed linen once a week. And leave them alone.

What you have is an artists' colony.

Does it sound like heaven?

It can be just that. Colonies—and 15 or 20 of them are scattered
around the country—exist to provide the creative artist with an ideal
environment for his work. During a residency, which may range from

a week or two to several months, all his needs are taken care of and he is blissfully removed from the sort of mundane matters that break one's concentration in the outside world. When he's in his studio, no phones ring and no one knocks at his door. Any real-world turmoil—a stack of unpaid bills, a turbulent relationship, a squalling infant—remains light-years away in the real world.

In addition to comfort and isolation, a colony provides one with the company of other people similarly committed to creative pursuits. There's conversation at breakfast and dinner, of course, and often in the evening a resident will present some of his work. Poets and fiction writers give readings. Artists show slides of their work, or invite their fellows to an open studio showing of what they've produced during their residency. Composers play tapes, or perform at the piano in the lounge.

And, of course, one is surrounded by the evidence of the accomplishment of past and present fellows; there's a library of books by people who have worked at the colony, and the walls throughout the studio barn and residence hall are hung with prints and paintings produced by fellows.

How much one participates in this cultural interchange is a wholly individual matter. Some fellows attend every reading and slide show and open studio, hold conversations far into the night, and find the company of fellow artists the colony's most valuable aspect. Others go back to their studios after dinner for more work. Indeed, it's possible to isolate oneself completely at a colony; there's frequently a bed in the studio for naps, and it's not unheard of for an artist facing deadline pressure to move in altogether, emerging only for quick, silent visits to the dining room.

Either mode of behavior, or anything in between, is considered acceptable. Work is a colony's whole reason for being, and it is axiomatic that it takes precedence over other activities. I won't take it amiss if you pass up my poetry reading; you in turn won't consider me a barbarian if I leave the table while you're in the middle of a sentence.

33 RPM

Before we go any further, I should emphasize that I am by no means an expert on the subject of artists' colonies. My experience has been limited to two month-long fellowships at a single colony. The first of these, in June of '87, was enormously successful as far as I was concerned; in February's column I described my experience, in the course of which I wrote a full-length novel, *Random Walk.* It was abundantly clear to me at the time that the atmosphere of the colony greatly facilitated the writing of the novel, and that the shared energy of my fellow artists helped me bring all my own energy to bear upon the project. Now, six months later, I am again in residence at the colony, and things could hardly be more different. I booked my stay here without a specific book in mind, trusting that I would be ready to write something by the time I got here. Nothing came to mind. On the second or third day here I started a short story and wrote half of it. The next day I reread what I'd done and decided that, if I were reading this particular story, I would probably quit about now; I couldn't see any reason why I as a writer should go further than I'd be prepared to go as a reader, and I laid the story aside.

I moped for a few days, then started a novel about Bernie Rhodenbarr, the burglar I've written five mystery novels about. After three days I had 33 perfectly acceptable pages. At the end of the week I still had those 33 pages, and I had too the realization that those five novels hold as much as I have to say about Bernie Rhodenbarr, and that while there may be nothing wrong with my 33 pages, neither is there any real reason to write page 34.

If June was heaven, the past couple weeks have been a reasonable facsimile of its opposite. This is a wonderful place to work; conversely, it's a perfectly terrible place not to work, and any day now I may quit punishing myself and cut my stay short. Meanwhile, perhaps I can improve the shining hour by answering a few questions about colonies:

How do you get to go to one? By applying. Different colonies have different application procedures, but all of them are designed to ensure that the artists in residence have some professional legitimacy. If you have not accomplished anything yet in the world of letters, you would probably have a tough time getting accepted.

This does not mean you have to be a self-supporting professional writer with a long list of publications and honors. You probably ought to have published something, and you probably will be asked to submit samples of your work, published or unpublished, along with letters of recommendation from someone with some standing in the field who can testify to your talent and accomplishment.

While most colonies operate year-round, they are harder to get into in the summer months when the demand for space is heaviest. If you can come off-season, and if you're generally flexible in terms of time, you stand a better chance of acceptance.

How much does it cost? That depends. Some colonies don't charge anything, and all of them are generally quite reasonable. The one where I'm staying asks fellows to pay $15 a day, more if they're able. However, some artists are accepted who cannot pay the basic $15 charge. Since this includes accommodations and meals, it strikes me as a pretty decent deal.

I should mention that a few colonies charge a considerable amount for room and board and operate to make a profit. They very definitely welcome amateurs and neophytes, and some of them provide some sort of instruction, even a structure of classes and workshops. While such operations may be just what you're looking for—and certainly easier to get into than a not-for-profit colony—they're quite different in atmosphere and caliber of resident.

Who gets the most out of a colony? On the basis of my two visits, I'd say the person with a clear idea of what he's going to write has a distinct advantage. On the other hand, going to a colony with a project in mind is no guarantee of success, nor is the lack of a project a certain impediment. Several people have told me that they've frequently gone to colonies with no advance agenda, drawn inspiration on the spot, and had productive residencies.

Colonies can be a godsend for somebody up against a deadline. The opportunity for truly concentrated work is unparalleled. It's not uncommon for a writer to complete a book or a screenplay in a month, or for a painter to complete a series of paintings for an upcoming show.

For those of us who don't ordinarily come into contact with other artists, a colony can be deeply energizing. A painter I met here first attended a colony four years ago. At the time she was living in a small city that was by no means a beehive of cultural activity, and the stimulation of the company of her fellows was heady indeed.

"I couldn't get enough of it," she told me. "I went to every open studio, I hung on every word at every poetry reading, I lapped it all up. And when my month was up I realized I didn't want to go on living in the middle of nowhere anymore. I went home long enough to pack and made a beeline for New York and I've been there ever since.

"Now when I come here it's different. I don't come for stimulation anymore. I get enough of that at home. I come here for a rest, and I pass up most of the readings and don't always get to the open studios, either. What you get from a place like this depends on what it is you're looking for."

A colony is probably not ideal for the sort of writer who prefers to write a page or two a day and complete a piece of work over an extended period of time. Still, writers who normally work slowly often find themselves putting in more time and getting more accomplished in the hothouse environment of a colony.

You've had two very different experiences at the colony. Would you go back for a third?

Absolutely. The only regret I have about colonies is that I didn't find out about them 20 years ago. They suit me perfectly, and I expect I'll do the bulk of my writing in them in years to come.

Assuming I ever write anything again, that is.

8

When I Get Like This I Can't Even Think of a Title

May 1988

AND COMING UP WITH A SUBHEAD IS NO JOY, EITHER.

Where do we get off calling it "Writer's Block"? That's what comes of playing with words instead of working with more palpable substances. We think we have the right to make words do what we want them to, rather like Humpty Dumpty.

I mean, does an out-of-work steelworker call it Steelworker's Block? The hell he does. He calls it Unemployment. He may not like it, he may gripe about it, he may go down to his friendly neighborhood tavern and tie one on, but he doesn't paw through the dictionary, haul out a couple of words, knot them together and proclaim himself the victim of some new metaphysical disease.

When the port is closed, do the longshoremen suffer from Docker's Block? During the NFL strike, did the offensive linemen complain of Blocker's Block? Of course they didn't. Only the writer, propped on a pile of unwritten words, uses two of them to hide the fact that he's just sitting around like a bum and not *doing* anything.

I don't know about this. I mean, talk about self-referential art. In high school I wrote a textbook-perfect sonnet (A-B-B-A-A-B-B-A C-D-C-D-C-D) about my inability to compose a sonnet. I don't for

a moment think I was the first person to do so. Poets have written vil-
lanelles lamenting the difficulty of creating a villanelle, and a couple of
years back Tom Disch wrote a really wonderful sestina on, you guessed
it, the composition of a sestina.

So I suppose there's ample precedent for a column on writer's block
(whatever that is) in the form of a struggle with the subject's topic. And
I'll grant that you can't fault such a column for lack of honesty. Because,
whether or not there's a condition deserving of the term writer's block,
I am one unemployed steelworker at the moment.

I have spent the past two weeks in residence at the writers' colony I
so glowingly described in last month's column. I came here with hopes
that seemed at the time not unrealistic. When I booked my stay here,
I thought I might have hit on a novel to write by the time I got here.
If that didn't happen, I was looking forward to the luxury of a secluded
month in which to write shorter fiction. I haven't written many short
stories in the past several years, and the thing is I *like* short stories, I
enjoy writing them and enjoy having written them. There's not much
economic sense in writing short stories, but I'm at the point where
mine have a chance of landing at better markets, and I've had the luck
to publish two collections of them, so their composition is not entirely
pointless from a dollars-and-cents standpoint. I certainly make more
money writing short stories than laundry lists or suicide notes, and have
a better time in the bargain.

So I got here and I wrote half a short story and threw it away. Then
I moped. Then I went to an art supply house and bought paints and
brushes and canvases and a $10 easel and a great many rolls of masking
tape and spent a couple of days painting, a pursuit for which I have no
discernible talent and precious little vision. The point of painting was to
have fun, but the fun was severely curtailed by the ever-present knowledge that I was not doing what I was supposed to be doing.

Then I spent three days on a new novel. It was to be the sixth book in my Burglar series, but it won't be, because it will never get past the 33rd page. There's nothing wrong with what I've written. There was nothing wrong with the 13 pages of short story, either. But neither is there any reason to go on with it. It's pointless. It's a waste of time. The words won't come, and there's no reason why they should. I don't feel like writing anything. I'm sick of writing, I've done enough writing, I've been writing one goddamned thing or another for more years than I can count. If I ever had anything to say in the first place, a hypothesis that strikes me as tenuous in the extreme, I've certainly said it by now.

In *The New York Times Book Review* recently was a remarkable article about Henry Roth, whose first novel, *Call It Sleep,* was published more than half a century ago. It was reissued in paperback in the early '60s, at which time it became a great bestseller, an undiscovered classic that got discovered in a big way.

Now, as if to prove he's no flash in the pan, its author has come out with a second book.

For more than 20 years after the publication of *Call It Sleep,* Mr. Roth didn't write a word. Call it hibernation.

Who knows why? It sometimes seems to me that we should marvel not when a writer stops writing but when he doesn't. And it's not that unusual for a writer to stop after one book. There seems to be such a thing as a one-book writer. If, as we're occasionally told, everybody has one book in him, why shouldn't there be some people who, having written that one book, have nothing more to offer?

The *Times* article suggests why Mr. Roth may have stopped. *Call It Sleep* is a novel of a young man growing up on New York's Lower East Side, written in an experimental, innovative style that owes something to James Joyce. Its author was at the time very much a political leftist, and his book was criticized by his fellows as being politically incorrect.

As he sees it now, Mr. Roth would have followed *Call It Sleep* with a second novel continuing the adventures of the book's protagonist. But his political orientation disposed him to regard such a sequel as unacceptable, and he was not artistically impelled to write something that he would deem politically desirable, and as a consequence he wrote nothing.

Now if Mr. Roth—

Leave it alone. What, after all, do I know about Roth? Only what I read in the article, and I don't have that at hand and will probably misremember some salient fact if I keep rattling on about him. I never read *Call It Sleep,* though not for lack of trying, and I don't know anything about Roth's life.

Even so, I find myself reminded of what happened to a friend of mine.

He's a science fiction writer. Years ago—*ages* ago—he was writing science fiction stories for the pulps. (This must have been in the late '40s, early '50s.) He sold what he wrote, and he wrote a lot.

Then one day his agent took him aside. "You know," he said, "you're doing pretty well, selling everything you write, but I think your career's on shaky ground. You've got all your eggs in one basket, and what happens if the basket spills? I think you should diversify. Don't just write science fiction. Develop a secondary area."

"Like what?"

"Sports stories," said the agent.

"Sports stories?"

"Right. For the sports pulps. Good solid market. And a really good sports story sometimes makes it into one of the slicks, which is more than you can say for science fiction. I think you should try your hand at sports stories."

"But I've never even read a sports story," my friend said.

"So read," said the agent.

"But I don't know anything about sports," my friend protested. "I was never good at sports. Even as a child—"

"You don't have to go out in the streets and play stickball," the agent said. "You're a writer, for heaven's sake. You'll read a few of the stories and you'll figure out how to write them. Look, give it a try. If it doesn't work out, what have you lost?"

So my friend bought a handful of pulp magazines and read sports stories, and then he sat down and wrote one. And the agent sold it. And he wrote another. And the agent sold that one, too. And he wrote, all in all, maybe half a dozen sports stories. Maybe a dozen. Who remembers?

The agent sold every sports story he wrote.

And then one day my friend found out he couldn't write another sports story, and neither could he write a science fiction story. And he didn't write a word for the next three years. (Or two years. Or four years. Who remembers?)

He never did write another sports story. (If he did, he would have had to eat it. The sports pulp market is right up there with the great auk and the passenger pigeon. The science fiction market, on the other hand, is doing very nicely, thank you.) After three years (or two or four) he resumed writing science fiction. But writing, which had been easy for him, was no longer quick and effortless. He was careful at it, as men who have had bypass surgery are careful at life.

OK, genius, do you want to tell the nice people what you're getting at?

I suppose my point might be that writing ability is a sensitive plant indeed, and we tamper with it at our peril. It seems to me to be danger-ous in the extreme for a writer to force himself to write what he does not really want to write, just as it is dangerous for him to refrain from writing what he really does want to write.

I think, not for the first time, of Stephen King's response when asked why he writes the kind of books he does. *"What makes you assume I have any choice?"*

I can envision Henry Roth, with one voice in his head telling him what to write and another telling him not to write it. What happens when an irresistible force meets an immovable object? Nothing happens. Nothing happens for years on end.

Let's keep all of this in perspective. If there is such a thing as writer's block, I don't think that's what I've got. What's galling is not that I'm not writing but that I'm doing this non-writing at a writers' colony. If I were elsewhere I would not characterize myself as being blocked. I would say that I was between books. I spend most of my life between books and I have generally found it a comfortable place to be. When it gets uncomfortable, that usually means it's time to write another book.

It's not time yet. I finished a major work, *Random Walk,* less than six months ago. It took a lot out of me (which is as it should be) and I have not yet filled up with whatever it will take to write the next book. That's fine. Recovering from a book is part of the process of writing the next one, and it takes as long as it takes.

To complicate matters, *Random Walk* was a profound departure from my previous books; having written it, I don't know that I can go back to the kind of books I used to write. Nor, at this point, do I know what other sort of books I might write instead. This uncertainty is not inappropriate, but it can be worrisome, especially if I'm at a colony and thus feel as though I ought to be writing something.

Interesting.

You've been here just over two weeks. You struggled through half of a short story and three chapters of a book—all wasted effort, and slow going, and agony to write. Yesterday you spent the entire day battling your way through last month's column, crumpling sheets of paper and throwing them away, pushing the typewriter aside, pacing the floor, making yourself nuts.

Today, writing a disorganized shriek of a column on writer's block (whatever that is) you've hammered out what certainly looks like a perfectly acceptable column in two hours flat.

Go figure.

9

Messages For Your Most Important Reader

June 1988

YOUR FICTION SOMETIMES CONTAINS CODED MESSAGES
INTENDED FOR YOU.

Why do we write?

Oh, you know all the usual reasons. First, the external ones. To make money. To win recognition. To gain respect. To escape from the rat race. To take up a freer and less confining life. To shake the dust of Ishpeming, Michigan, from our shoes and start hanging out with movie stars and international swindlers in Saint-Tropez.

Worthy ambitions, all of them. And each of them, to one degree or another, is part of what drives each and every one of us to the typewriter each morning. (Or to the word processor each evening. Or to the chisel and stone tablets every other Thursday. Whatever.)

And then, of course, there are the internal reasons to write, and while they may remain private, and occasionally secret even to ourselves, they are nonetheless compelling. We write, certainly, to prove to ourselves that we can do it. To demonstrate that our worst fears about ourselves are not true, that we are indeed good enough, that people really do want to hear what we have to say, that we are smart enough and decent enough to make it, that we deserve to succeed. That it won't hurt other people if we express ourselves. That we won't be destroyed if we let other people know who we are.

We write, too, to express ourselves, to take that which is unique within us and offer it up as a gift of self to the universe. We write to extend ourselves to others, to reach across the gap that seems to keep us separate. To heal that separation, to rejoice in the universality of our common humanity.

Profoundly idealistic motives, to be sure—and it may be difficult to believe that we're doing all this when we sit down to bat out a chapter of *Love's Lustful Lechery* or *Harrigan #19: Eaten Alive by Wild Pigs*. Doesn't matter. It's all the same trip, whatever our vehicle of the moment.

There is, I believe, a third sort of reason for writing. It is possible to see everything we write as a letter to ourselves, designed to convey to one portion of ourselves the lesson that another portion has already learned.

Sometimes these lessons are written in code. Sometimes, having written them, we neglect to read them.

Getting the Message

What am I getting at?

Well, let me tell you about a friend of mine. He has written perhaps half a dozen novels over the past 20 years. His first novel had a lot of impact—excellent reviews, strong sales. His subsequent books never did quite as well, but they were sound fiction, got a decent reception from the critics, and had respectable if modest sales.

I got to know the fellow after he'd done all this writing, and I came to know him quite well before I ever got around to reading any of his work. When I finally did, I was struck at once by the extent to which his work was autobiographical. Each of his novels featured a different lead character, but all of the leads were the same, and each of them was him. In all true and honest fiction the viewpoint characters are aspects of their author, but that's not what I mean. Each lead character was my friend, with his background, his views and attitudes, and his life experience. I had by this time heard him tell a nonfictional version of his life story on several occasions, and I recognized incidents and conversations and characters and situations when I encountered them again in his novels. He was not producing mere reportage in the guise of fiction, he had indeed crafted five or six genuine novels, but he had done so by taking big chunks of his life and slapping them down onto the pages. Everything was here, in one book or another—his family background, his relationships with his parents, his marriage, his struggles in his career, his spiritual life, his adventures with drink and drugs. Everything, transmuted slightly by the alchemic process that turns fact to fiction, but little different for the conversion.

I talked to him about the extent to which he had dealt with the events of his life by fashioning them into novels. And he corrected me.

"That's what I used to think I was doing," he said. "I saw myself as being enormously honest and daring, and I felt I was really dealing with things by writing about them. But lately I've been able to see that I was doing precisely the opposite. Writing wasn't my way of dealing with experience. It was my way of not dealing with it."

I asked him what he meant.

"Anything that ever happened to me," he said, "I turned around and put it in a book. I didn't have to figure it out. I didn't have to take the time and trouble to understand it. I didn't have to come to terms with it. I just took it and put it in a book and walled it off, and from that point on I didn't *have* to deal with it. Because as far as I was concerned it was a closed chapter. I had dealt with it by writing about it and now I was done with it. I isolated myself from my own experience the first time around by numbing my emotional nerve endings with alcohol and drugs—another great way of dealing with things by not dealing with them—and I isolated myself again after the fact by sealing off my experiences in fiction. Other people could read about them, and maybe they could deal with them, but I was done. For me the war was over."

Teaching and Learning

You teach, they say, what you most need to learn.

And the teacher is usually his own worst student.

This is not to say that people become fourth-grade teachers out of a deep need to acquaint themselves with the mechanics of long division, or that such arithmetical dexterity tends to remain forever beyond their grasp.

Even on that level, though, there's some truth in the principle. We are rarely terribly good at instructing others in that which comes effortlessly to us. In sports, there's a saying to the effect that natural athletes are no damn good—no good, that is, as coaches. Because they didn't have to learn how to swing a bat or perfect a swimming stroke or kick a football, because it came so naturally to them, they don't know how to teach the knack to others. Few Hall of Famers ever had much success as baseball managers.

As a teacher of writing, I find myself least effective when it comes to areas of style and technique. These were the aspects of writing that came most readily to me, the areas in which I was a natural, and so it's hard for me to tell anyone else how to do it. In those areas more concerned with the inner game of writing—overcoming fears and negative beliefs, sticking at it, dealing with rejection and apparent failure, accessing one's intuition and freeing one's imagination—I am a more successful teacher. Because these are things I have had to learn, and am still learning.

Every teacher is still learning; once the lesson is really and truly learned, the teacher is done teaching it. This helps somewhat to explain the evident contradiction between the teacher and the teaching. I know people who teach prosperity seminars whose own finances are periodically a mess. I know others who teach people how to manage their relationships yet have enormous difficulty maintaining relationships of their own. For all the books and columns I've written and all the seminars I've conducted, I certainly spend an unseemly amount of time trying to think of something to write, and start a disheartening number of books that I never trouble to finish. And the tabloids are forever overflowing with the examples of moral leaders whose own morality serves as an object lesson in how not to lead one's life.

"Do as I say, not as I do." Not because I'm a hypocrite, but because I have trouble learning my own lesson. We teach what we most need to learn, and we are indeed our own worst students.

Weaving the Code

The writer is a teacher, seeking to instruct himself at least as much as to impart his message to others. But this, of course, is not his primary conscious motive; if it were, he'd be writing a diary, or an extended letter to himself, instead of fashioning his lessons into the form of fiction. On a conscious level, he is striving to make a short or long story out of incidents and themes and characters that may appear to have come to him out of thin air.

So he creates a work of fiction. And, somewhere within it, he incorporates the lesson he wants to teach himself, often weaving it in so cleverly that it is quite invisible, looking for all the world like part of the design.

When I was a child (at a time which once seemed like only yesterday, but doesn't anymore) advertisers on the kids' radio programs offered premiums in exchange for a couple of box tops or labels from their products. Rings were a popular item, and every ring always had a secret compartment, where one could stow secret messages, preferably in code.

What does a ten-year-old need with a secret compartment for coded messages? Yet everyone wanted one of those rings, and would have wanted them less without their built-in hiding places.

Every work of fiction is a Captain Midnight ring, complete with secret compartment. Having tucked in the coded message, the writer forgets to read it. He may even forget where he left the ring. The message is sealed away, walled off like the experiences in my friend's six novels.

And this, I think, helps explain why some writers are so wise in their novels and seem so incapable of applying that very wisdom in their personal lives. An example who comes at once to mind is John O'Hara. His novels and short stories, in addition to telling an extraordinary amount about the nature of human lives in America over the past century and a half, reveal an exceptional wisdom about the way people behave in relationships, about the manner in which grudge-holding and bitterness rot a relationship and erode the soul. Anyone reading O'Hara with insight and perception will learn a lot about how to live in the world and get along with people.

Do as he says, not as he did. All of this wisdom seems to have gone directly into O'Hara's work, with precious little spilling over into his life. He was known as the master of the fancied slight, repeatedly taking offense where none was intended, nursing a grudge as passionately as anyone ever nursed a sick friend, refusing to speak to old friends and never even telling them why. The man wrote as brilliantly as anyone ever about the nuances of social behavior; he was, in many respects, a virtual social cripple.

A superb teacher. And his own worst student.

A Self-Taught Man

My own past work spills over with lessons, many of them unlearned. And so does yours, Gentle Reader, and so does every writer's. But we all of us manage to learn a little of what we are trying to teach ourselves, and write more books, and learn a little more.

All of this comes to mind partly as a result of a book I wrote half a year ago. It is entitled *Random Walk*, and I have written about it already in these pages; it will be coming out in October, published by Tor Books, and I have no qualms about urging you to buy a copy the instant it appears.

The main story line of *Random Walk* concerns a group of people who quite literally walk out of their lives and commence crossing the continent on foot. There is something sanctified about their joint venture, and miraculous things happen to them. Walking, they begin a process of healing themselves and their planet, and they do this simply by letting go of everything and walking out of the known and safe and familiar and into whatever the unknowable future may hold.

Having written *Random Walk,* I then allowed myself to examine a longstanding fantasy. For some time Lynne and I had told ourselves that someday we would like to shuck everything and just live for a while without a fixed address, going where the wind blew us, trying on different parts of the country and seeing what fit, and indeed letting go of the known and stepping off into the unknown. The prospect seemed no less attractive for having written the book, and indeed it appeared that there might be more of a purpose to the act than pleasure and adventure, just as there was in the novel.

And it seemed to me that I had written the book in part to prepare myself for the life change, but that I ran the risk of having written the book as an alternative to taking the action. When we did decide finally to go ahead and do it, I made the decision resolved not to be the one person who would miss the point of what I had written.

And yet, and yet. The teacher is so often his own worst student. We began by listing our house for sale and giving away many of our possessions, and somewhere along the line we found ourselves taking the house off the market and letting much of what we owned stay in cupboards and on shelves. This seemed appropriate to us; there were sound economic arguments against selling the house, good logical reasons to hold onto things, and we assured ourselves that, having become thoroughly willing to strip ourselves of house and holdings, it might no longer be necessary to do so in actuality.

Perhaps.

In any event, by the time you read this we will have been on the road for a couple of months, with a commitment to ourselves to go on living nomadically for at least two years. We have not even got out the door as I write these lines, and yet we already feel a certain pull to temper and qualify our commitment. To let *Random Walk*'s lesson stay walled off in its pages. To avoid getting it.

So we'll see what happens. Write for Your Life is out of business; we've let the book go out of print and closed the mail-order business, and what seminars we do will be a sometime thing if other people organize them for us. I will still be appearing monthly in this space—for a time that looked like something else that had to be sloughed off, but turns out to be something I want to keep. And letters to me c/o *Writer's Digest,* no doubt including offers of hospitality should we turn up in your part of the country, will be forwarded to me in the ordinary course of things. I may be somewhat capricious about answering my mail, but when was I ever otherwise?

Big changes. That's what happens when you let yourself read your own mail and become aware of the lessons you're trying to teach yourself.

Look at your own fiction. Crack the code, read the messages. And let yourself get as much of the lesson as you're ready for.

15 Things You Must Know About Writing the Short Story

July 1988

A PRACTICAL GUIDE TO WRITING SHORT FICTION, AND TO BEING A SHORT-STORY WRITER.

1

First of all, the short story is short.

That's pretty obvious, isn't it? Takes one back to the grand old days of the elephant jokes. Remember them? (If you're an elephant, you'll never forget them.)

> *Q: Why are elephants gray?*
> *A: So you can tell 'em apart from bluebirds.*

A short story is short so you can distinguish it from a novel. And that, it seems to me, is the only thing that absolutely sets the two apart. The novel has considerably more words to it than does the short story.

It may be indistinguishable from the novel in terms of its other characteristics. It may have as broad a canvas, as great a time-span, as extensive a cast of characters. All it necessarily lacks is length.

This is not to say that the *average* short story does not have a smaller canvas, a briefer time-span, and fewer characters than the *average* novel. But who cares about averages? If you've got one foot in a bucket of ice water and the other in a bucket of boiling water, on the average you're quite comfortable. Big deal.

Consider John O'Hara. Some of his short stories are no more than vignettes, illuminating incidents in the lives of his characters. Others are distinguishable from his novels only by their length; they observe a character over an entire lifespan, doing in a few thousand words what *From the Terrace* or *Ten North Frederick* does in a few hundred thousand. Any number of O'Hara's short stories could have been full-length novels if their author had chosen to tell them at that length. Conversely, most if not all of O'Hara's long novels could have been told as short stories; while I'd personally hate to see any of them shorter by as much as a word, I can readily see how a short story could be written about Alfred Eaton or Joe Chapin that would essentially tell the story now told at novel length.

Any number of writers have proved this point by telling the same story more than once, first as a short story, later as a novel. "Flowers for Algernon" began as a piece of magazine fiction, and was quite brilliant in that incarnation; when Daniel Keyes expanded it to book length it lost nothing, and to my mind gained from the transformation. (You may know the book as *Charly*, the title of the film starring Cliff Robertson.)

A couple of years ago I wrote a longish short story about Matthew Scudder, a series detective character of mine. It was my most successful short story, published in *Playboy* and anthologized in *The Eyes Have It*, the Private Eye Writers of America's first anthology. The story, which I had called "By the Dawn's Early Light," went on to win PWA's Shamus award as well as the Mystery Writers of America's Edgar award.

About a year after I'd written it, I transformed the story into a novel, which I retitled *When the Sacred Ginmill Closes*. I added a couple of plotlines, but basically I turned a 7,500-word story into a 90,000-word novel. The work succeeded just as well at its greater length; it sold well, was well reviewed, was reprinted in paperback as Berkley Charter's lead title for the month, and was nominated for both the Shamus award and the Anthony Boucher award. (And missed them both, dammit.)

The point of this is not merely to boast—although I don't doubt that's part of it. But I mention it primarily to demonstrate that the same material can serve as well at greater or lesser length. The plot and characters of my most successful short story became my most successful novel.

I hammer this point home because one so often hears people talking about the short story form. I do not believe that there is any such thing. The short story is not a form. The short story is a length.

2

We all know what a novel is. A novel, Randall Jarrell has told us, is a book-length work of fiction with something wrong with it.

One implication of this definition, as far as the short story is concerned, is that the short story need not have something wrong with it. A short story can aspire to perfection.

There is, of course, some hyperbole here. Some prosaic license, if you will. A novel does not *have* to have something wrong with it. Novelists are not like the pious weavers of oriental carpets, purposely incorporating an error in the design because only the Almighty is perfect. Nor does a short story have to be perfect—and a good thing, too, because so few of them are.

Still, the novel is ever so much more forgiving. In comparison to the short story, the tautest of novels is a brawling sprawling loose-jointed creature. It has so much space and so much going on that not everything has to be gemlike in its perfection and polish.

One poorly turned sentence, one ill-chosen word, does not in the ordinary course of things sink a novel. But such a weakness can utterly blunt the point of a short story.

I don't know that this makes one harder or easier to write. What it does mean, I think, is that a short story must reach a higher level of technical excellence if it is to succeed at all.

3

Faulkner said somewhere that every short story writer is a failed poet, and every novelist a failed short story writer. I think I know what he's getting at—we use more words to do what we could not manage with fewer. I wonder if he's right.

There are novelists who cannot write decent short stories. There are short story writers who are utterly at sea when they attempt a novel. There are some who seem equally at home at either length.

I suppose you could say that every poet is a failure, too, that the truly successful wordsmith would be one who could reduce his whole message to the world, his entire primal cry, to a single short word.

And there are days when I have a good idea what the word is.

4

Let's talk for a moment about the economics of short story writing.

If you don't care about money, skip this section. On the other hand, if you care only about money, skip the whole article. And forget about writing short stories. Because they don't make any real sense from a strict economic standpoint.

This has not always been the case. In the 1920s, back in the heyday of the slick magazines, short story writing could be enormously profitable. Some of the top magazines paid as much as a couple of thousand dollars for a story. The dollar has fallen on hard times in the past 60 years. It is now but a shadow of its former self, and yet only a handful of magazines pay that much nowadays.

There are good, sound reasons for this. It doesn't mean the world has gone to hell and the writers, as usual, are getting it in the neck. The role that the short story once played in American popular culture has been taken over by the television show. The sort of people who used to read four short stories and a serial every week in *The Saturday Evening Post* now watch *Dallas* and *Dynasty* and *L.A. Law* and look to magazines for topical nonfiction.

Similarly, the role of the pulp magazine, a training ground for a great many writers and a graveyard for a good many others, is filled by the paperback category novel. People who would have read western pulps 50 years ago now read western paperbacks. Yesterday's love pulp reader is today's reader of romance novels. And so on.

The result of all this is that there is not much of a market for short fiction. There are relatively few places to sell most stories and the rates of pay are, for the most part, nothing to get excited about. It is virtually impossible to make a living writing short stories nowadays.

(I cannot say it is flatly impossible because I know someone who has been doing it for years. As you might imagine, he writes a lot of stories.)

If you think in dollars-and-cents terms, as most of us have to do most of the time, you will very likely find better ways to spend your time than writing short fiction. Joe Gores, who writes short stories better than most people, told me a while back why he had largely stopped. It took about as much time, he explained, to write a short story as to write a teleplay. For the short story he might get two or three hundred dollars, plus another hundred or so every couple of years from anthology use. For the teleplay he'd get five or ten thousand dollars, plus residuals.

It seems to me, then, that the only real reason to write a short story is because you want to. And this, for a writer, is sometimes reason enough.

In my own case, I nowadays write a short story only when I happen to be struck by an idea that I genuinely like. I can't make a living this way, but in other respects it's not a bad state of affairs. Short story writing never feels like drudgery because I do it only when it's what I want to do. Not long ago, for example, I wrote half of a short story and decided I didn't like it much. There was nothing really wrong with it, and I knew how to finish it, but I wasn't crazy about it.

So I threw it away. Big deal. I wasn't tossing the rent money. I wasn't making a great sacrifice. As financially unrewarding as short stories are, I can feel free to abandon the ones I'm not crazy about.

And, if short story writing is a lousy way to turn a buck, it's a hobby with occasional rewards. In my own case, I've had two collections of short stories published in book form. They have not made me rich, but they came out in hardcover and got reissued in paperback, and in a sense every dime I get for them is money for old rope, as our English cousins say. Because I already got paid for these stories, some of which I wrote 25 years ago, and they don't owe me a thing.

And, once in a while, a short story brings in other income. After you've written enough of them, it becomes a frequent thing to get picked up for anthologies at $100 or so a shot. Sometimes a television show comes along and dramatizes a story, paying the author several times as much for the privilege as he received for the story's initial publication.

There are subtler financial rewards as well. Sometimes a short story will draw the attention of an agent or publisher who will want to know if the author has given any thought to the idea of trying a novel. Such an expression of interest is no guarantee of anything, but it doesn't hurt.

5

Is the short story a good training ground for the novel?

That depends.

In *Writing the Novel,* and before that in my *WD* column, I've argued that it's easier to get started writing novels than short stories. The novel is easier to sell and demands less in the way of technical facility to write.

That would certainly seem to make it a more inviting place to start, but that's just not true for everybody.

In my own case, I must have published 20 or so short stories before I wrote a novel. I could not possibly have done otherwise. When I first started taking perfectly good sheets of blank paper and marring them with words, I was able to write only very short pieces. It was difficult for me to sustain a fictional idea for as much as fifteen hundred words. I had read hundreds of novels, but I was a long way from having the sense of what a novel was and how a human being would go about fitting one together.

By writing a lot of stories for low-paying (and thus reasonably accessible) markets, I learned things. I discovered how to construct scenes, how to narrate, how to characterize. I didn't amass data on these subjects. I learned experientially, by doing it.

At the same time, I validated myself as a writer. I was writing stories and getting paid (if you can call it that) for them. I was seeing them in print, under my byline. I was developing a confidence in my ability to put words on paper in such a way that people would actually read them with something approaching pleasure. I would need every bit of this confidence when I leaped into free-fall and essayed my first novel.

And, while I was writing, I was reading other people's novels. The writing I was doing enabled me to see past the surface of the books I was reading. I read less as a pure reader and more as a writer, and I began to develop an intuitive sense of what a novel was and how a mere mortal might set about writing one.

Just about a year after I first sold a short story, I wrote my first novel and in due course placed it with a publisher. Perhaps I could have gotten to the same place by spending the same amount of time writing novels instead of short stories. But I don't really think it would have worked as well for me.

6

There's another way, too, in which the short story can constitute a superior training ground. And that's purely the result of its length.

Because short stories are short, you can write ten or twenty or thirty of them in the time you might spend writing a novel. And you will almost certainly encounter more variety in those ten or twenty or thirty stories than you would expect to encounter in a single novel. You will very likely employ different narrative voices, explore different fictional themes, try out different settings, and put together not one but ten or twenty or thirty plots.

This is not to say that you will learn more from those stories than you would from a novel. You might. You might not.

In a classroom situation, however, I've come to believe that short story writing makes for a much more interesting and stimulating couple of months. I proved this to my own satisfaction a few years ago when I conducted a three-month workshop under the auspices of Mystery Writers of America. The first time I led the workshop, most of my students were working on novels. Each week they would bring in another chunk of their novel and everyone would read it. In several instances they had been working on their novels long before the workshop began, and they would still be at work on them after it was over.

It made for a dull and static class. The weeks went by and the manuscripts got longer, farther from their beginnings if not discernibly closer to their ends. I never felt that Student A would learn a great deal from Chapter 14 of Student B's novel that he hadn't learned anywhere in Chapters 1 through 13. And God knows I got bored reading the same stuff week after week; I can only assume everyone else did, too.

At the short story workshop, everybody brought something new each time. Occasionally I would give assignments, so that a week's work would be united by subject or theme or some technical aspect. The students got much more involved in the class; it may not be entirely co-incidental that, unlike the first group, they bonded early on and took to going out for coffee in a body after the class session ended. And, while this is by no means the only criterion, or even the most important one, several of the students sold stories written for the class.

And I had a good time, and learned a lot—which was why I had gotten involved in the class in the first place.

7

To write short stories, read short stories.

That ought to go without saying. To write anything, one is well advised to read deeply and widely in one's field. The object is not merely to see how other people do things but to install in one's subconscious mind a synthesis of what works and doesn't work.

It's also sometimes important to know what has already been done. This is more often the case with short stories than with novels, because some short stories work largely because they incorporate a wholly original idea. (A novel generally depends less upon its central idea.) If you are going to write short fiction in a particular category—mystery-suspense, say, or science fiction—you will have a better chance of selling if you are familiar with the greater body of work in the field.

What should you read?

Not just the best stuff. If you just read classics, you may despair at ever producing anything a fraction as good. And, because the very best short stories seem to have sprung all of a piece from their authors' foreheads, or even to have been dictated by some celestial being and only transcribed by the human whose byline they bear, it's often hard to learn from the very best work. The bones don't show. You can't see how it was done.

Mediocre work is easier to learn from.

Similarly, the best way to get a sense of how some admired author does what he does is to read a whole ton of his work, one story after the next. This, incidentally, is often a very ill-advised way to read for pleasure. Subtle ways in which a writer repeats himself, imperceptible when the stories are read at intervals, become apparent when you read them one after another.

I recall reading a collection of Flannery O'Connor's short stories, one right after the other. A character in one story had lead-colored eyes. I thought it a nice touch. A character in the next story had eyes the color of pewter. A few stories later, someone was described as having eyes the color of yet another base metal. Antimony? Tin? I don't remember. What I do recall is that what had looked like acute observation initially soon began to look like a trick, and none too subtle a one at that. And I would never have noticed if I had read the several stories a few days apart.

8

When a story runs to no more than 1,500 words or so, it's called a short-short.

Once again, one hears talk about the short-short form when what we're really dealing with is not a form but a length. It's a popular length with both readers and editors, and you often hear editors complaining that they don't see as many good short-shorts as they'd like.

Readers like them, too. They seek them out, anyway. How many times have you picked up a collection or a magazine of short fiction, checked the contents page, and read the shortest stories first? You are not alone. Millions of people do this. They don't necessarily enjoy the shorter stories more, or even expect to enjoy them more. Perhaps the underlying thought is, "If this is lousy, at least it'll be over soon."

Short-shorts are at once easier and more difficult than short stories. Easier and more difficult to write, easier and more difficult to sell.

Just as the novel is a more forgiving form than the short story, so is the full-length short story more forgiving than the short-short. With only 1,500 words to play with, you had better make sure they're the right words, and in the right order.

In addition, a short-short often isn't much more than a developed idea. Since the idea plays so great a role in the short-short, it has to be a strong one.

(In a novel you barely need an idea. "A boy grows to manhood." "A family evolves through five generations in a Texas town." "A marriage falls apart and then is saved." Twenty people could sit down at the same time and pick one of those ideas, and twenty publishable novels might result. With hundreds of pages to move around in, it doesn't matter how many times the idea has been used, or how ordinary it is.)

The same elements that make the short-short difficult also make it easy. Because the idea is so important, a sufficiently good idea can sometimes make up for weak execution. Similarly, with so little space to move around in, the unpolished writer has less room to make mistakes. His story may be no more than one extended scene, and in any event will probably not cover a great timespan or carry a large cast of characters. For the new writer who finds it difficult to get his arms around a big story, the short-short may feel safer and more comfortable, more manageable.

A large proportion of short-shorts have a surprise ending of one sort or another. A surprise ending does not have to be wholly unpredictable to every reader in order to be successful. The more sophisticated readers—and editors certainly belong to this group—know that a surprise ending is nothing to be surprised about, and tend to anticipate them; thus an editor may purchase (and a reader enjoy) a story whose ending he sees coming, as long as the story remains effective and as long as the ending seems to be one that will take *most* people by surprise.

Sometimes, though, a particular editor will see your ending coming all the way from page 1, and will consequently be unfavorably disposed

toward your story regardless of its other excellences. Conversely, sometimes a rather pedestrian surprise ending will take one particular editor
utterly by surprise, and will do so without seeming to have come from
out in left field, or to constitute cheating the reader. The editor will buy
the story—and it may be the same story the first editor rejected.

Which goes to show that, once having decided you're happy with a
story, you must market it relentlessly.

9

Speaking of surprise endings. If you are just starting out, or even if
you're not, you may someday write a story—probably a short-short—in
which we find out at the end that the characters are a) dead or b) a dog
and a cat or c) Adam and Eve. Or d) all of the above.

Don't ever do this.

10

You don't need an agent.

Nor, if you are only writing short fiction, does an agent need you. If,
as we've already established, there's no really sound economic basis for
writing short stories, what do you figure 10% of that economic basis
amounts to? If you write a story, send it around to half a dozen markets
in turn, and finally sell it for $300, at least you've got something to
show for your efforts. You won't rush out and buy a Corvette, but it's
something.

If an agent does this, he makes $30. If he's one of those grasping
swine who charge a 15% commission, he gets $45 for his troubles.

Not too surprisingly, most agents don't want to bother doing this.
An agent may accommodate his book-writing clients by marketing
what short fiction they also happen to write, but he's doing them a favor. And it's not always all that much of a favor; since the agent doesn't
deal much with magazines, he may not be as closely in touch with the
market and its requirements as the writer himself.

Some magazines, however, have announced that they are unable to consider unagented manuscripts. What's a short story writer to do?

Don't rush out and tell everybody, but I'll let you in on a secret. Just because a magazine says this doesn't mean it's 100% true. If you present yourself properly, if you know how to back in the door so it looks as though you're on your way out, if you can slither in through the keyhole instead of dropping down over the transom, you can get read.

I'm not going to spell out how to achieve this. If you can't figure out a way, you probably don't have a sufficiently inventive mind for fiction-writing anyway.

11

One more thing about agents. Just because an agent won't drool at the prospect of marketing your short fiction doesn't mean he won't be impressed by it. He'll only want you as a client if you've written or are writing a novel, but he may be more favorably disposed toward you as a novelist if you've amassed some decent credits with your short stories.

The late mystery editor Lee Wright told a friend of mine some years ago that anything you happen to publish in a magazine can't hurt you, but that it might help you. In other words, if someone in the business reads a magazine piece of yours, fiction or nonfiction, and thinks it's lousy, he won't hold it against you. He'll figure maybe the editor screwed it up, or maybe it got cut too severely, and anyway it's only magazine writing, it's ephemeral, it doesn't matter. But if he reads something and loves it, it's to your credit.

12

Short stories should be fun.

They're demanding, certainly. All good writing is demanding. Even when it flows effortlessly, he who writes it is taking pains, consciously or unconsciously, to get it right.

All the same, a short story rarely involves the sort of drawn-out exhausting labor of a novel. While novels, too, can be fun, they typically include stretches that are about as enjoyable as trench warfare, long hard sessions of slogging through mud. Novels, too, commonly contain chunks where the writer has some trouble figuring out what to do next. (An outline is no sure protection against this. You wind up trying to figure out what to do now that you realize the outline doesn't work. Same difference.)

While short stories can similarly evolve as they are written, and ought to hold some surprises for their authors, it is possible to hold an entire short story in the mind in a way that one simply cannot with a full-length novel. The author may not be wholly in control—I suspect you are never entirely in control of good writing, that it must have a life of its own and be given its own head—but he has less sense of being out of control. There's the story, clear in his mind, scene by scene. All he has to do is write it down.

And it won't take forever to do it, either. Some short stories are written in a single session. Others take a few days. It is, of course, possible to spend an infinite amount of time on any piece of writing, but unless something goes awry it rarely takes a productive writer longer than a week to finish a short story. It is thus possible to complete the work before any of the initial inspiration and enthusiasm for it has faded.

It is also possible to take greater pains with a short story. Stanley Ellin, an absolute master of the short story, would rewrite endlessly as he went along. He wouldn't write page 2 until page 1 was just as he wanted it, and confessed that he had once rewritten his opening paragraph more than 40 times. Mr. Ellin went on to write hefty novels, and abandoned his perfectionism when he did. You can't work that way on a novel—you'd never finish it—but you can if you write short stories, and are willing to spend a great deal of time on each of them.

13

If you want to sell a mystery short-short to *Woman's World,* pick up the magazine every week and read the short-short. Buy every back issue you can get hold of and read those short-shorts, too. Subscribe to *Ellery Queen* and *Alfred Hitchcock* and read them cover to cover. Go to the library and read detective story anthologies and single-author collections. Get *Woman's World*'s guidelines and study them.

When ideas come to mind, play with them until you see how you can fit them into the framework of a *Woman's World* short-short and tell them in however many words the stories run. Work on each one until it's just right, and then send it to *Woman's World.* When it comes back, send it someplace else. If it sells, congratulations.

14

If you want to sell a short story to *The Atlantic,* read all kinds of short stories. Chekhov might be a good place to start. Read novels, too. Also cookbooks, encyclopedias, back copies of *TV Guide,* and the backs of cereal boxes. Look at sunsets. Cultivate your garden.

When you get an idea for a story, write it. Don't pay any attention to whether the theme or length or style is appropriate for *The Atlantic,* or indeed for any particular market. Concentrate exclusively on making it the very best story you can write. If it gets completely out of control and runs on for 80,000 words, do not despair. You have not failed as a short-story writer. You have succeeded as a novelist.

This probably won't happen. In all likelihood you will wind up with a short story. If you think you could improve on it, do it over. When it's as good as you can get it, stop.

Then read it and try to guess what magazine's requirements it comes closest to fitting. Submit it—to *The Atlantic,* perhaps, and then to *The New Yorker,* and to *Harper's,* and to *Esquire* and *Playboy* and . . . well, it's your story. You figure out where to send it. After the higher-paying markets have all returned it, try the low-pay ones. When you run out of them, send it to the ones that pay in copies.

If, somewhere along the line, it sells—congratulations. And, if it doesn't, so what? You've written a good story, and that's largely its own reward.

15

Meher Baba, the Indian holy man, was a powerful spiritual leader and teacher. He was also the sort to make Calvin Coolidge look like a blabbermouth. At one point Meher Baba did not utter a sound for 18 years.

The greatest teachers don't really have to say a whole lot; much of their message seems to be transmitted at the psychic level, and being in their presence is of itself a transformational experience. Nevertheless, when a fellow goes 18 years without saying a word, his occasional utterances get listened to with respect.

One thing Meher Baba liked to say was: "Don't worry. Be happy."

If you're going to write short stories, those words belong on the wall over your desk.

By the Time I Get
to Phoenix I'll be Working

July 1988

A NOVELIST TAKES TO THE ROAD, AND WRITES BY NOT
WRITING.

Good morning, boys and girls.

Good morning, sir.

And what a glorious morning it is! Here I am, standing up in front
of you and conducting this class (or, if you want to be painfully literal
about it all, sitting at my desk writing this column) on the morning
of Super Bowl Sunday. The sun here in Fort Myers Beach is shining
brightly enough to gladden the hearts of the tourists, not to mention
the local Chamber of Commerce. As they say in the cat food commercials, it doesn't get a whole lot better than this.

By the time you read this, however, some of you may have to stop
and think for a minute to recall who won the Bronco-Redskin face-off
this afternoon. And Fort Myers Beach will long since have faded in my
rear-view mirror. Four days from now, we're out of here. We're taillights.
We are, like, *gone.*

Where are you going, sir?

Anywhere and everywhere, Rachel. But I suppose that's a little vague.
That's not entirely inappropriate—our plans are deliberately vague, in
order to allow plenty of room for the unexpected, but we have a fair

idea of what's on our immediate agenda, albeit it's subject to change without notice.

When we leave here Thursday morning we'll be heading north as far as Buffalo, Alabama. (We're collecting Buffaloes this trip. I was born in Buffalo, New York, and there are a lot of other towns in America named Buffalo, most of them the merest dots on the map, and we want to see how many we can get to. Don't ask why.) Then we'll cut down to Mobile, and then up to Meridian, Mississippi, to check out the Jimmie Rodgers museum, and then across to Natchez, and then down through Buffalo, Texas, to visit a friend in Austin. And on into New Mexico to see kin in Roswell and Albuquerque, and on to Santa Fe and to Denver, where we'll be taking a seminar.

Then we fly to New York to participate in the Mohonk Mystery Weekend Donald Westlake produces every year. Then off to Egypt for a two-week spiritual retreat on the Nile. Then back to Albuquerque to pick up the car and a quick trip west to Sedona, Arizona. Then back to Santa Fe, where we'll conduct a two-day Write for Your Life seminar at Sunrise Springs. Then out to Anaheim, California, for the American Booksellers Association convention, and then—

Sir?

Yes, Arnold?

I hate to bring this up, sir, but the question does arise.

I'll bet it does.

So I'll ask it. When are you going to be doing your writing, sir?

Ah. I'm glad you asked me that. (There was a President once who said that to give himself time to think of an answer.) But I really am grateful for the question, because it's one a great many people have been asking me upon hearing about the trip, and it gives me a chance to make a point.

I'll be writing all the time.

Or, more accurately, I'll be pursuing and advancing my writing career all the time. Because, the way things stand right now, the best thing I can do for myself *as a writer* is what I'm setting out to do—going new places, seeing old and new people, taking seminars, expanding psychic and spiritual horizons, and letting all those elements flow into me that will, sometime in the future, find expression in something I come to write.

When will I do my work? *This* is my work—to recharge those creative batteries that have been quite properly exhausted in my work to date. Or, to vary the metaphor slightly, there is a time to drive and a time to fill the gas tank. You don't reach your destination faster by running on empty; indeed, you may not get there at all.

Hang a Write at the Corner

Sometimes the most important thing a writer can do is write.

This is most often the case at the onset of one's writing career. Many of us start out not so much wanting to write as wanting to *be* writers, and published writers at that. I had a note the other day from a friend of a friend, explaining that he was 40 pages into his first novel and wanting to know what agent to send it to. He had no prior writing experience, he had ten or fifteen percent of the book done, and he was in a rush to get it sold. I told him to finish the book first, and this was by no means what he was hoping to hear.

For most of us, the thing to do when we're starting out is to write. It scarcely matters what we write, or how well we write, and it certainly doesn't much matter what we do with what we write. In fact, the less we focus on the whole idea of publication, the better off we probably are. What's important is that we write a lot, and on a daily basis.

But there are other times when too strict a focus on production is an impediment to growth. Writing every day keeps one writing much the same thing every day.

An example from my own career comes readily to mind. I spent my first several years as a writer turning out soft-core sex novels for a couple of paperback houses. I produced a lot—a book a month minimum, and sometimes as many as 20 books a year—and I can see now that I was using the quantity of my work to keep me from focusing on the quality of my work. As long as I was producing salable pages every day, I didn't have to try something more ambitious with the attendant risk of failure and embarrassment. The more I wrote, the less opportunity I gave myself to grow and develop and extend my success.

If I had any doubts about what I was doing, I told myself I had no real choice, that I needed the sure money that was mine if I wrote what I knew I could sell. I have since seen a great many writers make this kind of choice at one or another stage of their careers; they tell themselves they can't afford to take risks, or to write less, or to stop writing one kind of book and move on to another, because they need the money.

Similarly, I watched a friend of mine use that sort of excuse to avoid being a writer altogether. The author of several published novels, he kept insisting he wanted to quit his hated job in advertising and write full-time. His wife finally made him believe she meant it when she said they could both live on her salary while he established himself as a writer; the next thing you knew, they were expecting a baby. As soon as she was ready to function as a working mother, and once again prepared to support the family while he got going as a freelance writer, he moved them all from an affordable apartment to an expensive house in the suburbs. He kept insisting that financial considerations kept him from taking the plunge, but in point of fact he kept *creating* financial considerations to keep himself safely out of the pool.

Five-Speed Transmission

There's a process we sometimes recommend at the Write for Your Life seminar. You do it every night before going to bed. At the top of a sheet of paper you write: *Five Things I Did Today to Advance My Writing Career.* And then you list them.

The point of this process is two-fold. First, it lets you acknowledge yourself for actions you've taken during the day on your own behalf as a writer. This is always valuable, but it is especially so on days when nothing got written. The poisonous guilt with which we afflict ourselves on nonwriting days is lifted somewhat when we allow ourselves to see that we have indeed been busy as writers, even if no words got on the page.

Second, the process allows you to program yourself subconsciously; during the day, a part of your mind is busy leading you to perform actions that will belong on the list you'll be making that night. Thus you're that much more likely to do things to advance your writing career.

Sometimes you'll have the sort of list Isaac Asimov would be proud of:

1. Wrote 60 pages of *Three if by Air.*
2. Sent query letters to *Modern Bride, Mausoleum Manager's Digest, Let's Crochet* and *The Virginia Quarterly.*
3. Read three books for research on space satellite novel.
4. Interviewed county coroner for background for short story.
5. Had lunch with editor and grabbed check.

On other occasions your list will require more in the way of imagination, and calling it things to advance your writing career may seem like the best fiction you've written all day:

1. Read the morning paper.
2. Went for a long walk, thought about a short story idea, and decided it wasn't worth writing.
3. Called my agent to keep him from forgetting that I'm alive.
4. Read through *Writer's Market,* trying to figure out where to send

the piece that just came back from *Mausoleum Manager's Digest,*
and couldn't find anything.

5. Watched *Wheel of Fortune* and concocted elaborate if unprint-
    able Vanna White fantasy.

The point is that, on the worst of days, you will have taken some positive actions (or avoided some negative actions) on behalf of your career
and identity as a writer. *Decided not to smash my typewriter. Thought about
killing myself but didn't.* I have had days when these items would have
been on my list, and a good thing, too; where would my career as a
writer be otherwise?

At the Wheel

Writing, like just about everything else, is a holistic pursuit. You
don't do it just with your fingertips. You use your entire body and mind
and spirit. And you don't do it just when you're putting words on paper.
You do it every minute of every hour. If you are a writer, you are literally writing whenever you are being yourself. And, of course, the more
completely you are being yourself, the more effectively you are writing.

When will I write during my travels? All the time, obviously. And
when will words get onto the page?

I don't know. Some words will get onto some pages once a month
when I write this monthly letter to all of us. The typewriter will be in
the trunk of the car, and barring bumpy roads it will continue to function. And, bumpy roads or no, so will I.

It is my sense that it will be a while before I'm ready to write my next
novel. *Random Walk* drained my batteries, and it seems nothing less
than appropriate to let them draw a long charge. But at the same time
I have come to know that changes happen very quickly sometimes, and
that books can suggest themselves at a moment's notice. When it's time

to write the next book, I'll probably know it; knowing it, I'll probably do it.

In the meantime, I've got things to do. There are a lot of Buffaloes out there.

12

No, But I Saw the Movie

August 1988

Just recently I was reading a novel called *The Color of Money*, by Walter Tevis.

This was my second reading; I read it for the first time right after it came out. It was published in 1984 as an original Warner Books paperback. I'm not entirely sure why the book didn't appear in hardcover first. Most if not all of Tevis's previous novels did, including, most recently *The Queen's Gambit*, which sold well and garnered good reviews not long before the publication of *The Color of Money*.

The decision to go paperback original may well have been based on the nature of the book. *The Color of Money*, as you may know, is a sequel to *The Hustler*, taking up the life and career of pool hustler Fast Eddie Felson some 25 years later. (Right around the same time, several contemporary novelists produced sequels to books they had brought out 20 or 25 years previously. Sloan Wilson, for example, brought us up to date on *The Man in the Gray Flannel Suit*, while Hal Dresner wrote an as-yet-unpublished sequel to *The Man Who Wrote Dirty Books*. And there are more examples, could I but summon them to mind. Why so many writers should spontaneously choose to renew acquaintance with their long-lost fictional friends is something to ponder. Sixties nostalgia? Some arcane line-up of the stars and planets? Beats me.)

In any event, the publisher may have wanted to skip hardcover publication on the grounds that the book's great audience was in paperback, that the continuing popularity of the Newman-Gleason-Scott film guaranteed a large paperback readership, and that a sequel might get short shrift from reviewers anyway. Walter Tevis died around the time the book came out; his health may have been a factor in the decision.

Meanwhile, Back at the Column . . .

As I said (pages and pages ago, it seems), I read *The Color of Money* when it appeared. Then I saw the film version when *it* appeared; it was released late in '86, so that Paul Newman could pick up an Oscar for his role in it the following spring. Then I read the book again, just a couple of weeks ago, and I'll tell you something. The book is better.

I should point out right away that I'm prejudiced. For one thing, I've had three books of my own filmed, two of them fairly recently, and if they weren't better than the movies made from them, I ought to get into another line of work in a hurry. For another, I'm a book writer; it's very much in the natural order of things for me to prefer a novel to the film made from it. Finally, I read the book first, and I've observed that most of us tend to prefer a story in whichever form we first make its acquaintance. (I saw *The Manchurian Candidate* before I read it, for example, and consequently believe John Frankenheimer's film is superior to Richard Condon's novel; had I read the book first, I might think otherwise. And, for that matter, I saw Robert Rossen's film of *The Hustler* before I read the Tevis novel, and at the time preferred the film. Since then I've reread the book and reviewed the movie, and I think they're both just fine.)

In respect to *The Color of Money*, however, the book and film are so utterly different that comparing them may be instructive.

In the book, Fast Eddie has been anything but fast since his retirement from pool a quarter of a century ago. He quit hustling rather than share his winnings with a criminal syndicate, and he married and opened a pool room in Lexington, Kentucky. The book opens with the marriage over and the pool room closed; the tables themselves are being sold off piecemeal as part of the divorce settlement.

Fast Eddie coaxes Minnesota Fats out of retirement so that the two of them can participate in a series of exhibitions sponsored by a cable TV network. In each match, Fats beats Eddie badly, but Eddie is spurred to practice again and work on his game.

Meanwhile, he meets a woman, the ex-wife of a professor at the University of Kentucky. She's a folk art expert, and Eddie responds strongly to the work of some of the local folk artists she has discovered. With his capital and hustling ability and his willingness to plunge in support of his hunches, they buy up the work of several of the best artists and open a gallery. The same characteristics that made Eddie successful as a pool hustler work for him here, and we see him exercising the same muscles.

The exhibition matches end one day when Eddie discovers Fats dead in bed in his hotel room. Eddie, playing pool for money again after all these years, finds that the world has changed. All the action is in nine-ball, a game he has always despised and one he now finds out of his reach. The younger players who win the nine-ball tournaments can do things that seem to be beyond him. At the same time, Eddie finds that playing pool for money is quite simply his life. He unaccountably lost it for 25 years. Now he's found it again, and they've changed the rules, and the kids are better at it than he is.

The denouement, at a top tournament in Nevada, is just wonderful, and I'm not going to spoil it for you.

The Colorized Version

The film is completely different. Fast Eddie 25 years later is still a hustler type, making his money as a liquor salesman. In a bar one night he meets a brash, cocky pool player he recognizes as an enormous natural talent and a reminder of his own younger self. He takes the kid as a protégé. The kid has a girlfriend who is smarter than he is, which is not all that hard to believe, and there's a triangle, and the kid gets jealous. He's also unmanageable, winning games when he's supposed to lose, letting his ego get in the way of his hustle. Tom Cruise plays the role well enough, even as Newman plays Fast Eddie capably. Richard Price's script is good, with some crisp dialogue, and there are some nice scenes and good moments, and if the ending is not terribly illuminating, neither is it a great disappointment. It's not a bad movie. It may even be a good one. But it has nothing to do with the book beyond the fact that it too is a sequel to *The Hustler*, and that it's about pool.

Does that make it a travesty? Did the film's makers do something unconscionable to Walter Tevis's book?

You could argue the point. But you could argue as well that they only did what had to be done in order for the book to work on the screen. After all, when you opened up the book and looked at it, what did you have? The early business with Minnesota Fats doesn't lead anywhere; halfway through the story Fats dies of a heart attack and you're nowhere. Besides, Jackie Gleason isn't about to play the part, and Newman wouldn't work with him anyway, and how are you going to do a sequel with someone else playing Fats, after Gleason made a meal of the part the first time around?

And the whole business of the love story and the folk art gallery, that entire subplot, doesn't go anywhere either. You deal with characters there who don't reappear. It's interesting stuff, but it would just get lost on-screen without advancing the story at all.

No, forget all that. Stick with something you know will work. Keep all the same characters on-screen for the whole movie. Use a nice Oedipal situation, something tried and true. Make Cruise's part almost as prominent as Newman's, so that it comes down to a contest between them and a buddy picture at the same time. Have Paul get drunk in one big scene; after all, he should have gotten an Academy Award for *The Verdict*, so give them a scene to remind them of what they overlooked last time out.

And, whatever you do, keep the whole thing simple. Fast Eddie in the novel has a great deal of dimension. He's more sophisticated than you'd expect in some areas, far less so in others. You don't want to confuse the popcorn-munchers. Keep it all simple, and every once in a while come in tight on Paul's blue eyes, and they'll love it.

Cut! Print It!

I don't mean to imply that *The Color of Money* was filmed quite so cynically. I do know that the people who made the film felt the book did not have a usable storyline, and perhaps they were correct. Perhaps what worked so superbly in the novel would not have survived the transition to the screen.

I wish they'd tried. Tevis was an extremely cinematic writer, given to writing in strong scenes, and it wouldn't be hard to show everything that takes place in the novel. You could change Minnesota Fats to another old-time pool player and get around the Gleason problem easily enough. The folk art scenes could be marvelous, and if you handled it right you could do them justice without losing the audience.

On the other hand, if I had money in the film I probably would have made the same decisions the screenwriter and producer made. Because it costs millions and millions of dollars to make a movie, and do you really want to increase the odds against you just for the sake of aesthetic considerations? Are you going to plunge that heavy on a hunch, a whim? Fast Eddie Felson would, but he's not running a studio.

And what's my point?

I suppose what I keep becoming aware of is what I would call the natural superiority of print to celluloid, of the novel to film. As a book, *The Color of Money* was able to be done as its author wanted it done. As a film, it had to be changed into something altogether unrecognizable, and for what may well have been valid reasons.

Novels are so much richer. There's so much more in almost any book than can possibly wind up on the screen. This is not to say that a book is always superior to the film made from it—on the contrary, sometimes a good film is made of a terrible book, and occasionally a novelist's pedestrian writing and cardboard characters turn into something wonderful on screen. But every halfway decent novel has a slew of bits and elements to it that you have to leave out when you film it. And that's one reason, incidentally, that novelizations of original screenplays are almost always anemic; there's nothing there that wasn't in the film, and there's not enough in a film to make a book of substance.

Is all of this an argument against becoming a screenwriter? No, of course not. You write what works best for you, and what yields the most satisfaction.

But do have a look for yourself at the work of Walter Tevis, a fine novelist who died too young. *The Queen's Gambit,* the story of a female chess prodigy, is a masterpiece, and you no more need to be a chess player to love it than you need to hustle pool to read about Fast Eddie Felson.

Read it and see for yourself. And read *The Color of Money,* too, even if you've seen the movie. *Especially* if you've seen the movie.

13

Prejudice and Pride

September 1988

CATEGORICALLY SPEAKING, WRITERS TEND TO BE KNOWN
BY THE COMPANY THEY KEEP. BUT YOU NEEDN'T BE
LIMITED BY THAT.

This past October I flew to Minneapolis to attend Bouchercon, an annual colloquy of mystery fans and authors. Every year one mystery writer is selected as Guest of Honor, a process of wining and dining and all-around lionizing that is enough to turn the head of a marble statue. Last year was my turn in the barrel, and it was pleasant indeed.

Then in January I was one of a great flock of mystery writers who descended upon Key West for a literary symposium on the mystery novel. Like everybody else, I appeared on a couple of panels. One of mine was called "Western Cultural Attitudes as Reflected in the Contemporary American Mystery Novel." (As you may imagine, this was a topic close to my heart; rarely do I sit down to the old Smith-Corona without asking myself, "Well, old horse, what are you gonna do today to reflect Western cultural attitudes?")

It's the end of February now, and I'm in New Mexico, typing these lines. In a week or so Lynne and I fly east to spend a pair of weekends at Mohonk Mountain House, up the Hudson from New York, where we'll be participating as suspects in one of Donald E. Westlake's annual mystery weekends. (The guests, divided into teams, try to solve an original mystery by grilling the suspects, who remain in costume and character during this process. Then the teams put on original skits of their own advancing their respective solutions. It is, I assure you, more fun than it sounds.) The play this year is a takeoff on '40s private eye films, and I play a nightclub bouncer named Wilmer Gunsel, while Lynne is typecast as Helen Hunt, a torch singer. (Westlake's the private eye, and *his* name is Phillip Screwdriver, and I wish I'd thought of that.)

After that's over, or possibly between the two weekends, I'm supposed to participate in some sort of transatlantic conference call with British mystery writer P.D. James and with mystery critic and journalist Marilyn Stasio, who will be writing up our exchange. Then, in May, I really ought to attend the annual Mystery Writers of America get-together in New York, especially since it's an international meet this year.

At the end of June, if all goes well, I'll be spending two weeks in Spain and Italy as an American representative of the International Association of Crime Writers. In mid July there's a writers' conference in Rochester, New York, focusing on the mystery; I may turn up there, if I can fit it in.

In October *Random Walk* comes out.

It's not a mystery.

The Making of a Mystery Writer

The point of the foregoing is not to impress you with how well I'm doing or what an exciting life I lead. (Actually, if you live long enough and keep on writing the damn stuff, and if you're not too offensive to too many people, and if word gets around that you don't eat your peas with your knife or pass out at inappropriate moments, you get your share of these perks. It helps if somebody somewhere likes what you write, but it isn't always absolutely necessary.)

Anyway, my motive for boring you with all this is to stress the extent to which I am identified as a writer of mysteries. This is to be expected;

the great proportion of my work over the years has been in the field of mystery and suspense. The books, to be sure, have differed considerably from one another, ranging from lighthearted mystery through hard-boiled private eye and foreign intrigue to psychological suspense. Still, in the mystery house are many mansions, and most of what I've written can find a room therein.

A friend of mine, a woman with a checkered career in film and publishing, most recently settled in as the proprietor of a Greenwich Village shop that sells exotic soap. When an assistant asked her how she'd gotten into the business, she replied in some temper that no one ever set out to become the keeper of a soap emporium, that one did not graduate from college and move to New York with the goal of purveying scented soap to yuppies, that on the contrary it was the sort of thing one found oneself doing when one realized that Other Things Had Not Worked Out.

My own emergence as a mystery writer was not quite so unintentional, but I can't say that I set out specifically with that goal in mind. As best I recall, I initially wanted to be up there in the pantheon of great American realists, a linear successor to Stephen Crane and Sherwood Anderson and Wolfe and Hemingway and Farrell and Steinbeck and O'Hara. At the same time, I was willing—nay, eager—to write absolutely anything that someone would actually print. I sold my first story to a mystery magazine (although in its initial version the story was by no means a mystery story) and its acceptance had something to do with the direction of my future efforts. I didn't go on writing mysteries simply because I found some measure of acceptance in the field. I also found that the kinds of stories I wanted to tell lent themselves to the genre. And, after enough years of this, I turned around one day and discovered that I was a mystery writer.

Prejudicial Treatment

What does it mean to be a practitioner of a particular genre of fiction?

For one thing, it means that certain people who otherwise wouldn't read your books will, and that others who might otherwise read them with pleasure will carefully avoid them. There is a reason why bookstores and libraries put all the mysteries in one place, all the westerns in another, all the science fiction in a third. Many readers are categorically inclined; while they will occasionally pick up a plump bestseller, or a work of capital-L Literature, the bulk of their recreational reading will be confined to one or two categories. One person will read almost any science fiction novel, unless it is by an author he has learned to detest, but would never bring home a western no matter whose name is on the cover. Another will read anything *but* science fiction.

"I have to confess I'm not familiar with your work," I've heard more than a few times, "because I never read mysteries." The admission always strikes me as curious. I can no more imagine a reader who would dislike all mysteries than I can envision one who would like everything published in the field.

Not long ago I was talking with someone who had recently discovered Elmore Leonard, and who had read his way through all of Leonard's contemporary novels and couldn't wait for the next one. Had he read any of Leonard's westerns? He had not, and shook his head at the suggestion that he try them. "I don't read westerns," he said.

My Uncle Hi is a very different sort of reader. When he finds a writer whose work he enjoys, he reads everything the person has written. It doesn't matter what category a book is in; what matters to him is the style and sensibility of its author. "I read authors," he says.

For my part, I can't imagine how anyone could enjoy Dutch Leonard's contemporary suspense novels and fail to enjoy his westerns. The only difference between the books is their setting. Leonard always

writes the same sort of book, a story of more or less ordinary human be-
ings caught up in a more or less desperate set of circumstances. Whether a particular story is set in Detroit in the 1980s or Arizona a century
earlier seems a relatively unimportant distinction. If you like the one,
you'll like the other.

Same goes for other writers who labor in more than one vineyard.
Loren Estleman, another Detroiter, writes westerns when he's not
chronicling private eye Amos Walker. Bill Pronzini, best known as a
mystery writer, has written some fine westerns that are not unlike his
mysteries in structure and style. Brian Garfield began as a writer of
westerns and has moved into the suspense field. Isaac Asimov is equally
at home in science fiction and mystery, and has written some books that
fit both genres at once.

If you like any of these writers in one genre, you'll like him in another. Unless, of course, you look at the label instead of the cloth, and
make your judgment in advance. (That's what prejudice is, of course.
Pre-judging.)

And all of us do this to some extent, in some area or other. Not long
ago, dial-hopping on the radio, I picked up a station and found myself
enjoying the record that was playing. Then I realized it was Punk Rock,
and I remembered that I hate Punk Rock, and I stopped enjoying the
record. I know that's ridiculous, but it's no more ridiculous than ruling
out westerns or mysteries or science fiction or romance or historical
novels or whatever you're convinced you don't like. I think it's legitimate
to say that, all things being equal, I'm more likely to enjoy one genre of
fiction than another. But all things aren't equal, not when you get down
to individual cases, and if I let myself rule out certain books categorically I'm as much handicapped by my prejudices as if I operate that way
in the field of interpersonal relationships.

Another prejudice relates to category fiction as a whole. Many readers, including some who read category fiction as well as many who

don't, take it for granted that mysteries and westerns and science fiction novels and so on are automatically less consequential than mainstream uncategorized fiction. The genre novel is presumed to be of less substance, to have little purpose beyond escape and entertainment, and to be a far cry from Art or Literature.

At the same time, some of the people who read and/or write in a category, will argue that mysteries (or westerns, or whatever) are intrinsically *superior* to mainstream writing, that they are more honest and less pretentious, that they have more right to be taken seriously than do those books and writers that take themselves so seriously.

I think either position is fundamentally silly. According to the first point of view, there is no such thing as great category fiction because, once a book is great, it stands outside of its category. *Hamlet* is a detective story, *Les Misérables* and *Crime and Punishment* are crime fiction, but because these works are Literature they are no longer considered mysteries.

(The publishing world operated under a similar Catch-22 until recently. A mystery, it was generally acknowledged, was a book that sold between 4,000 and 6,000 hardcover copies irrespective of who wrote it or how well it had been written. Whenever a mystery writer sold 15,000 or 20,000 or 50,000 copies, he or she ceased to be a mystery writer and became instead a brand name. Conversations like this ensued: "We're not going to bother advertising your book because we sell 4,000–6,000 copies of a mystery whether we promote it or not." "What about Agatha Christie?" "Oh, that's Agatha Christie." "What about Ross Macdonald?" "Oh, that's Ross Macdonald." "Well, what about me? What am I, chopped liver?")

I suppose it is legitimate to say that *most* category fiction is of less consequence than most mainstream fiction, if only because a book can be published in any of the genres that has no purpose beyond escape and entertainment. Once this was true of mainstream fiction, but now, with the near-disappearance of the midlist book, a mainstream novel has to be more than a pleasant little read to get itself published. It must have either a strong topical hook or genuine bestseller potential or at least the illusion of true artistic merit. It is still enough that a genre book be entertaining, and thus some of them are not much more than that.

Making Your Own Choice

These are all thoughts that may be of some value in helping you decide in what area to concentrate your own efforts—to whatever extent these are choices we get to make. Over the years, it seems to me, I've pretty much written the books I wanted to write, or was given to write. I'm sure some of my books turned out the way they did because I had come to think of myself as a mystery writer, but I can't recall ever taking a story that I'd have preferred to write without a mystery-suspense element and forcing such an element into it.

I wonder now, with *Random Walk* soon to be published, whether its reception will be adversely affected by the general perception of its author as a mystery writer. As far as a segment of the reading and reviewing public is concerned, to be sure, a writer of category fiction is not to be taken seriously, even when he steps outside of his category. This may not seem fair, but whoever said life was fair? I know several writers who've used pen names on noncategory books, not out of lack of pride in them but to avoid being the victims of just the sort of prejudice we've been talking about.

I never seriously considered doing this. It's my book, and the last thing I want to do is hide the fact. Besides, I want the people who've liked my other books to have a chance to see if they like this one. I'm hoping a lot of them are like my Uncle Hi, who reads writers, not categories.

14

The Ripening Process

October 1988

TIPS FOR MAKING YOUR FICTION AS TANTALIZING AS FINE
WINE.

I always liked those dotty wine commercials Orson Welles used to do.
In a tone we might properly label stentorian, he would announce, "We
will sell no wine before its time." He managed to convey the implication that such a policy represented the highest possible moral and ethi-
cal stance on the vintner's part, that there was even something self-sac-
rificing in postponing immediate sales for sake of the consumer's palate.

If Mr. Welles were here, I might just quote William Blake at him. "If
you trap the moment before it's ripe," the poet noted, "the tears of re-
pentance you'll certainly wipe." Now it seems to me that—yes, Arnold?

I didn't realize that Blake wrote for the Hallmark people, sir.

The couplet does have a sort of greeting card cadence to it, doesn't
it? I'd say it's as well for Mr. Blake's reputation that he also wrote other
things. But never mind. The point here is that it's no more than en-
lightened self-interest to sell no wine before its time, lest you wind up
peddling wine that no one much wants to buy. The ripening process is
an essential one, and to cut it short is to court disaster.

And this, I would suggest, is as true for fiction as for claret. A story
must ripen in the mind as surely as must wine in a cellar. The metaphor goes only so far, because the ripening stage comes at a different
time with the two delicate commodities. Wine is aged after it has been

produced, while fiction often needs aging while it is in the idea stage, before a single word has landed upon the page.

I was not born knowing this. When I first began writing, shortly after the invention of movable type, I would generally sit down at the typewriter as soon as an idea came to mind—or even before. A few years ago I went through a batch of my early stories while putting together an anthology, and in a few instances it was easy to see that I had not given my ideas time to ripen. The stories were thin; one idea imperfectly grasped had been rapidly spun into a story. And in a couple of instances it looked to me as though I had started *without* an idea, simply sitting down and writing a scene and letting a plot find its way to me. Sometimes this had worked well enough so that a marginally publishable story had resulted, but I could see the story's genesis in the finished work; it took too long getting started, and it wasn't shaped and crafted as well as it might have been.

Rachel, you look troubled.

Sir, I just wonder if you should be telling us all this.

Admitting I have in years past occasionally written a less than perfect story?

No, sir. I think we all knew that. But you seem to be saying there's an advantage in putting things off, and I think it's dangerous to give that sort of advice to people for whom procrastination is so often a problem. Sir.

Procrastination's not a problem, Rachel. I've told you that. Procrastination is a symptom. When you have a cold, Rachel, sniffling isn't the problem. The infection is the problem, and sniffling is the symptom. Writers do often procrastinate, and we do tend to think that's the problem, when the real problem is the particular self-doubt or anxiety or fear or mental conflict that leads us to procrastinate. But I've told you all that before.

Repeatedly, sir.

Letting a story idea ripen isn't procrastination—or, if it is, it's what I called it in an earlier column, "Creative Procrastination," which you can find as a chapter in *Telling Lies for Fun and Profit* (Arbor House). I find myself returning to the theme because of experiences I've had writing a pair of short stories this past month.

Several months ago I got the idea of writing about a grown man who sleeps with a teddy bear. I wasn't sure—

Sir, how did you happen to get the idea?

That's none of your business, Arnold. As I was saying, I wasn't sure what it was an idea for. I thought it would probably work best as a short story, then gave some consideration to the idea of writing it as a novel, then decided I'd probably been right the first time, that it would go best as a short story.

But it wasn't a story yet. It wasn't even the plot for a story. All it was, really, was the tiniest germ of an idea. A good idea, it seemed to me, and one that might well develop into something nice, but a long cry from a blueprint for a successful piece of fiction.

Fortunately we were traveling at the time, somewhere between Buffalo, Mississippi, and Buffalo, Texas. Otherwise I might have tried to write the story then and there, and I don't think I would have done a very good job of it. Instead I thought about it for a while, and then I forgot about it.

Some people would criticize this last step as unnecessarily perilous. I could have made a note to myself, as I occasionally do and often recommend to others. Lately, however, I find myself rarely making notes of ideas, trusting that the good ones will linger in some dark corner of the mind while the rest are better off forgotten. I'm by no means certain this is true, but it's the way I seem to operate.

In this instance, I did not completely forget the idea. It would come now and then to mind, occasionally after a glimpse of a stuffed animal, but sometimes with no obvious circumstantial prompting. All that happened on such occasions was that I would recall the idea and agree that it was a sound one, and that someday I would have to do something with it. But further plot elements did not surface. It remained, to all outward appearances, the same mere fragment it had always been.

Then in May I found myself in Sedona, Arizona, with a month to work on a novel. After a few days it became clear that I was not really ready to write the novel. I sifted through that rag-and-bone-shop I call my mind, and the teddy bear idea presented itself.

I thought about it. And, mysteriously, a plot began to form itself. I still didn't really know exactly where the story was headed, but I had a sense of who the lead character might be, and what kind of circumstances would lead him to start sleeping with the bear, and what effect this might have on his life.

The next day I sat down to write the story, and within the week I had finished it. It was, I am certain, a vastly superior effort to what I would have turned out if I'd gone to work on it earlier, and not because of anything I had done. Because, in point of fact, I hadn't done anything—not on a conscious level, at least. I had simply allowed the idea to ripen, and some other-than-conscious area of my mind had taken the opportunity to work on it. And, when I was ready to write it, there was something there to write.

"Some Days You Get the Bear" was one of two stories I wrote in Sedona. The other, "A Date with the Butcher," was supposed to be a novel. It illustrates another stage in the ripening process, and I think it may be instructive.

Early in April I spent a sleepless night on a train. While it was not an experience I would hasten to repeat, some good did come of it; as I lay there bouncing around, the plot of a mystery novel came to me. It came in a flood, as such things sometimes do, with scenes and characters all vitally alive. I had the feeling that, if I were able to sit down immediately in a room with a typewriter and a stack of blank pages, I could turn out an entire book as rapidly as I could type.

Well, I often have that feeling, especially when I dream an idea or hatch it during a sleepless night. There's a certain suspension of the critical sense that may be essential in order for creativity to surge that way, and as a result I may think I have a more fully developed notion than I do, or that everything's sound when in fact there are some snags. In this case I did indeed have a good plot, and it was indeed quite well developed, but when I settled in to write it I found out I wasn't really ready. I didn't know as much as I ought to have about several of the characters. And the book needed a strong secondary plotline or it was going to be awfully thin. I found this out after I'd written 30 pages of it, and I think I probably could have pushed on and finished the book, and that it probably would have been acceptable, that I would have been able to publish it. But I was able to visualize a better book than I was at that stage able to write, and I knew the only way to realize that better book was to let the story ripen.

In this instance, I decided to aid and abet the ripening process by writing the idea right away—but as a short story. By condensing my central plotline into a long short story (it ran about 9,000 words by the time I was done with it), I was able to strengthen my grasp of the story enormously. I knew a lot more about the characters, about the pace and mood of the story, about its whole shape and tone and flavor, than I had known before I wrote it. And, by writing it as a short story, I programmed my subconscious to play with it in the coming months. Sometime in the fall I'll probably be ready to write the book version, and at that point I hope and trust it will be ready for me to write it.

Flourishing on the Vine

Sometimes this same ripening process happens with projects that look as though they've been abandoned. As I've noted often enough, I have on many occasions had books go dead on me after 20 or 50 or 100 or even 200 pages. There's something wrong, with either me or the book, and there's no point going on. Sometimes I save those stillborn darlings, hoping there'll be a way to save them. More often I toss them.

Years later I'm apt to find that what I thought was rotting actually was ripening. In 1977 I wrote almost 200 pages of a book about a pimp; four years later elements of that failed effort transformed themselves into elements of *Eight Million Ways to Die*. Similarly, a key component of "A Date with the Butcher" had its origin in a detective novel that petered out after 40 pages back in '83.

This is not uncommon, and it's one reason why many writers save every scrap they write. I tend to take the opposite tack, feeling that what's worth saving is not what I've put on the page (which after all didn't work in the first place) but what remains rooted in the subconscious. Even when I do save aborted manuscripts, I've found I almost never reread them before using the material anew. The manuscript of my pimp novel was right there in the drawer while I wrote *Eight Million Ways to Die*, and I never once hauled it out and looked at it.

I suppose there's a moral to all of this. Can any of you think of it? Yes, Rachel?

We will publish no fiction before it's ripe.

I'm not altogether sure I like the sound of that, Rachel. Arnold?

Never put off until tomorrow what you can postpone indefinitely.

Ah, there's the rub! Because I quoted only part of Blake's poem to you: here's the complete quatrain:

> *If you trap the moment before it's ripe,*
> *The tears of repentance you'll certainly wipe;*
> *But if once you let the ripe moment go,*
> *You can never wipe off the tears of woe.*

The trick, of course, lies in judging the moment of ripeness, and different fruits have different ripening times. *Random Walk*, my latest novel, was ready to be written ten days after the idea for it flashed into my mind. It would have been folly to delay. On the other hand, one major component of *Random Walk* had its origin in a novel I tried to write four years ago, and discarded after 140 pages. I suppose the answer may be that none of a writer's time is wasted—not the time you spend writing, and not the time you spend not writing, and not even the time you spend writing stuff that doesn't go anywhere. It's all part of the process, and perhaps it's the nature of the process to remain mysterious.

15

Fiction to Order?

November 1988

SHOULD YOU CONSIDER SLANTING YOUR FICTION TO
SPECIFIC MARKETS, THE WAY THE NONFICTION WRITERS
DO?

Just when do you start marketing your story? To what extent is a piece of fiction affected by where you plan to submit it?

These questions came up for me while writing a couple of short stories. In each, considerations arose that had to do with more than pure literary artistry. I found myself thinking not only about producing the best possible story, but also of what I would do with the story after I'd written it, and how to so write the piece as to facilitate its sale.

Now if you, Gentle Reader, are primarily a writer of magazine nonfiction, you'll probably greet the last paragraph with a yawn and a big "So what?" Magazine articles are almost always slanted, their style and substance deliberately tailored to meet the needs of a specific targeted publication. Most are written to order, a query letter has led to a firm assignment to write the piece or at the least an invitation to proceed on spec. One of the chief reasons for querying nonfiction editors is so that one can feel free to slant an approved piece strongly in the direction of the editor who has approved it. Having secured this approval, the writer can produce a piece neither longer nor shorter than the editor would prefer, taking an approach the editor favors, and matching the tone and style and thematic approach of the magazine itself. If the piece doesn't work out, if the editor winds up rejecting it, the author might indeed rewrite it substantially before submitting it elsewhere, with the aim of reslanting it for a new prospective buyer.

As fiction writers, we like to think we are above this sort of thing. Our stories are works of art entire unto themselves. Not that we're ivory tower airheads; once we've written the stories our way, we take a hard line on reality when it comes to marketing them. But the marketing is the cart, and we take care not to place it before the horse. First we write, and then we market.

Or do we?

Let's get specific. The first of my two stories is a whimsical yarn about a grown man who sleeps with a teddy bear. I got the idea for the story a few months back when I found myself in bed with just such an animal for reasons I don't care to go into just now. (I have, let it be said, shared similar quarters with less appropriate companions in my day, so I make no apologies for this latest instance.) At the time I knew no more about the story than my one-sentence description conveys, so I let it brew for a while, until I felt ready to write it.

Now I was unquestionably willing to write the story for its own sake. If you're not, you really shouldn't be writing short stories. The paying market is so small, the rates of payment so low, and the odds against publication so high, that the entire occupation is commercially indefensible. The only way to make the business of short-story writing cost-effective is to rechannel your energies elsewhere.

All this notwithstanding, I did not even sit down to the typewriter without considering where I might place my as-yet-unwritten story. I took it pretty much for granted that the first publisher to see the story would be *Playboy*. I have sold there, and the magazine's fiction editor, Alice Turner, has long been enthusiastic about my work. Moreover, *Playboy* is at the top in terms of payment and prestige. Even if my story should turn out to be a very unlikely bet for them, I would automatically give them first look.

The story was begun, then, with the expectation of its submission to *Playboy* and the hope of its acceptance. Did this influence the personality of my lead character?

I think it must have. I didn't know much about him when I sat down to write the thing. I made him a film critic, divorced, with an apartment in New York's Greenwich Village. Did the *Playboy* image and the *Playboy* audience profile induce me to equip him with a glamorous career and a sophisticated lifestyle? I made his marriage a childless one. Did I do so out of some unconscious conviction that a *Playboy* reader would sooner identify with an unencumbered bachelor than a weekend father?

When I began the story, I had no idea how it would end. (I barely knew how it would open.) The ending to which the story found its way involved my hero's beginning a relationship with a provocative young woman with her own nocturnal idiosyncrasy. Had I had a different destination in mind for the piece, I might well have been led to a different ending. For a more determinedly serious market than *Playboy,* I might have rejected this ending as too pat and might have ended the story with my lad socially and emotionally isolated from others, his involvement with the bear having facilitated a process of withdrawal that began with his divorce. For a science fiction and fantasy audience, I might have had the bear take on a personality of its own, even manipulating my character emotionally and interfering in his relationships with women.

I don't think I compromised my story's artistic integrity by writing it as I did. I can't think of an ending I'd be happier with, irrespective of marketing considerations. I don't know of anything I included to make Alice happy (although as I wrote certain lines I let myself imagine her chuckling over them), nor did I leave anything out for fear of alienating her.

Still, the whole shape and texture of the story owes something to my thoughts about its future. It is true, certainly, that I wrote the story for myself. But it is also true that I wrote it for *Playboy*.

Now that it's written, there'll be no more slanting. If "Some Days You Get the Bear" leaves Alice Turner underwhelmed, I won't revise it before submitting it elsewhere. It is not that sort of a suit of clothes, to be retailored for each prospective customer. But I can't deny that there was some tailoring in advance.

Trains of Thought

The other piece didn't set out to be a short story. It was going to be a book, but it wound up 300 pages too short.

A month earlier, rattling along one night from Luxor to Cairo in what the Egyptian railroad dares to call a sleeping compartment, I got an idea for a book. (I'll write about this one of these months; it was an interesting example of how plots come to you.) As soon as we got back to the States, I set about finding a place to pitch camp and write the thing. We're nomads these days, but I wanted to light long enough to get all or part of the book done.

Ah, well. Like the best-laid mice, this plan went astray. We settled down in Sedona, Arizona, in a rented condo, and I wrote 30 pages of the book and discovered that I didn't have a full enough plot yet. It needed more time to fill out.

Then I remembered something. A couple of years ago I wrote a long short story about my detective hero, Matthew Scudder. (It was, coincidentally enough, my previous sale to *Playboy*.) Subsequently, I greatly expanded that story, from 8,500 words to perhaps 90,000, and it was published as the novel *When the Sacred Ginmill Closes*.

The new plot, hatched on that lousy train, also involved Scudder. While it had begun as a book idea, why couldn't I write it first as a short story? It struck me that this could serve to tighten my grip on the plot, and to stir my subconscious so that, in a couple of months or so, I would have the secondary plot line that was lacking.

And perhaps the short story might do me some good in and of itself. "By the Dawn's Early Light," the predecessor to *Ginmill,* netted me the Shamus and Edgar awards and a place in the first Private Eye Writers of America anthology; while you can't make a living writing short stories, this is not to say that they don't ever pay their way.

How did I slant "A Date with the Butcher" (which is what I called the new story)?

Again, I wrote it knowing that Alice Turner would be the first editor to see it, and in the earnest hope that she would like what she saw. I also knew that I could expect a receptive reading at *Ellery Queen,* where a majority of my stories over the last decade have appeared, and at *Alfred Hitchcock,* where two previous Scudder novelettes have been published.

With this particular story, length looked to be a consideration. While *Playboy* has no strict length requirements for fiction, my sense of things was that a detective story that ran much past 7,500 words might seem disproportionately long. I could allow myself more room as far as the two crime fiction magazines were concerned; my earlier novelettes for *Hitchcock* had run 12,000 and 13,000 words.

"A Date with the Butcher" wanted to run long. Remember, it had been an unwritten novel before it decided to become a short story. I had an elaborate main plot line and I couldn't abridge it too radically without sacrificing something.

From the first sentence, I made a conscious effort to keep it short. I left out bits of business I knew I would eventually include in the book. I skipped some scenes and summarized others.

At the same time, I tried not to leave out too much. I kept reminding myself that my paramount goal was to produce the best possible story, that if I stuck to that goal, everything else would sort itself out. The story, when I was done with it, ran around 9,000 words. It is, on the one hand, rather longer than what I would think would be ideal for a *Playboy* submission. At the same time, it is shorter than it would be had I intended it for submission initially to *Queen* and *Hitchcock*; I might very well have written it 15,000 words long. (This is not to say that those magazines publish many stories that long, but that I would have felt comfortable submitting this particular story to them at that length.)

I think that the story is best at its current length—but perhaps I'd just prefer to see it that way. I wouldn't like to think that I did less than my best work out of commercial considerations, yet I can't deny the presence of such considerations in my consciousness while I wrote the thing.

Another judgment call in "A Date with the Butcher" concerned language. Neither of the crime fiction magazines tend to print the unprintable words, or examine unpleasant subjects and details with an excess of candor. (*Queen,* at least, seems to be loosening up in this area; it seems to me that Eleanor Sullivan has been printing stories with themes and lines and words of late that would have been proscribed a few years ago on grounds of taste.)

I allowed myself the same license in the story that I grant myself in my novels, employing what we might in *these* hallowed pages call "the F word." Again, I decided I'd write the thing my way; if an editor liked it, she could make changes, and if she didn't like it enough to do so she probably didn't really want it in the first place.

Earning One's Foolishness

This column, like both of the short stories, is running longer than the publisher might prefer it. But I can't end it without pointing out that I would not have taken the same stance 20 years ago.

Not because I've learned something I didn't know then— although I sincerely hope I have. But because I am in a position now to allow myself a little more in the way of artistic integrity.

If I were just starting out in the business, if editors did not know my work and view it with affection and respect, I would be a damned fool to send *Playboy* a 9,000-word short story, or *Ellery Queen* a novelette with the F word in it. At the current time I know my work is going to get read, and that the reader, while she very well may return it, will at least be reading it in the hope of being able to buy it.

Twenty years ago this was not the case. Twenty years ago my stories had to clear the dreaded First Reader before a top editor ever saw them. First readers have to wade through crap all day long, and they reject hundreds of stories for every one they approve, and if you give them a reason to stop reading your story, stop they will. Twenty years ago, if I had a story where I wanted to use the F word, I might have used it to submit to a magazine with no taboos against the word—but I would have retyped the manuscript before submitting to a magazine with different requirements.

"Some Days You Get the Bear" has some passages and paragraphs that are by no means essential to the story. It's a long story, and I could cut them without hurting it, and it might even be better for their excision. But I like them, and I like the story's pace, so I left them in, trusting that this wouldn't predispose an editor to reject the story. If a new writer showed me the same story, I'd advise him to make the cuts.

Why didn't I make them, if only to increase the story's chances for acceptance? Because the test I applied, finally, was to ask myself what version I'd want to include in my next collection of short fiction. I decided I wanted those passages in, so it seems to me they belong in the manuscript.

It's worth noting, I think, that the better a magazine or book market is, the less necessary it generally is to slant for it. It is the crummiest of genre fiction that is prepared with rigid guidelines in force. And it is the best of editors who let their own sense of appropriateness replace strict guidelines in determining what they publish, and it is the best of publishers who employ good editors and give them their head. If you're trying to sell to a medium that operates within guidelines, obviously you have to follow them—at least until you reach the stage where you can start selling to better markets.

16

Is it Time to Quit Your Day Job?

December 1988

FOR ANSWERS, APPLY WITHIN.

Dear Geoffrey,

I enjoyed our lunch the other day, and, as always, I enjoyed the conversation. Since then I've found myself thinking about some of the things we discussed. I find myself moved to write to you. I also find myself facing a deadline—it's time to write this month's column. A single stone ought to do for both birds; with your indulgence, and my readers', I'll write my column in the form of a letter to your estimable self.

As you'll recall (though it will be new information to the eager multitude of *WD* subscribers), at lunch you recounted some of your recent successes. An article placed here, a short story sold here and anthologized there, another story nominated for a major award in its genre, and a book just published and well received.

Then you went on to mention a letter you had lately received from a novelist friend. He too had been apprised of your recent successes as a writer, and he had some advice. "Geoffrey," he wrote, "it's time for you to quit your day job."

Don't quit your day job, of course, is what a musician says to let another musician know he thinks he's of less than professional caliber. Your friend was telling you that you are indeed ready to join the pro ranks; beyond that, he was saying that the crutch of steady employment was one you no longer needed. Once it had helped keep you steady on your feet, but now it was only slowing you down and holding you back.

But, you went on to say, you had thought it all over and decided you were not about to quit your day job. Full-time freelancing was definitely something you wanted sooner or later, but you were not ready to take the plunge, not just yet. You spoke of rent increases, of the cost of putting children through school, of all the thousand financial ills that flesh is heir to.

And I've been thinking about our conversation ever since.

There are moments when the answer seems very clear to me. "He's absolutely right," I'll say to myself. "He should keep the job. Among other things, it enables the man to enjoy writing. He gets home from the office, he plugs in his word processor, and he's as happy as a buffalo in chips. If he didn't have an office to go to, if he had to start each morning by facing the high-tech equivalent of a blank sheet of paper, he wouldn't be so sanguine about it. Anyway, security's not the worst deal around. Assuming that discontent is inevitable, part of the human condition, isn't it better to be discontented with a steady income than discontented without it? Better to be gainfully employed in an engaging profession and wishing you were writing full-time than hacking away day and night and wishing you had a steady paycheck coming in?"

Another day the opposite answer will seem every bit as self-evident. "He's sick of the damned job," I'll tell myself, "and he's learned as much as he can learn from it and gone as far as he can go with it, and now it's only hobbling him. He's waiting for a perfect time to quit, a safe time, and there is no such thing. You can't step safely into freelance writing. The place is an economic lion's den. Insecurity comes with the territory. But he wants to be sensible and responsible, and he wants to look like (and even to be) a good father and family man, and in the process he's letting his life slip by and missing out on what he really wants to do."

Most of the time, however, I'm not so sure. After all, I rarely know for certain what I should do, so where do I get off making major decisions for other people?

Still, the question demands consideration. Most of us at least start off doing something else for a living, launching our writing careers early in the morning or late at night or on the weekends. Most of us dream of quitting our day jobs, and very likely wonder whether we've held onto the thing too long or let go of it too soon.

In my own case, it took no particular courage for me to begin writing full-time. I started publishing fiction while still in college, and by the time I left I had a publisher who was eager to take a book a month from me. This may sound like guaranteed wealth, but in fact it was hardly that; the fellow paid me $600 a book, or $540 after agent's commission, and this is not a great deal of money now and wasn't great wealth even back then.

Still, it was a living. More to the point, it was at least as much as I could have been confident of earning by any other lawful means. I had left college without a degree, and had never held anything but a menial position, and there was really not a great deal that I was qualified to do.

As you can see, there was an obvious dollars-and-cents argument for my writing full-time. But dollars-and-cents considerations are rarely the primary determinant. The writer's temperament, it seems to me, plays a greater role.

Two contrasting examples spring to mind, both of them writers of thrillers. First let me tell you about a fellow I've known for years. When I first met him he was a couple of years out of college with a gradu- ate degree in history. He was newly married, living in Manhattan, and employed as the slightly underpaid editor of a trade journal. He had recently become friendly with several novelists, myself among them, and decided that he liked the life the rest of us appeared to be living. (He only saw us at parties, at which time we tended to be carefree and drunk, so he very likely thought we were like that all the time. Which, come to think of it, we pretty much were.)

He had never tried writing anything before, but he put his mind to it and came up with what struck him as a good idea for a book. Then one Monday morning he called in sick and started writing, and he kept at it all day. He did the same thing Tuesday, and Wednesday, and on Thursday he called the office again and told them he was quitting. He stayed at his desk five or six days a week for the next six or eight weeks, and at the end of that time he had finished a book.

Well, it was terrible, but that's beside the point. He went on to write a second book, which was still unpublishable but was light-years ahead of the first effort. And he wrote a third book, and that one sold.

And he has been writing and publishing ever since. Not without misadventure—there was a stretch when nothing went right and several books in succession went begging, and he had to take a bartending job. But that was just a bad patch, of the sort to be found in most writing careers. The fact remains that he had managed to go from a standing start and make of himself a published full-time writer in a matter of months.

My contrasting example is an even more successful thriller writer who began publishing while teaching at a large university. While his first few books did not make him rich, his sales increased sharply, and a couple of movie sales boosted his income dramatically. His agent was soon urging him to quit his day job, as it were, especially in view of the fact that he had no deep and abiding love for teaching but had been staying with it because it was steady and secure.

And he had a great deal of difficulty letting go of it. Writing part-time, he was making a healthy six-figure income, yet he found reasons to hang onto his professorship. "I'm not sure I should let go of this," he told a mutual friend. "You know, they've got a really good medical insurance set-up here."

I suppose a big factor in this equation is just how comfortable you are with risk. I don't think there's any way to make freelancing altogether risk-free. Even the writer just mentioned, with his high income and his receptive market, could not insure against the possibility that his creative well might run suddenly dry. As a tenured professor, he could count on a lifelong good income so long as he showed up each day, whether or not he came up with anything inspiring to say to his classes. But writers don't get paid just to show up. They have to produce.

There is no particular virtue in being comfortable with risk; indeed, the world is awash in degenerate gamblers who are distinctly uncomfortable without it. It's true, though, that we're always much quicker to applaud the person who takes a chance than the one who plays it safe. The studio audiences at television game shows always cheer for the lady who gives up the washer-dryer to go for what's behind Curtain Number Three.

It must have been more than 30 years ago that I read an article in *Writer's Digest* by Richard S. Prather, creator of Shell Scott, surely the greatest of the soft-boiled private eyes. Mr. Prather wrote of his decision to quit his job and give writing his best shot. He had realized, he wrote, that nobody starves to death in America, and so he'd set up housekeeping in a trailer and kept at it until, miracle of miracles, he'd written and sold a couple of books.

Nobody starves in this country. That impressed me enormously at the time, and I rather suspect that I've been a little more of a risk-taker for having internalized this bit of wisdom. I don't know that it's as true as it was 30 years ago; the throngs of homeless people on the city streets suggest that, if people don't literally starve to death, some come rather closer to it than I would care to. Still, I know dozens of people who have supported themselves solely and exclusively by writing for a substantial number of years, and none of us has missed meals or been forced to sleep on the subway. Almost all of us have done without things we would have enjoyed having, and almost all of us have gone through times when the wolf was encamped on our doorsteps. And, while I have no hard data on this, it seems to me that almost all of us would do it all again.

Ah, Geoffrey. My conclusion—and it was probably a foregone one—is that I don't know whether or not you should quit your day job. How could I know? How could anyone know but you yourself?

There are, God knows, reasons beyond security for holding onto a job. Some writers go nuts without the human contact that regular employment provides. Some of us draw input from our daily work that enriches our writing. Some of us are freer to take risks in our writing because we've elected to play it safe vocationally. (When I'm tempted to congratulate myself for my daring in setting out as a freelancer, I have to remind myself how long I went on doing sure-thing formula paperback fiction for $600 a book. That was the day job that I had trouble walking away from.)

When all is said and done (and it certainly seems to be), the only advice I'm comfortable giving you is that you do what you want. Not what you feel like doing. Not what you think you should do.

Good luck with that—whatever it turns out to be.

Yours,
Lawrence Block

17

Bouncing One Off the Fourth Wall

January 1989

THE IMPORTANCE OF AN INTIMATE AUDIENCE FOR YOUR STORIES.

A few hours after I finish writing this, my wife, Lynne, will read it.

It doesn't always take a few hours. In the ordinary course of things, I'll type *The End* at the bottom of the last page, put the pages in order, give the thing a cursory proofreading, change a good word to a better one and carry the manuscript to wherever she is. (If we're staying someplace with a washing machine, that's where she can generally be found, feeding socks to the monster.)

"I just finished my column," I'll say. "Wanna read it?"

"Sure," she'll say. Then she'll drop everything (especially socks) and read it, and she'll assure me that it's terrific, and I'll photocopy the thing and ship it off to Cincinnati, where Bill Brohaugh may or may not agree with her.

In the current instance the column will have to wait a few hours before Lynne reads it, and I'll have to wait a few hours more to be assured that it's terrific. That's because it's midnight as I write these lines, and Lynne has quite sensibly gone to sleep. I have no less sensibly gone to work, and shall most likely finish up shortly before dawn, when they say it's always darkest. I'll go to sleep, and a while later she'll get up and read what I've written, and a few hours after that I'll get up and be reassured that I haven't lost my touch, that I can still turn out a column with the best of them and that the world is a better place for my presence in it.

Months later, you'll read all this. And right about now you'll very likely be wondering why I'm telling you all this. "He probably wrote this in the dog days of August," you'll say to yourself, "and the heat must have addled him. How could his wife tell him it was terrific? I mean, what's the point?"

The point, I guess, is that the task of writing this column is not truly complete until Lynne has read it and pronounced it satisfactory. (Oh, in a sense it's not complete even then. The columnization process continues through its submission, through receiving galleys and returning them with corrections, through receiving my check, through seeing the magazine in print and reading letters from grateful or irate readers. But the writing part of the process ends when Lynne reads it.)

Why?

Beats me. I don't suppose I'm any more insecure than the next garden-variety neurotic. I don't sit around trembling until she pronounces my work fit for human consumption. I'll go to bed as soon as I finish this, and concern about her reaction won't keep me awake. As a matter of fact, I don't really need to be concerned about her reaction. Nothing's all that certain in this vale of tears, but I can be reasonably confident that she'll tell me it's a good column. She always does. She may like some of my columns more than others, but her reaction to each of them is invariably positive.

In any event, what does her opinion of the work signify? Unlike the good Mr. Brohaugh, she's not in a position to say yea or nay to the piece. And, unlike you, Gentle Reader, she has no particular interest in the technical problems of the fictioneer; she has sufficient problems, I have no doubt, in living with one.

This is not to say that she never offers any advice. Sometimes she spots a typo that I've missed. Sometimes she'll notice that I've repeated a word or phrase. Sometimes she'll call my attention to an infelicitous turn of phrase or an ambiguous construction. This is helpful, no question, but it's not why I make such a point of having her read it.

Her reading it completes the writing process. Until she reads it, it hasn't really been written.

She's the fourth wall.

The Final Ingredient

The fourth wall.

That's what theater people call the audience; without its presence, the performance is not framed and is consequently incomplete. A piece of fiction (or, in the present example, a magazine column) is similarly incomplete without an audience; like Bishop Berkeley's tree, if it falls unheard, does it even make a sound?

All art is communication, but in none is communication more inherent than in writing. I've discussed this before, in pondering the paramount importance most writers attach to publication. Even those of us for whom writing is very clearly a hobby, a leisure pursuit, are quite single-minded about wanting to see our words in print. If they are not in print, how are they to be read? And, if they are not read, have they truly been written? Do they make a sound? Or do they fall unheard?

Of Compulsions and Collaborators

All of this came into focus for me a week ago when Lynne and I visited Barbara and Max Collins in Muscatine, Iowa. Al writes the Dick Tracy comic strip, along with a prodigious amount of high-quality crime fiction, including a wonderful series of period novels about one Nathan Heller. He works nights, and every morning Barb reads what he's written the night before. She tells him what she thinks of what he's done, and they discuss it, and then he goes on.

As Al explains it, Barb's a sort of collaborator. He has learned over the years to value her input and rework passages and chapters on the basis of her reactions. While he may not always regard her response as the final word, he never takes it lightly.

I couldn't do this. For one thing, I'm too damned pig-headed; when I've managed to get something on paper, the last thing I want is someone telling me how to fix it. To have someone offer suggestions on a work in progress would drive me around the bend.

More to the point, I wouldn't want Lynne (or anyone else) to read chapters of a novel I hadn't yet finished even if she said nothing whatsoever about them. As compulsive as I am about getting her to read my stuff as soon as it's finished, I'm at least as compulsive about keeping her from reading work in progress.

I'm not sure just why this is so. Perhaps I don't want anyone else's mind groping the material until I've finished shaping it. Maybe I'm afraid I won't be able to finish the thing, and I'll be less embarrassed if I haven't already shown some of it to someone. Whatever the underlying reason, for years now I've avoided showing work in progress, and the whole idea of someone reading chapters of an unfinished work gives me the willies.

Some years ago, on two or three occasions I showed chunks of unfinished novels to my agent. In each instance I had gotten stuck on the book and wanted his opinion. Each time he pointed out several serious problems in the work in question and expressed reservations about the project. Each time I sighed, thanked him, nodded thoughtfully, and abandoned the work.

A while later I realized what was going on. I was showing him work in progress only when it was quite emphatically work that had ceased to be in progress, and when I was looking for an excuse to put it in a trunk and slam the lid on it. My agent was cast in the role of Mikey in the cereal commercial. I showed it to him, secure in the foreknowledge that he would hate it, and his negative reaction would absolve me of the need to do any more work on it.

Ever since the penny dropped I've ceased to show him anything until it's finished. He's still apt to dislike it, but by then it's too late.

A Little Bit Nuts

Once I've finished a piece of fiction, I can't wait until it's read.

Lynne is my first reader. When I finished *Random Walk,* I literally could not wait until she read it. I wrote the book at a writers' colony in Virginia, and I drove all the way back to South Florida nonstop. That's around 900 miles, and you have to be a little bit nuts to drive it in one stretch, and I was. I didn't just want her to read the book—I missed the woman, for heaven's sake—but I couldn't wait until she read it.

Part of the intensity of my desire can be attributed to insecurity. The book was a departure for me, and I wanted to be assured that it worked. I knew, too, that she was more likely than anyone I could think of to respond favorably to this particular book; if she didn't like it, I was in trouble.

More than that, I wanted to share the book with her, and to share myself through it. In the deepest sense, everything I write is written in an effort to let people know who and what and where I am. The more important people are to me, the more urgently I want them to become acquainted with those aspects of myself that my work reflects.

Now that I think about it, I showed *Random Walk* to more than the usual number of people. Two of my daughters read it, and my son-in-law, and my mother, and three writer friends. I don't know whether I was moved to show it to so many people out of a greater than usual insecurity and the concomitant desire for reassurance, or because I was working deeper veins of self in this book and felt especially moved to show what I'd unearthed.

A little of both, probably.

Critics and Contracts

I haven't conducted a survey, but it seems to me that most writers show their work to one or more people before trotting it off to market.

Even for those for whom the reaction of a particular agent or editor is of the greatest critical importance, a spouse or friend or lover will commonly serve as a first reader. Most of us have some sort of fourth wall, and most of us have learned to compose that wall of persons who can be expected to look with favor upon what we've produced. Not blindly, not sycophantically, not uncritically—but, yes, favorably.

It's different, of course, when we sense that something's wrong and genuinely need to be told what it is. That's the time when we have to seek out someone on whose critical acumen and integrity we can rely. In ordinary circumstances, however, we want to be told that what we've done is marvelous. Since we don't want to be lied to, we take pains to pick readers likely to love what we've written.

I suspect this kind of fourth wall is at least as important to the un-established writer. When everything you write is coming back from publishers by return mail, it may be cold comfort to know that your husband thought the description of the desert was right on target, that your girlfriend cried during the death scene, that your sister couldn't put the book down until she'd read the last page. None of these readers has the authority in your eyes of an agent or an editor. They can't offer you a contract or write you a check.

But they can make you aware that you are writing, and that your writing is communicating, that you are indeed being read. They can even make you feel better.

And that's not bad.

18

Lies, Lies, Lies

February 1989

FICTION IS FIBBING: HERE'S HOW TO FIB WELL.

Fiction is prevarication. The accomplished fictioneer is a very good liar.

And what brought this on?

Reflection, I suppose. Reflection upon good news. Any day now, barring a foul-up in production schedules, I'll be receiving my author's copies of the new edition of *Telling Lies for Fun and Profit.* The book, published by Arbor House in 1981, has been out of print for several years and was hard to find for some years before that. Now the good people of Albuquerque's CompuPress have arranged to make it available again, and I couldn't be more pleased.

I was thinking about that, and wondering what the cover might look like, and hoping the text would hold up fairly well, when it struck me how fortunate I'd been to come up with such an eminently serviceable title. From the beginning it had been that rare article, a title that everybody liked. People who hadn't read the book, even people with no interest in writing, have come up to me over the years to mention the title with approval. While I'd like to think the book's text may have had something to do with its sales, I know the title has been a strong factor.

Along with being catchy and provocative and irreverent, the title contains a fundamental truth that serves it well. Fiction is indeed untruth in the form of a prose narrative, and the fiction writer is a professional teller of lies. While there are some, I'm sure, who would see this as pointing up the essential immorality of what we do for a living, I can't say that I see it as a moral problem. It strikes me as more of a technical one. How can we become better liars, so as to produce better fiction?

Purely Coincidental

This has been a busy month. Along with *Telling Lies,* I've had two other books published. Writer's Digest Books has brought out *Spider, Spin Me a Web,* a new collection of columns and occasional writings about writing, and Tor Books has published *Random Walk,* a new novel I've mentioned all too frequently of late. This is all very exciting, or it would be but for the fact that I've spent the month in residence at a writers' colony, where I've been entirely occupied with writing a new book, so much so that I haven't even driven to a bookstore to see what the cover of *Random Walk* looks like.

The book I'm now writing is a detective story, the seventh volume to date chronicling the life and times of a chap named Matthew Scudder. (Regular readers of this space may recall a column within the past year wherein I explained why I would never be able to write more books about Mr. Scudder. That, it turns out, was a lie, albeit not the sort fictioneers deal with. It seemed like the truth at the time.)

One morning, struggling to get a scene right on the page, I thought to myself something along these lines: "Dammit, I know what happened. Why can't I just tell it?" And I looked up, struck by a thought.

Because what I wanted to get on paper was not something that had happened. It was something I was attempting to fabricate out of whole cloth. As they say in disclaimer notices, neither the events nor the characters portrayed in the book had their counterparts in real life. The whole book, along with the scene I was agonizing over, were solely the products of my admittedly overactive imagination.

Because I am always and forever your faithful servant, because column-writing for *WD* is a task on which the sun never sets, I took up a pen and wrote down the following:

"The superior fiction writer is the superior liar. When I write a novel, I am trying to report honestly and accurately about an event that did not happen in the lives of people who do not exist."

Having jotted this down, I heaved a sigh of accomplishment, pushed the sheet of paper aside, and resumed work on my novel. Once or twice over the days that followed I glanced at the sheet of paper, read the two immortal sentences, and told myself that a fine column would eventually spring from them. They seemed to me to embody some important truth.

Well, we'll see about that. Novel-writing takes place in a slightly altered state, and what looks good in that state doesn't always hold up later on. Years ago I heard the story of a chap who liked to smoke an unlawful herb in the evening. He would always have these profound thoughts late at night, just as he was drifting off to sleep, and he was sure he had a handle on the meaning of the universe, but the thought was always gone the next day. So he took to keeping a pad and pencil on the bedside table, in the hopes of capturing the next smoke-induced insight and fixing it upon the page like a fly in amber.

Several times he had great brilliant thoughts but nodded off without getting it together to write them down. Then, at last, he caught himself at the last minute, scribbled a few words upon the page, and slithered off into unconsciousness. When he awoke the next day he grabbed for the pad, eager to find out what brilliance had come to him, what distillation of pure knowledge, what rubric from the philosopher's stone.

What he had written was, "This room smells funny."

This Column Smells Funny

Now, my own novel completed, I can only hope that my kernel of truth is of a little more value than his. It strikes me that it might be useful to look at some of the qualities that make a good liar, and see how they might be employed by a good fiction writer.

1. *The ideal liar can lie as easily as he can tell the truth.* For most people, lying is more difficult than telling the truth. The greater difficulty of lying is what allows a polygraph to work. The liar experiences more stress than the truthteller, and this stress is physiologically palpable.

Adepts at Neuro-Linguistic Programming employ a nonmechanical means of determining whether a person is lying or telling the truth. They keep track of the subject's involuntary eye movements. When we are recounting something, we tend to glance to one side to access memory and to the other side to access imagination. If you ask me where I was on the night of October 11th, and if I seek the answer not in memory but in imagination, you can logically suspect me of lying.

There are liars who can routinely beat polygraph tests, and I shouldn't wonder if they can escape NLP detection as well. It is easy for them to lie. It places them under no greater stress. The lie, which may have come originally from imagination, has become part of their memory. They believe it now.

It seems to me that writing fiction is always hard work, and I'm here to tell you that it doesn't get any easier over the years. For the most part, though, it's not the lying that's hard for me; writing nonfiction is at least as difficult for me, and a good deal more difficult to get right.

When I am writing well, when a book is going smoothly, it is rarely all that hard for me to know what happens next. It is as if the book's scenes and chapters are a series of darkened rooms already furnished and occupied in my mind; all I have to do is open their doors as I get to them, turn on the lights, and describe what's going on inside. I know what my characters look like, and how they talk, and where they're going. I may not see around corners, but I can be confident that more will be revealed when I need to know it.

I don't always see everything. To belabor the metaphor, some of those rooms are lit in a chiaroscuro fashion, with a slender ray of light falling on one object and everything else shrouded in darkness. So I may know that a character has a broken nose or an uncertain smile without knowing his height or ring size.

2. *The liar doesn't doubt that he'll be believed.* Occasionally, reading a story or novel, I get the feeling that the writer is trying too hard. He doesn't think the reader is going to buy a particular scene, and so he pushes to make sure it goes over, and that just makes it that much less effective. I've done that myself when I lacked confidence in what I was writing.

Adequate research is one way to guard against the fear that your lies in a given area are insufficiently believable, but sometimes research doesn't do the trick. I've read books where the research showed, books where you could tell the author was throwing whole libraries at you to bolster something he still didn't feel altogether right about.

Similarly, it isn't always necessary for the author to be informed about a given area, as long as he genuinely believes that the character is sufficiently informed. For example, I've written five mystery novels about a burglar, Bernie Rhodenbarr. The fellow is a wizard at getting through locks, and any number of people has understandably assumed a similar knowledge on the author's part. Well, I have on occasion opened a door without its key, but I'm the furthest thing from an expert. Joe Gores once gave me a set of picks as a present; I was delighted to have them, but I have to admit that I never took the trouble to learn how to use them, and there's precious little information on locks and lock-picking in my books. What is present is the utter certainty that Bernie knows what he's doing. Readers believe this of Bernie, and draw their own conclusions about his creator.

3. *The liar is flexible.* Mozart wrote down the music he heard in his head. Michelangelo looked at the block of marble and cut away the part that wasn't David.

Similarly, the writer sees the story and its characters whole in his mind, and tells the reader what he sees.

When things go perfectly (and sometimes they do) that's all there is to it. The artist is given to hear the music in the mind, to see David whole within the stone. But our vision is usually imperfect, or more accurately incomplete, clouded. We have to vamp a little.

A plot idea comes to mind, and I start following it, writing a scene. Then I realize that it will throw off something I've already foreseen coming up in a later chapter. For a moment, the intellect has to be brought to bear to see if the two conflicting elements can be reconciled. If not, it weighs them both. Can I think up something better for the later chapter? Or would I be better advised to scrap the new development and devise an alternative?

It is useful to be able to perceive alternatives. Sometimes I'll write a scene, and I see it so clearly on my field of inner vision, and it writes itself so effortlessly, that I can easily overlook the fact that it's not a useful scene, that it takes the book in the wrong direction. I can, if I find my way to it carefully, uncover another scene that I will be able to visualize and to write about just as vividly, a scene that will have the added virtue of fitting the book.

Writing—indeed, all art—is a matter of making one choice after another. Sometimes, when everything is clear-cut, when each sentence in a book seems to have a sort of inevitability about it, it merely means that the choices are all being made on an unconscious level. More often we choose constantly—whether to write a scene long or short, whether to summarize an event or illustrate it, whether to reveal certain background facts we know about a character or leave them forever unreported. Even when we are never in the slightest doubt as to who these people are or what they're doing, we make choices all the time.

The best liar is giving a full and accurate report of something he has managed to let himself believe, but he is keeping one eye all the while upon his listener. If something's not going over, he shifts gears and finds something that will. Similarly, the writer keeps an ear to the ground, hearing what the reader will hear and seeing how the sound registers. If it sounds off, he looks for another approach.

Blake, who reminded us that

> *A truth that's told with bad intent*
> *Beats all the lies you can invent*

also advises us, in *The Marriage of Heaven and Hell,* that if a fool would persist in his folly he would become wise. If we persist in our lies, if we pursue them honestly, they lead us to truth.

Go figure.

19

Not Enough Rain

March 1989

SHOULD YOU READ FICTION WHILE WRITING IT? THE
ANSWER DEPENDS ON HOW PARCHED YOUR SOIL IS.

Long ago, the Australian writer Peter Carey was interviewed on American television. In the course of the program he explained why he avoids reading other people's fiction while in the process of composing his own.

"Otherwise," he explained, "I'll read a particularly good description of a storm. And I'll put the book down and say to myself, 'Damn, that's my problem—I haven't got enough *rain* in my book.'"

The foregoing is not a verbatim quote. It's not even a close reconstruction from memory, because I never saw the program in question. I had it recounted to me by my friend Philip Friedman, author of the about-to-be-published courtroom thriller *Reasonable Doubt.* I am reconstructing from memory Philip's reconstruction, so Mr. Carey's actual words may well have been something rather different.

No matter. They amount in any case to an excellent argument against reading while you're writing. "Not enough *rain* in my book." Says it all, doesn't it?

Except that Philip, reporting the incident, drew quite the opposite moral from it. "I thought about what he'd said," he told me, "and I realized that's precisely why I *do* read other people's fiction while I'm working on a novel. Because, if I don't, there really *won't* be enough rain in my book."

We had this conversation back in September, when Philip and I were both coincidentally in residence at the same writers' colony. He was finishing up *Reasonable Doubt,* while I was at work on *The Cutting Edge of Death,* a detective novel featuring an ex-cop named Matthew Scudder, of whom I have written on several occasions over the years. (Faithful readers of this column will perhaps recall my explaining a year or so ago that I would not be able to write any more books about Mr. Scudder. Obviously, this turned out to be every bit as premature as Mark Twain's obituary. How all of this came about may prove instructive, and I'll very likely write about it sooner or later. Stay tuned.)

After Philip and I had our conversation about Mr. Carey, I shrugged it off and went back to work. I did notice over the next several days that I was paying rather more attention than usual to the weather—not the weather there at the colony, which I recall as wildly variable that month, but the weather Scudder was encountering in New York. There was, that is to say, quite a good bit of rain in *The Cutting Edge of Death,* and I couldn't help wondering if some of what was splashing on the page was a result of our discussion.

More to the point, I found myself thinking about the whole question of reading while you write, of bombarding the senses with another writer's fiction while endeavoring to produce one's own. I myself have addressed the issue in several different ways over the years, and with varying results.

Early on, it would have been inconceivable for me to have avoided reading while I wrote. During my 20s and 30s, I was always at work on one book or another. While I did not work every single day, neither did I take a great many days off—and, when I finished one book, I was hard at work upon the next within a week or so. I was not quite the drudge Trollope was—he reportedly would write the last sentence of a long novel, draw a line, heave a sigh, and jot down the first sentence of his next novel, starting work not only on the same day but, God save us, on the same *page*.

Not me. I would waste a few days, and I'd be profligate enough to begin the new opus on a fresh sheet of paper, but it must be said that I was not much given to long vacations. Had I eschewed reading while I wrote, it would essentially have meant not reading at all.

And that was out of the question. Reading was then at least as important to me as writing, and no more to be done without than food and water. I was always reading something, and commonly had a few books going at once. (And, in those days, I finished everything I started—as a reader and as a writer. This surely has changed. I discard a large number of books half-read nowadays. And, alas, I discard more than I'd prefer half-written. I don't mind being free of my old reader's compulsion to finish everything on my plate, but I sometimes wish I were a little more compulsive still about finishing what's in my typewriter.)

As a general rule, reading in those days was something I did when I was finished with the day's work—or, less frequently, before I started it. While I was actually physically present at the typewriter, banging out something immortal, I didn't have somebody else's book in my hand.

My chief reason for not doing so had precious little to do with the presence or absence of rain in my work. On a more mundane level, I learned that reading would very simply take time away from my writing. I might indeed have the need to draw my mind away from my work for a moment or two, but reading at such times was a dangerous diversion. Either I wouldn't get drawn into the book at all, in which case it was not doing what I wanted it to, or I would be utterly absorbed by it, in which case it would be doing its work far too well. I would have wanted a five-minute respite from my own work, and before I knew it an hour would have vanished. The better the book, the greater the danger—and, if I got sufficiently engrossed in it, I could not even escape by closing it and setting it aside. Even then, I'd still have my mind caught up in its force field, and would be hard put to concentrate again upon my own book.

Sometimes, too, what I was reading would have a direct influence on what I was writing. Once, reading a Rex Stout novel while at work on something of my own, I looked up from a sentence I'd just written and realized with a start that it had more of the cadence of Archie Goodwin than of my own narrator. I don't know that anyone else could have noticed this, and there wasn't anything sufficiently wrong with the line to make me go back and change it, but it was there, and it got my attention.

Finding the Message

In recent years I have increasingly tended to make writing a less frequent and more concentrated experience. Sometimes I isolate myself—in a motel room or rented apartment, or, as with my last two books, at a colony. I work rapidly, put in long hours, take no days off for the duration, and produce a large quantity of work each day. I wind up completing in a month what might take me three or four months under more ordinary conditions. I don't get more work done overall in this fashion; having finished a book in a month, I may go three or four or six or eight months before getting to work on another. But I like working this way, and it seems to me that I'm better able to concentrate on my work and to bring all of my resources to bear on it.

Because the success of this method depends upon the intensity of my concentration, I certainly don't bring novels to the typewriter. It's true that I seem to require frequent breaks from my work, interruptions during which my conscious mind can yank itself away from the manuscript while, presumably, the unconscious mind goes on sorting things out, sifting alternatives and solving problems. As I reported some years ago in this space, my choice for such interruptions is solitaire, and I will commonly wear out a deck of playing cards almost as quickly as I'll exhaust a typewriter ribbon. (That used to be true. The new cartridge ribbons, however, are ready for the garbage can after 30 or 40 pages, while I can still get a whole book out of a deck of cards.)

During my hours away from the typewriter, I don't have anything as fixed as a rule about avoiding the reading of fiction. On the contrary, I'm perfectly willing to do anything that will pass the time agreeably between one day's writing and the next. I have found, though, that I am rarely receptive to fiction at such times, or at least that I have trouble concentrating on a novel. (Short stories are more apt to hold my attention, since they aren't called upon to hold it for very long.) I must have picked up six or eight novels while I was writing *The Cutting Edge of Death*, but I didn't get all the way to the end of a single one of them.

It seems to me, though, that there's a larger question here. It's not just a matter of whether or not to read fiction while writing fiction. Beyond that, one has to decide what input of any sort is to be allowed. Anything—a movie, a television game show, a conversation with a passing stranger—can call into question the amount of rain one has in one's book. Any new element in one's surroundings can alter one's own mental state—and can thus affect what winds up on the page.

Consider, if you will, the writing method of Georges Simenon, an archetypical role model for all of us who would write rapidly and in isolation. Typically, Simenon takes himself, his suitcase and his typewriter to some European capital, where he checks into an agreeable hotel, hangs the "Do Not Disturb" sign on the knob, and produces an Inspector Maigret mystery in 12 days. (Let it be said that these books are short. This is not to minimize M. Simenon's achievement, but to keep the task from appearing even more Herculean than it already is.)

After Simenon has done his first day's work, he goes for a walk, buys a packet of tobacco, has a cup of coffee, and otherwise amuses himself. There is nothing terribly remarkable about his course of actions, except for the fact that, on every subsequent day until the book's completion, he follows the same unvarying routine. He walks the same route, patronizes the same tobacconist, sips coffee at the same café, and consumes the same evening meal.

His object, as I understand it, is to avoid any change that might touch off a corresponding change in his own mental environment. His goal is to remain all of a piece while he writes the book, so that the book itself will similarly be all of a piece.

I've found that I tend to create a routine away from the typewriter while I'm engaged in writing a book, though it's not nearly as elaborate as Simenon's. Often, though, I'll have something I make a point of doing on a daily basis, some exercise regimen or some form of meditation. I'm not sure, though, that I do this for Simenon's reason. I have the feeling that I take up such rituals for their own sake, much in the manner of a baseball player who won't change his socks during a hitting streak, if with less fragrant results.

As far as maintaining my own mental environment in an unvarying state, I don't really think that's possible. And, even if it were, I'm not sure it's desirable.

The impossibility seems clear enough. As Heraclitus told us, we can never set foot twice in the same river, because other waters are flowing. By the same token, Simenon can never truly retrace his steps from one day to the next, for he can never step twice into the same street, or drink coffee twice at the same café. Other waters are flowing. Different people are walking in the street, or sipping their own coffee at nearby tables. Even those persons and objects that remain unchanged will impinge differently upon his consciousness from one day to the next.

I don't have to pick up someone else's novel and read about a storm to become concerned, for good or for ill, that there's not enough precipitation in my pages. If that's the message my mind wants to receive, I'll find some way to receive it. If there's no fictional storm on hand to bring me the message, the skies will very likely open up while I'm walking to my studio some morning. Or they won't and the very *lack* of rain will deliver the same message.

Thanks, Oprah

And sometimes, as Philip suggested, that message is precisely what I need to hear. Because there really is too much or too little rain in the book, and it's my own conscious awareness of this lack or glut that brings some outside element into my awareness.

It was last May when I began preliminary work on *The Cutting Edge of Death*. I was in Arizona at the time and I was writing the book in novelette form, as a way of allowing the story to develop, (I eventually decided against publishing the novelette, but having written it that way helped me greatly when it was time to write the full-length novel.)

My plot called for the death of a character by what might or might not later turn out to be suicide, and I was having trouble with the scene. I wrestled with it for a while, then did something quite uncharacteristic. I walked over and turned on the television set. *The Oprah Winfrey Show* was just coming on and I sat down and watched it. The subject turned out to be autoerotic asphyxiation, and it was exactly what I needed to see at that particular moment, because autoerotic asphyxiation was precisely the plot element my story required, the very rain my book was lacking. I watched the whole program, and then I sat down and wrote the scene.

Should you read fiction while you're writing it? I don't know. But, whether you do or not, your mind will inevitably—and quite properly—be influenced by everything around you while you're engaged in the organic process of composing fiction. The rain will sink in or run off, depending upon what you do or do not require of it. If you're open to it, you'll get what you need.

20

Ten Percent of Your Life

April 1989

How come you never write a column about agents?

For a couple of very good reasons, I think.

First of all, this column is not about marketing. It is unquestionably true that marketing is of more than casual concern to most writers, new or old, of fiction or nonfiction. Happily, other departments at *WD* cover the subject more than adequately. When this column began appearing in the magazine, around the time the last dinosaurs were dying out, its focus was centered on the techniques of fiction writing. Over the years my scope has widened some, to the point where I find myself as apt to write about the mental and emotional preparation for putting words on paper as the actual process of putting them there. Other aspects of the writer's life, too, have seemed to fall within the column's purview. Writing, after all, is a holistic activity, one performed with the entire self, not just the tips of the fingers. I've written about dealing with rejection, for example, because it can inhibit one from putting other words on other pieces of paper. I've written about the art of surviving on a writer's income, and risk-taking, and lying fallow. I have even, Lord save us, had the temerity to write a column some years ago about the importance of regular exercise (and it probably wouldn't hurt me a bit to go through my files and read that one myself). But I have tended to avoid writing about the whole business of selling one's work, and I think I should keep it that way.

But that's what your readers want to know about.

No kidding. Sometimes I think it's *all* anybody wants to know about. You expect the question at writers' conferences, but I get it other places as well. I was on a panel in Miami a couple of years ago at a book fair. Several of us were discussing crime fiction. The whole show was for readers, not writers, and during the question-and-answer session a couple of people kept relentlessly demanding to know how they could get an agent. I won't take questions like that at a general gathering—I think they're out of place and of precious little interest to the nonwriters who comprise the bulk of the crowd—but at writers' conferences they're impossible to avoid.

And what do you say when people ask how to get an agent?

That I'm the wrong person to ask, because my agent is not open to new clients and I don't know a great deal about other agents. And I have that in common with most writers. It's rare for a writer to know anything about agents other than his own, and it's not uncommon for the writer to know precious little about the relative merits of his own agent, either. After all, what basis of comparison does he have?

If I can't ask you, who can I ask?

Someone in publishing. That's what I did the last time I made a change of agents. I talked to four or five friends who'd been in various areas of publishing for a fair number of years and who had consequently worked with a good many agents on a daily basis. They also knew me, knew what my work was like and knew what sort of personality I had. (And, knowing this, they still remained friendly with me. Go figure.)

Each of my friends suggested three or four agents they thought I might work well with, and I sifted the possibilities and made my selection accordingly. It was a far more informed choice than I could have made by talking to other writers.

But suppose I don't have any friends in publishing?

They don't have to be bosom buddies. Sometimes a slight acquaintance is enough.

For instance, let's say you've managed to find a publisher for your novel without having an agent in the first place. It's time to sign a contract, and you realize that you don't know how to negotiate or what rights to ask for. You ask your new editor to recommend an agent. He'll very likely recommend several, and they will all be people he's worked with successfully in the past. His recommendation, backed up by the solid fact that he's already committed to buying a book from you, will certainly get you a sympathetic reception from these agents, and the odds are that one or more of them will want to represent you and will suit you in turn.

Well, of course I can get an agent if I've already got the book sold myself. But what do I need him for then? Why should I give away 10% of my income?

First off, forget that "of course." You could have a book on the bestseller list and still get turned down by certain agents, not because they're high-hat but because they may not respond personally to some element of your writing style. A good agent knows that a successful writer-agent relationship requires both that he like your work and that he feel it's salable. Either without the other is just not enough.

More to the point, an agent is most valuable *after* the book has found its publisher. That's when he earns his 10%. He'll make sure you wind up with a higher share of subsidiary rights, strike out the unfair clauses that appear in almost every publisher's standard contract forms, and generally earn his keep by asking for concessions you wouldn't know to ask for.

Good for him. My problem is I haven't sold a book yet, and that's what I really want an agent for. I don't really care whether I wind up with 50% or 80% of Dutch language rights.

You will when the guilders start pouring in, but I get your point. You don't have to have sold a book to get a publisher to recommend an agent.

Selling something else might help. Suppose you've sold a few short stories. (You don't need an agent to sell short stories. Most agents really don't want to market short fiction; they may do it as a favor to clients whose books they represent, but it's not something that thrills them.) So you ask the editors who've bought short fiction from you to recommend agents, and you take it from there.

Far as that goes, you don't have to have sold anything. All you need is to have come close.

Huh?

If you're getting nothing but form rejection letters from publishers who have seen your novel, this approach won't work for you. But suppose a couple of editors have taken the time and trouble to write you thoughtful letters, explaining why your book doesn't quite work for them but saying nice things generally about the way you write. Write back to them, thanking them for the kind words and adding that you feel unequal to the task of marketing your novel yourself. From what they've seen of your work, could they suggest a few agents who might be receptive to your writing? You might not get an answer, but then again you might.

None of these approaches will get you on the client list of an agent who doesn't like your work or doesn't think he can sell it. But that's as it should be; better no agent at all than one who does not believe in you and your work.

What about reading fees?

Well, what about them?

Some people say they're reasonable compensation for an agent who takes the trouble to read unsolicited submissions. Other people tell me they're a swindle. What do you say?

I used to say they were a mistake and let it go at that. Now I'm less sure of my ground.

All of the agents who charge fees to read manuscripts from unestablished writers will tell you that they're just doing this to cover expenses. Some of them are telling the truth. Some of them are lying.

Back in 1957–58 I worked for an agent who charged reading fees and advertised extensively for new clients. At that time there were three or four of us employed to read the slush and respond with encouraging letters, detailing the story's faults, advising against revision, and inviting the writer to send more stories with more fees. Our letters followed a carefully delineated form, always praised the writer's talent and style, explained that the plot of the story in question had structural flaws, and went out signed (and presumably written) by the agent himself. While a slushpile writer was occasionally "discovered"—I found a couple myself during the year of my employment—this whole department existed not to find new clients but because it was enormously profitable. I've always felt that submitting to that agency was an utter waste of money, although I have since met people who actually considered the criticism they received worth their investment.

On the other hand, I know a couple of agents now who will read the unsolicited offerings of unestablished writers but charge what strikes me as a nominal fee for the service. They don't offer lengthy reports and analyses—the charge is a reading fee, and all it guarantees is a reading, followed by a letter either offering representation or politely declining the manuscript. The agents in question explain that they cannot afford to give slush a thoughtful reading without this compensation, and that seems reasonable to me.

Agents who don't charge a fee will generally take a look at what's sent to them, even if they may publicly deny their willingness to do so. However, they probably won't prioritize it; slush gets read when there's nothing else to do, and there's usually something else to do. They're more apt to resent unsolicited manuscripts and to give them short shrift. But if they do get around to your manuscript, and if they do really like what they see, they'll be every bit as eager to represent you as someone to whom you've paid a fee.

How much creative help does an agent provide?

Depends on the agent—and on the client. Some agents see it as their function to get the client's work in the best possible shape before submitting it, and their role may include detailed criticism and revision suggestions. Some will originate book ideas and hand them off to their writers, even plotting the book along with the writer.

At the other extreme, one of the hotter agents in the trade these days is a former lawyer whose boast it is that he never reads his clients' work. His role, as he sees it, is not to evaluate or improve their work but to sell it, and this he does superbly.

Some writers treasure the creative input they get from their agents. Others regard any suggestion as interference. You pays your money and takes your choice.

Speaking of money, I notice that some agents charge more than others. What's the difference between an agent who gets 10% and one who gets 15%?

What's the difference? The difference is 5%, dummy.

In the past ten years or so, a number of agents have raised their rates from 10% to 15% of sales. I had one agent explain to me that this was in response to inflation. My rejoinder was that if his clients' income kept pace with inflation, so would his—all without a raise in commissions.

Another agent—who did *not* raise his rates—pointed out to me that every year a few more publishing professionals give up their jobs and set up shop as agents. They don't need to demonstrate any qualifications in order to do so, all they need is for someone to paint their names on their office doors, and almost all of them remain agents and make a success of it.

"There are only two reasons for raising commissions to 15%," this man said. "One is greed. The other is incompetence."

Some years ago, Raymond Chandler wrote a bitter piece on agents and called it "Ten Percent of Your Life." Thinking of an agent's commission in those terms is a little unsettling, but "Fifteen Percent of Your Life" doesn't sound a great deal better. There are agents who can make a good case for the higher rate, I know, but there are people who can make a pretty good case for anything.

That may be true, but at this point I don't care too much whether my end is 85% or 90%, because right now I've got 100% of nothing. I guess the most important thing is to get a good agent.

No, the important thing is to write a good book.

And *that's* why I object to the endless questions about agents. The presumption seems to be that an agent will make all the difference, that you can't fail with one or succeed without one. And that's nonsense, and when it leads people to place marketing considerations ahead of creative considerations, it's dangerous nonsense. And it's one more reason why I absolutely refuse to do a column about agents.

And there's no way to get you to change your mind?

Sorry. This is one point I'm firm on.

21

Inspiration is Where You Find It

May 1989

TRAVEL, CHANGE AND OBSERVATION GIVE YOU FRESH
MATERIAL AND A BROADENED WRITER'S PERSPECTIVE.

Time for a progress report.

It was in February of '88, as some of you will recall, that my wife, Lynne, and I became nomadic. We closed our house, pulled up metaphorical stakes, folded our metaphorical tent, and Took Off. Ever since then we have been living without a fixed address. It is late November as I write these lines, and in the past nine months we have put 25,000 miles on the car and considerably more than that on our own internal odometers. We've been out of the country twice, traveling first to Egypt, later to Italy and Spain. (We also walked across the Mexican border twice, for about a half hour each time, and we spent a few hours in Canada, driving from Detroit to Buffalo, but those brief excursions somehow don't seem to qualify as Foreign Travel.) We've hit 29 states, including Confusion and Anxiety, and we've spent the night under some 80 different roofs. We have, incredible though it may seem, visited 23 different towns and hamlets named Buffalo, which would surely appear to constitute a record.

While not everyone can see the point of our pursuit of the elusive Buffalo, almost everyone does respond to the romance of the nomadic lifestyle. And most see it as serving a valuable vocational purpose.

"You must be getting great material," they say.

Am I?

I wonder.

Travels with Larry

I could, of course, write an account of our travels. The public has an extraordinary appetite for such books, no doubt because the nomadic fantasy has such a strong hold on the American imagination. I could write my own version of *Blue Highways* or *Walking Across America,* a sort of *Travels with Charlie* without the dog. The Buffalo hunt would give the book an overall theme, and a laudably eccentric one at that.

There's only one problem, and that's that it's just not my kind of book. I'm a fiction writer, and I'm out of my element when I try to write nonfiction. There's one exception—I seem endlessly capable of writing about writing. But other nonfiction is less successful for me. I have to struggle with it, and the results almost always disappoint me and everyone else.

One of the most important lessons I've learned—and I've had to learn it more than once, I'm sorry to say—is to distinguish between books that ought to be written and books that I ought to write. I may try a magazine piece about Buffalo hunting, but I suspect that's as far as it'll go.

Am I, then, finding other inspiration? Settings for stories? Characters with which to people them? Incidents with which to enliven them?

I must be, but I probably won't know it for a long time, because that's how it seems to work for me. All of my observation and experience gets piled up in a great compost heap, and eventually something springs out of the soil.

Inspiration's a curious thing. Writers are always seeking it, and in a myriad of ways. Somerset Maugham looked for plots in the South Seas, and some of his most successful stories amount to little more than the artful retelling of some anecdote related to him on some tropical island. James Jones, feeling burned out, took up scuba diving in the hope that he would be moved to write fiction about a scuba diver; ultimately he returned to the Second World War, always the setting for his best fiction. Searching for inspiration, some of us look afar, some look within, and some simply look around, finding that proverbial acre of diamonds close at hand.

Some of my own thoughts on the subject were triggered by a recent letter from my friend Tom Williams, a writer and bibliophile who lives in Oakley, California. "A while back," he wrote, "my wife Kathy asked her paternal grandmother a routine question about her long-dead paternal grandfather, all in connection with school records for our own children. Her grandmother reacted as if she'd been asked to strip naked and roll around on a bed of broken glass. Kathy found this curious, but her grandmother had always been a bit reserved. And, since the woman was deaf, it was not easy to communicate with her.

"Earlier, after Kathy's father had died, she'd received the impression that her grandfather had not indeed died in the war, as she'd been given to understand as a child. But she was never able to find out what actually happened. Recently, when her grandmother passed away, the whole question came up again, and I decided to see what I could find out. The two of us went down to sunny Fresno to play detective.

"What we were surprised to discover was that this little lady who'd kept so much to herself most of her life was in fact a murderess. Kathy's grandfather had died in 1921 of a gunshot wound to the head fired by his spouse with the intent to commit homicide. That's what we learned in the County Building, where we read the death certificate. We went from there to the library, where we learned from microfilmed records that the grandmother and her children were allegedly victims of abuse, that Grandpa had also been deaf mute, that Grandma shot him three times from behind, firing through the back porch window as he hunched over his breakfast, and that she went to trial with the prosecution trying for the death penalty."

At this point Tom sent for the trial transcript, only to learn that no trial records seem to exist. "We have heard that Kathy's great-grandfather bought his daughter's way out of it," he wrote, "but it seems funny that there's no record of any disposition of the case. In any event, the most eye-opening part of all this is not the detail of what happened but that it even happened at all to such a seemingly normal, everyday kind of person.

"You're probably wondering why I'm telling you all this. First, I wanted to sort through it, and what better way than to write it all out? Second, I've learned something from the whole affair. As a writer, as well as personally, I've been a fool to dismiss Old Maiden Aunt Mildred, Goofy Cousin Cecil and Weird Uncle Rick as dull, lifeless people that I'm simply obligated to visit once in a while. Probably (and hopefully) none of them is a serial killer or a pygmy rapist, but they might just have some past or present aspect of their lives that is worth knowing. They might even provide inspiration enough to yield up an idea that can blossom into a bestseller.

"What I turned up in Fresno may or may not find its way into my writing someday. I have a good visual sense of the shooting itself, and the image of two deaf people playing out such an intrinsically noisy scene gives the whole thing an especially stark reality for me. But, whether or not I make direct use of what I learned, I think the overall lesson is an important one."

Change Changes

I would agree. And I would think it's the kind of lesson that can't fail to find its way into one's writing because of the extent to which it changes one's perceptions. Tom may not write about his wife's grandmother, or about a woman shooting an abusive husband, or about a bullet fired through a porch window, or about one deaf person dying noisily at the hands of another. But whatever he writes about will be different for having been written by someone whose own horizons have been extended. Our writing is always changed when our view of the world changes.

I have to believe that my own wanderings will change the way I see the world, and that this will be somehow reflected in what I write. But this doesn't mean I'll go to Wyoming and then write something set in Wyoming. That might happen, but it's not the way I most frequently process experience.

A couple of months ago, after all that time in transit, I holed up at a writers' colony and wrote a book. The book was set in New York, in those side-blocks west of midtown where my series detective Matthew Scudder lives and works. The book, *The Cutting Edge of Death*, was one I had been trying to write for more than five years, a sequel to *Eight Million Ways to Die* which continues the adventures of Scudder after he has stopped drinking. (*When the Sacred Ginmill Closes*, written after *Eight Million Ways to Die*, was actually what Hollywood types call a prequel; it was set back in time several years before *Eight Million Ways*.)

This past April, riding a horrible square-wheeled night train across Egypt from Luxor to Cairo, unable to sleep and raddled with dysentery, I suddenly knew how to write a new book about Scudder. Characters took shape and scenes played themselves out in my mind. For perhaps an hour I lay there in creative ferment, and at the hour's end I felt as though I could sit down and write the entire book straight out.

A month later, in Arizona, I worked on the book. I saw that I wasn't quite ready, that I needed a secondary plot line, so I developed what I already had into a novelette. Several months later, when it was time to write the book, I had ideas and characters for the secondary story line, and, in rural Virginia, I wrote the book.

What does it owe to my travels?

I don't know. At a glance, it wouldn't seem to owe anything to them. The plot is an invention, and it is very much a New York story. I rarely take people and plunk them down in the middle of my stories, so the characters, too, are my own inventions. I can see antecedents for parts of the plot, and for some of the characters, too. The back story for one of the female characters is part of the life history of a friend of mine. Another character owes a lot physically to a man who used to own a couple of saloons in the Village; no one would recognize him from the physical description I provide, but his was the face I had in mind when I wrote about the character.

Another character remembers how he once voted 15 times for a New York mayoral candidate; years ago I heard a fellow tell how he and some friends had similarly voted early and often in Philadelphia, and the incident now found its way into my book. I could point to another half dozen bits and pieces of the book and explain where they came from, how something I once heard or saw or read about got transformed into fiction.

And, as I mentioned last month, while I was writing the novelette in Arizona I turned on the television set and watched an *Oprah Winfrey Show* about autoerotic asphyxiation, and that gave me just the plot element I needed.

As far as I can make out, that was the only part of the book I got by traveling, and I could have traveled anyplace with a television set. It didn't have to be Arizona, any more than it had to be an Egyptian train that got the whole process started.

Footloose Change

Am I getting a lot of material?

I don't know. I'm seeing a lot of the world, and meeting some interesting people, and having the mind turned both outward and inward in ways that I have to believe will be valuable. Perhaps all of this will be reflected in books set in some of the places we've been. Perhaps whatever I pick up out here in the world will be mysteriously transformed into still more books set in New York.

It probably doesn't matter. Tom Williams will be somehow changed, somehow enriched as a writer, because he knows the truth about his wife's grandmother; this is so whether he writes about her or not. And I'll be changed for having driven across the desert and climbed a mountain and collected a couple dozen Buffaloes, whether I write about any of it or not. Change the writer and you change the writing. How, really, could it be otherwise?

22

It's Your Book

June 1989

AND YOU CAN CRY IF YOU WANT TO. YOU WOULD CRY TOO IF IT HAPPENED TO YOU.

Good morning, boys and girls.

Good morning, sir.

I'd like to begin today by telling you a story. Once upon a time—yes, Arnold?

Sir, if it's the one about the actress and the bishop, you told us last week.

It's not, Arnold. As a matter of fact—

Or the one about the soldier, the sailor, the marine, and the independent businesswoman. That was the week before.

Ahem. This week's story concerns a young man who grew up secure in the knowledge that he wanted to become a playwright. His first work, however, was not for the theater. It seems he got an idea for a novel and thought it would be enjoyable to write and good training for writing plays. And so he wrote it, and a publisher brought it out, and it garnered excellent reviews, sold very decently, and ultimately won the Mystery Writers of America's Edgar award for best first mystery of the year. Rachel, you look troubled.

I was just thinking that this can't be a true story, sir. Good things like that don't happen to writers in real life.

Sometimes they do. This, most assuredly, was a good thing, and you can be sure that it did indeed happen. It made the young writer very happy, but it by no means dissuaded him from his initial notion of writing for the stage, and that's just what he proceeded to do forthwith. He wrote several plays, and no doubt his novelistic experience served him well in their construction, even as his success with the novel gave him better access to producers. In short, he had several plays produced, and some of them did quite well.

After he'd been doing this for several years, he had a play in rehearsal and another germinating in his mind. I don't know anything about the play in rehearsal, but the other concerned a young couple living in a glamorous if somewhat spooky building on the West Side of Manhattan.

One day during rehearsal for the other play, an actress interrupted a scene and approached the footlights. "That line's impossible," she told the director. "Get the writer to change it."

The writer looked up, and Something Happened.

Here's what happened: he remembered when he'd placed that first novel with a publisher. Lee Wright was his editor, and she made a few revision suggestions, the most significant one calling for the repositioning of two of his early chapters. He went home and thought about it for a week or a month or whatever it was, and then he went in to see his editor. He felt diffident about this, he knew she knew ever so much more than he did about the construction of mystery novels, but he just didn't like the change, and he managed to tell her so.

"All right," she said. "After all, it's your book."

And she published the book with the chapters in their original order.

"After all, it's your book." And now, years later, some . . . some *actress*, some actress who couldn't even be bothered to call him by *name*, could screech to a director and make him change his lines.

He made an acceptable change, because after all that is what you do in the theater. And then he went home, and he sat down and went to work on that story of the couple in the apartment house, but for some curious reason he decided he'd have more fun writing it as a novel. Then once again he went back to writing plays, because after all that was his true calling in life, but in the meantime he had managed to write *Rosemary's Baby*.

Ira's Baby

The writer, of course, was Ira Levin. (The first novel was *A Kiss Before Dying*, and it's a honey. I don't know which play was in rehearsal when Mr. Levin had this particular epiphany, but he's written a number of them, including *No Time for Sergeants* and *Deathtrap*.) Mr. Levin told this story some years ago to a friend of mine, who just a week ago passed it on to me, so some of the details may have lost or gained something in the translation, but you get the point.

A couple of days after I heard the Ira Levin story, I read an item in *The New York Times* about a songwriter named Bart Howard, whose biggest hit over the years has been "Fly Me to the Moon." The song was recorded by a variety of singers over the years after Kaye Ballard first put it on the flip side of "Lazy Afternoon," and it became a hit when Joe Harnell and his orchestra released a bossa nova version in 1963. Since then it has been recorded more than 300 times, and has never earned its author less than $50,000 a year.

Mr. Howard wrote the song in 20 minutes. "The song just fell out of me," he recalled. "One publisher wanted me to change the lyric to 'Take me to the moon.' Had I done that I don't know where I'd be today."

Oh no? Well, I have a fair idea. Rather than reach the moon, I suspect the song would have fizzled out on the launching pad. But Mr. Howard told that publisher to take a flying jump at the moon, so to speak, and kept the song the way he wanted it. The publisher had objected to the improper usage of the verb *fly*; Mr. Howard, sticking to his guns, wound up adding that usage to the language.

Editorial Direction

At a glance, the point of all of this would seem to be clear enough. It's your book, it's your song, and if anybody wants you to change so much as a comma, tell him to go climb a tree. The late John O'Hara even went so far as to make of this a pronunciamento. "Once you've finished a story," he thundered, "the only way to improve it is by telling an editor to go to hell."

Well, yes and no.

Some writers like to get suggestions from editors, ideas on how they can revise what they've written. I've had writers tell me how grateful they are for a particular editor's participation in their work, as if they regard the books as essentially collaborative ventures. They themselves are very much open to suggestions, and delighted when another person can come up with a way to improve what they've done.

I have to admit that I'm not so constituted. On the contrary, I'm a lot closer in temperament to Mr. O'Hara. I don't welcome a great deal of editorial input, and I rarely look with favor upon the suggestions I get. I don't think of my editors as my collaborators, and indeed I've had to learn not to regard them as adversaries. Well, what the hell; when I was a kid I never got high grades in *Works and Plays Well with Others*, and one of the attractions of writing was I figured I could do it alone.

The trouble is, sometimes editors are right. (And even a blind sow gets an acorn once in a while.) I don't just mean that an editor may come up with a good idea that doesn't happen to be right for the book I happen to have written. That, alas, happens all the time. But sometimes an editor comes up with an excellent idea, and one that improves and enhances the very book I've written. The only thing wrong with such an idea is that the editor thought of it and I didn't, and that I may consequently be too pigheaded to embrace it to my bosom, or too lazy to do the requisite work.

My most recent novel, coming to you from Morrow in October, is

Out on the Cutting Edge. It's a detective novel featuring Matthew Scudder, of whom I've written half a dozen prior volumes. My editor at Morrow is Liza Dawson, and she wrote me a thoughtful letter suggesting what she thought might be problematic aspects of the book, and some ideas she had for their resolution.

I was able to agree with Liza's analysis. The book involves two linked cases. One concerns a young actress who has disappeared, and we never see her directly. The book's pace while Scudder hunts for her is measured, and while it doesn't drag, there's no great sense of urgency.

I called Liza after I had digested her letter and we talked about it without really getting anywhere. She suggested I might want to start the book with some sort of third-person prologue in which I could bring the girl on and give the reader reason to give a damn about her. "No," I said. "I really don't like third-person prologues tacked on at the front of a straight first-person detective narrative."

A week or so later, driving through Texas, I saw how to handle it. And a few days after that I sat down and wrote a prologue for the book, but a *first*-person prologue, with Scudder imagining a scene that comes later on in the book, and at which he was not present. It reads like this:

> *When I imagine it, it is always a perfect summer day, with the sun high in a vivid blue sky. It was summer, of course, but I have no way of knowing what the weather was like, or even if it happened during the day. Someone, relating the incident, mentioned moonlight, but he wasn't there either. Perhaps his imagination provided the moon, even as mine chose a bright sun, a blue sky, and a scattering of cottony clouds.*
>
> *They are on the open porch of a white clapboard farmhouse. Sometimes I see them inside, seated at a pine table in the kitchen, but more often they are on the porch. They have a large glass pitcher filled with a mix of vodka and grapefruit juice, and they are sitting on the porch drinking salty dogs . . .*

And it goes on like that, for perhaps another 400 words. Reading it, you don't know just who or where these people are, or what they're up to. But it works. It shifts some weight toward the front end of the book—I can't think of a better way to explain it—and it makes us care more about what happens to the girl, and makes it reasonable to us that Scudder cares.

Most important, *I* like it. I have over the years made changes in books to keep editors happy, and I've almost always regretted it. In this instance I'm frankly delighted with the change; it's something I would have done of my own accord if I'd had the wit to think of it myself.

Another change in *Out on the Cutting Edge* came in response to a reaction of my agent, Knox Burger. There is a character in the book named Mick Ballou, a saloon owner and racketeer, and Knox was very much taken with the fellow. While he's an off-stage presence in the book from fairly early on, he doesn't come on until fairly late in the proceedings. In an earlier book, *When the Sacred Ginmill Closes,* Scudder spent some time at an after-hours joint run by the Morrissey brothers, and Knox wished too that some of the ambience of that place could have been included.

Again, I was able to agree with the analysis of the problem. And, going over the book, I found a scene early on in which Scudder was alone in his hotel room after a discussion with a character in which Ballou's name and career came up. It made perfect sense for him to sit on the edge of his bed and recall having met Ballou at Morrissey's some years previously. I added about a page, maybe a little less, and it fits in so perfectly you'd have thought it had been there from the beginning.

Sometimes in the past year or so I've enjoyed imagining that my books already exist in some other dimension in perfect form; when I write them, it's just a matter of trying to come as close to those perfect books as I can. In this particular instance, you might say that Liza and Knox each helped me bring over another piece of that "real" book from the other dimension.

Cutting Other Edges

Just a few days ago I got a call from Knox. Last spring I wrote a story called "Some Days You Get the Bear"—I think I mentioned it in a column some months ago. Now it seemed that *Penthouse* wanted to buy the story, but in order to do so they would require two major changes.

First of all, the story opens with the protagonist in bed with a woman to whom he has just made love, and he realizes that he wants a cigarette, although he hasn't smoked in years. But he thinks about it. The *Penthouse* editor explained that they didn't want him to think about a cigarette. I don't really know why, and I don't much care; it had struck me, in a recent rereading of the story, that the cigarette bit was trite and dopey anyway, so if they wanted it out, I certainly was not inclined to fight for it.

The other change was more substantial. There is a female character in the story with a pet snake, and she confides that the snake shares her bed. She and the snake don't do anything, uh, weird. The snake gets body warmth from the relationship, and the young woman gets a sense of abiding security. Even so, the scene would violate an evidently important editorial taboo at *Penthouse,* so they wanted her to go on having a pet snake (a reticulated python, if you must know) but they didn't want her sleeping with it.

Now I could not think of this as a change for the better. So what do you suppose I did? Rachel?

You stood up for the story, sir. You told them to take it or leave it.

Mimi?

I'm sure, sir, you found a way to satisfy their editorial requirements without compromising your artistic integrity.

Arnold?

How much were they offering?

A lot.

Then I figure you knuckled under, sir.

Absolutely right, Arnold. I told them to do whatever they wanted. I did so because, while *Out on the Cutting Edge* is indeed my book, and while "Some Days You Get the Bear" is my story, *Penthouse* is not my magazine. Magazines have a right to be a good deal more arbitrary in such matters than do book publishers. I, in turn, have the right to be intransigent, but I have to weigh matters first. If a market that paid $100 insisted upon such a change, I would very likely tell them to go to hell. But *Penthouse* was offering a good deal more than that, and the change they would be making was not impossible to live with, and it was a very easy decision for me to make.

Down the line, when I next publish a collection of stories in book form, I'll restore the snake cut. (I'll probably leave out the cigarette business; I think that's a cut I should have made myself.) The book version is the one that lasts, and it's the one over which I legitimately have more control.

In the meantime, I can live with the cut and rejoice in the sale. I'm glad to be in *Penthouse*. After dating their models for so many years, it'll be nice to have something in the magazine.

23

Piping Them Aboard

July 1989

C'MON UP THE GANGPLANK, GANG. OUR THREE-MONTH
FICTION-TECHNIQUE CRUISE IS ABOUT TO BEGIN.

There are really only three things you have to do," I heard a man say.
"First of all, you have to get them on board. Then you have to make
sure you keep them on the ship. And finally, you have to kill them at
the end."

I thought at first that I was overhearing a declamation from *Every
Boy's Guide to Piracy,* and my head swam with visions of peglegged par-
rots wearing eye patches and Hathaway shirts, brandishing cutlasses
and leaving no swash unbuckled. But I was not tossing on the high
seas, or tossing 'em back in some waterfront dive. I was at a party in
Greenwich Village, and there was not a pirate in the room. (There were,
however, a couple of agents, and the distinction between the two is a
narrow one indeed.)

But the speaker was neither pirate nor agent. He was Donald E.
Westlake, the prominent mystery novelist and occasional screenwriter,
and the violent criminal activity he was advocating was strictly metaphoric, and to be perpetrated on dry land. He was talking about writing,
and the intended victims were readers.

"First you've got to pipe them aboard," he explained. "You've got to
hook them good and get them into the boat. Then all you have to do
is provide enough shipboard activity to keep them there. Decent food,

plenty to drink. Entertainment in the evenings—a juggler one night, some played-out operatic soprano the next. Remember, you've got an essentially captive audience here. They'd just as soon stay put.

"And then, at the end, you've got to kill 'em. Or the whole cruise is a failure."

Threes

For years I've watched speakers stand up in front of rooms full of writers and explain that every story has a beginning and a middle and an ending. While I've never had occasion to argue with this bit of wisdom, neither have I ever seen what good it does anyone to know it. A story has a beginning and a middle and an ending. Terrific. A person has legs, a trunk, and a head. So what? Now that we know that, what do we know?

Listening to Mr. Westlake, however, it struck me that dividing a story like Gaul into three parts might be of value in detailing what we must do to make the fiction we write satisfying to those who read it. Our obligation would seem to vary with the portion of the story, and we have to focus on different considerations depending on whether we're dealing with the beginning, the middle, or the end.

To depart from our nautical metaphor, the beginning of a story is a snare. We have to engage the reader's attention. We have to draw him in and trap him, and the more effective is our trap, the more likely we will be to have him with us for the duration.

The middle of the story is a joyride. We don't have to be so competitive now because there's less competition out there. With every paragraph, the reader considers himself to have a greater investment in what he's reading. It's easy for him to quit on the first or second page, much harder to jump overboard and start swimming when we've had him with us for half a dozen pages of a story or as many chapters of a novel.

The ending of the story is the payoff. It's the promised destination that drew him onto your boat in the first place. (The nautical motif seems inescapable, doesn't it? I can't manage to shake it.) If the ending doesn't deliver, the reader feels cheated by the entire experience. He may have enjoyed himself all along, but he's apt to forget that now; all he'll recall later is that he finished with a feeling of considerable dissatisfaction. "The first chapter sells the book," Mickey Spillane has said of his own work. "The last chapter sells the *next* book."

Let's talk about beginnings.

First Things First

The first chapter sells the book. The first page sells the story.

And it is there at the beginning that good salesmanship is most important.

In the introduction to one of his books of poetry, E. E. Cummings explained that his poems were in competition, not only with other poems but with flowers and balloons and mud puddles and train rides and, indeed, with everything that might occupy a prospective reader's attention. Our fiction is similarly competitive, and it is essential for me to remember that nobody has to read something simply because I had to write it. A couple of people—my agent, my editor—have to go through the motions, but if their eyes glaze over, they can turn the pages without paying too much attention to the words contained thereon. Nobody else even has to turn the pages. No one has to print what I've written; once it has been printed, no one is obliged to buy it; the person who buys it can stop reading after a paragraph and pick up something else instead, or watch television, or go out and mow the lawn.

It is my job to keep this from happening, and I can best assure this by starting out right.

Sometime last year I picked up *A Study in Scarlet,* Sir Arthur Conan Doyle's classic novel of Sherlock Holmes. I blush to admit that I had never read it before. (I do a lot of this sort of blushing. The list of acknowledged literary masterpieces that I have unaccountably missed is a lengthy one. The books could fill a library—and, come to think of it, often do.)

The first thing that struck me about *A Study in Scarlet* was that it could never have been published today in the form in which it appears. The book takes forever to get underway. Watson talks about how he met Holmes, describes their lodgings, and provides a wealth of admittedly absorbing detail before anything happens. That a novel should take so much time getting started seems incomprehensible to us a century later, and it becomes even more remarkable when we recall that *A Study in Scarlet* first appeared as a magazine serial. I don't know just where the first installment ended, but it's unlikely that it could have contained more than a bare hint of the story itself.

Would a contemporary editor reject Conan Doyle's novel? Not necessarily. The writing is so good and the characterization so engaging that a good editor might well stay with the book through its desultory opening, and then get wholly caught up in the book's narrative flow. But that same editor would certainly insist that the author refashion the opening in order to make the story more accessible to the reader.

Ought the book to be revised today to accommodate the tastes of modern readers? No, certainly not. *A Study in Scarlet* has been in print since its first appearance, and it seems likely to remain in print as long as people read books in English—or in any of the dozens of other languages into which it has been translated. It does just fine in its present form, and it would be a travesty to alter a word.

But today's reader knows what he is getting when he picks the book up. He knows, for openers, that the book is a classic, that it has delighted generations of readers, and that he can be certain of a rousing tale and a fascinating cast of characters. He knows who Holmes and Watson are, and knows that at least half of the pleasure of the book will be the delight of their company during its reading. He is, in short, presold. The book could open any damn way and he's going to stay with it.

You and I are not in that enviable position. (Neither, when the book first appeared, was Conan Doyle, but he lived in different times. Readers were less hurried, and they very likely had fewer alternate pastimes available to them. Even so, he would not have been ill-advised to get the game afoot a little closer to page 1.)

In a couple of columns over the years I've written about opening paragraphs and their function in getting things off to a good start. But the beginning of a story or novel amounts to more than a couple of paragraphs. It is, indeed, as much as it takes to pipe your reader aboard, to get him hooked even as you get the story going.

You have to manage several things at once. First, of course, you have to attract his attention and draw him in. You may try to accomplish this by beginning with the action already in progress; later on, you and he will both have time to take a breath and put your feet up, and you can then fill him in on the whys and wherefores of what he's been watching.

This is a handy device, but it's not the only way to start quickly. You can open with a provocative statement about the story or one of its characters. ("Most people take a lifetime to learn life's most important lesson. Jack Bayliss learned everything he had to know in five minutes one September afternoon on the leeward side of a West Virginia mountain.") You can use a background anecdote. ("When Audrey was a baby she was always a picky eater. Years afterward, her mother would tell anyone who listened about the day she tried to get the child to eat an artichoke . . . .")

At the same time that you engage the reader's attention, you want to let him know what kind of a story he's reading. This task is not a burden to be carried exclusively by the beginning of the text. The title will share the load, along with the blurbs, the jacket copy, the cover art, the promotional campaign, and whatever reputation your previous work has earned you. All of these elements have combined to give the reader an idea of what to expect from your book, but he will still not entirely have made up his mind when he reads your opening, and it can either increase his appetite for what follows or put him off altogether.

Some years ago a friend strongly urged me to read *Another Roadside Attraction*, Tom Robbins's brilliant first novel. I dutifully picked up the book in a store, read the first two pages, and put it back. A few weeks later my friend asked if I'd read the book.

"I started to," I said, "but I could tell it wasn't my kind of thing."

"It is absolutely and unequivocally your kind of thing," he said. "I'll bet you got bogged down in the first two pages, didn't you? I should have warned you about that. Pick it up again and bull your way past the first two pages, or skip them if you have to. They're false advertising, because the book's completely different from what they'd lead you to expect."

A further chore of the beginning is to make you care about the story, to convince you that you ought to give a damn how it turns out. In a recent column I mentioned how I'd had a slight problem in this regard with my latest novel, *Out on the Cutting Edge*, due from William Morrow in October. While the beginning was smooth enough, and while there was enough movement to keep the reader from dozing off, the book seemed to my editor to lack a sense of urgency. She felt the reader would wonder why my detective hero, Matthew Scudder, would care all that much about the fate and whereabouts of a young woman he's hired to find. We've never seen the woman, and neither has he, and we're thus not all that concerned about her, and wonder why he would be.

I solved this problem by adding a prologue in which Scudder imagines the woman's last day. The chapters that follow are unchanged; we still don't see her, and neither does Scudder, but we've had a strong hint that something terrible will turn out to have happened to her, and we've established that there's some kind of psychic bond between her and the detective. We believe that he feels as though he knows her, and we even feel as though we've met her—but of course we haven't.

Setting Sail

Are you on board now? Can we hoist the gangplank and put out to sea?

I hope so. Next month we'll be ready for the second leg of our three-part voyage, considering how to keep the reader on board and how to amuse him during the cruise. And the following month we'll discuss how best to kill him at the end.

Stay right where you are.

24

Keeping Them on the Ship

August 1989

LAST MONTH WE DISCUSSED PIPING THE READER ABOARD
THE "SHIP" THAT IS YOUR STORY. NOW THE CRUISE BEGINS.

Good morning, boys and girls.

Good morning, sir.

Our lesson this lovely morning is a continuation of what we were talking about last month. Now I certainly hope you all remember where we left off. Who would like to summarize what we discussed? Rachel?

Sir, you began by quoting some writer named Donald E. Westlake. You said that he said that a writer's job is like that of some sort of homicidal cruise director. First you have to get them on the ship, he said, and then you have to keep them on board, and then you have to kill them at the end.

Very good, Rachel. It seemed to me that Mr. Westlake's observation provided us with a convenient framework for considering the three parts of a story or novel, which are, as I'm sure you recall—yes, Arnold?

The pitch, the deal, and the sub rights?

Not exactly. Mimi?

The beginning, the middle, and the ending, sir.

Quite right. Last month we began at the beginning, curiously enough, and talked about just what the writer must do to open his story in a manner that will get the reader caught up in the story. In short: What can he do to pipe those potential travelers aboard his frail vessel?

Today we'll talk about the middle. Once you've got them on board, how do you keep them there?

All Aboard

Of our three lessons, this has been the most difficult for me to prepare. And that seems appropriate, because for a great many writers, the middle of a story presents the greatest problem. This is less noticeably the case with short fiction, where there's simply less ground to be covered between the start and the finish. (The shortest of stories may be said to have no middle; the beginning leads almost directly to the ending.) In the novel, however, most of the book is middle. A chapter or two gets the book underway, and a chapter or two later on will finish it off, but between the two stretches an endless tunnel, a bottomless abyss, a vastness beyond measure. Page after page of innocent paper has to be filled with words, all of them well-chosen and placed in some presumably agreeable order.

The most self-assured of writers is apt to suffer a crisis of confidence during a book's lengthy midsection. His nightmare tends to be two-fold. First, there's the mounting concern that the book will never be done, that the middle will extend forever, that each new page he writes will bring him farther from the beginning but not a whit closer to the end.

(There is, incidentally, an alternative to this concern. The writer becomes anxious that the middle will be too short, that he cannot possibly pad it out long enough to fulfill either the general requirements of the fiction market or the specific ones of his own contract. I have on occasion had both of these worries at the same time, and have sat at the typewriter simultaneously alarmed that my book was going to be too long and that it would wind up too short. It is, let me assure you, a curious matter to write scene after scene not knowing whether you should be padding them or cutting them short. If you induce a comparable neurotic state in a lab rat, he sits down in the middle of the maze and chews off his own feet.)

Besides worrying over the long and short of it, the writer is typically concerned that what he's shouting is going to fall on deaf ears, or on no ears at all. The reader, cunningly hooked by the book's beginning, will dislodge that hook and swim off into the sunset.

And, indeed, this happens. I don't finish every book I start reading, and I somehow doubt I'm unique in this regard. While I once felt some sort of moral obligation to wade through every book I picked up, somewhere around age 35 I outgrew this foolishness. In this world, one of many books and little time, I feel comfortable occasionally leaving another writer's book unfinished.

But the thought that someone—anyone!—would abandon one of *my* books . . . well, that's another matter entirely.

Some of my concern in this regard may derive from my own literary apprenticeship. I started off writing soft-core sex novels, and the experience left me imprinted with the notion that, if I ever let a whole chapter go by without someone either making love or getting killed, I was waving a beige flag at the reader's attention span.

While this left me with some bad habits that I had to learn to break, I think I was probably luckier than some writers who emerge from an academic background and start off writing thoughtful, introspective novels in which there is not a great deal of dramatic incident. All things considered, I would rather give too much than too little attention to holding the reader's interest.

The Ride of Their Lives

How do you keep the reader aboard? How do you keep him reading?

The first thing to remember is that he *wants* to keep on reading. He picked up the book in the hope that it would engross him utterly. The most compelling blurbs in ads and on book jackets are those which assure you that the book, once begun, cannot possibly be set aside. I know any number of people who read books in order to get to sleep at night, yet no one would try to sell a book by hailing its soporific properties.

"This book kept me up all night" is a far more effective promotional claim than "This book lulled me right into a coma."

More than he wants insight or laughter or tears, and far more than he wants his life changed, the reader wants something that will keep him reading. Once hooked by your opening, he has an investment of time along with his investment of money in your book. Every additional page he reads increases his investment and commits him more deeply to finish what he has started.

So you have a lot going for you. The reader would prefer to stay with you, to see the book through to the end, to have a good time on the way.

All you have to do is keep him amused.

And how do you do that? Here are a few ways:

• *Have interesting things happen.* Most of the books I've written in recent years have been detective stories. While the category is broad enough to embrace a wide range of novels, a common denominator exists in that a lead character is almost invariably called upon to do a certain amount of detecting. This very often involves going around and talking to people.

When my detective hero, Matthew Scudder, goes around knocking on doors and asking questions, he's acquiring information that serves to advance the plot. But if these scenes did no more than provide him with data, they would make very tedious reading indeed. It is not enough that they be functional in terms of the book's plot. It is also essential that they be interesting.

In *Eight Million Ways to Die,* for example, Scudder is hired by a pimp to investigate the murder of one of the pimp's girls. He pursues the investigation by interviewing each of his client's surviving girls. Writing these scenes, I took pains to make each interesting in and of itself. I did this by letting the women emerge as individuals, with their own separate histories, personalities and current lifestyles. Their different perceptions of the pimp enlarged the reader's understanding of that enigmatic character, too.

Every scene you write can be more or less interesting depending on how you write it. Not every scene deserves full treatment, and there will be times when you'll hurry things along by summarizing a scene in a couple of sentences. But the more space you give to a scene and the more importance you assign to it, the greater is your obligation to make that scene pull its weight by commanding the reader's attention and keeping him interested and entertained.

• *Keep the story moving.* The reader will accept a lot of diverse scenes, if they're diverting enough. But you don't want to do such a good job on this that he forgets the point of the whole thing.

In the broadest sense, fiction is about the solution (successful or not) of a problem. If the reader loses sight of that problem during the book's vast middle, he ceases to care. He may keep reading out of inertia if you provide enough entertainment along the way, but if anything comes along to break his attention, he may not get around to picking the book up again. Even if he does keep reading, you may lose your hold on his emotions.

Several times in recent books I've stopped along the way to rewrite a chapter, cutting scenes down or chopping them out entirely. They were entertaining enough as written, and I had to chop out and throw away some nice snappy dialogue that I felt rather proud of—because it was slowing the book's narrative flow. I feel the need to do this as I go along because I'm not comfortable otherwise, but many writers find it works better if they let their scenes run on and do their cutting after the first draft is finished. In either case, the same considerations operate.

• *Pile on the miseries.* One thing you want to do in the book's middle is turn up the gain on your narrative. You do this by making the problem more of a headache. This makes its solution more essential.

In suspense fiction, a standard way to do this is to toss another corpse on the floor. The reader is already committed to the idea that the initial murder must be solved and the murderer apprehended. When someone else dies, such a resolution becomes even more imperative. Furthermore, you've introduced an element of urgency; the hero must act not only to restore balance to the universe, but also to prevent the death of other characters, including some who may by now have become important to the reader.

Similarly, you can raise the stakes for the reader by making the problem's solution more difficult. In *A Ticket to the Boneyard,* a just-completed novel about Scudder, he is trying to apprehend a particularly vicious killer. While he is struggling to track the man down, several things happen to heighten the tension and raise the stakes. There are additional murders. Scudder gets severely beaten. And his closest friend on the police force turns on him, denying him support he'd come to take for granted.

• *Enjoy the trip.* Some people enjoy writing. Others hate it. As far as I can tell, there's no real correlation between the pleasure the author takes in a book's composition and the pleasure a reader will take later on.

Even so, I suspect we're well advised to have as much fun with all of this as we possibly can. And it's the middle of the book that is most apt to appear burdensome when we're bogged down in it. If writing a book is driving across America, the book's middle is an endless highway across Kansas, and there are days when every sentence is as flat as the unvarying landscape.

There are, to be sure, a lot of interesting things in Kansas. But you won't enjoy them much if you spend every moment telling yourself you can't wait to get to California, and if you're twitching with anxiety that the book will be too long or too short or just plain lousy.

Forget all that. Stay in the now. Enjoy the trip.

The Final Leg

Are you still with me? Have you read this far?

Good. But if you're waiting for a big finish, I'm afraid you'll have to keep on waiting.

Until next month.

25

Killing Them at the End

September 1989

PART III OF OUR SERIES ON GRABBING AND HOLDING READERS EXAMINES THE IMPORTANCE OF POWERFUL ENDINGS.

A while back a friend of mine was flying from Los Angeles to New York. He was in the first-class section, a luxury to which he is not much accustomed, and the chap seated beside him was some sort of yuppie businessman, on his way to or from some sort of hostile takeover. The little swine had a clear enough conscience to lose himself altogether in the inflight movie, a pleasure my friend was willing to forgo.

The yuppie laughed immoderately all through the film. When he unplugged his earphones even as they rolled the final credits, my friend asked him how he'd liked it.

"Not so great," the young man said.

"But you laughed your head off," my friend protested. "If you hadn't been belted in you'd have fallen out of your seat."

"Oh, I'm not saying it wasn't funny," the little shark replied. "There were some great laughs in the thing. But, you know, it just wasn't a very good picture."

Now this story might do little more than illustrate the perversity of the Young Undeservedly Prosperous but for the specific film involved. It was *Burglar*, the Whoopi Goldberg vehicle based (more or less) on a book called *The Burglar in the Closet*, a mystery novel written by, uh, me.

And the chap seated beside the chortling little chiseler was my agent, the redoubtable Knox Burger.

And, worst of all, the damned whelp was right. *Burglar* was a million laughs, but it just wasn't a very good movie. And virtually everyone who saw it reacted pretty much the way Knox's seatmate did. They roared while they were in the theater, and then they told their friends not to bother going. This was true of the insider audiences; laughter was riotous at the large Manhattan house where I saw the film screened, and the very people who laughed the loudest then went home and wrote scathingly negative reviews. The reaction was the same at the theaters in suburban shopping malls. Everybody had a good time for 90 minutes and went out shaking the old head in disgust.

Why should a film—or fiction in any form—provoke this sort of contradictory response? How could audiences have such a good time with the picture while it was going on and respect it so little once it was over? In the particular case of *Burglar,* I think there are several answers. The gags were too easy, the characterizations were shallow, the relationships were too hard-edged—there were lots of things wrong with this movie, and most of them need not concern us here. But one factor that I'm sure contributed to the film's failure to generate good word-of-mouth was the relative weakness of its ending. The ending was soft, and it left the audience unsatisfied.

"The first chapter sells the book," Mickey Spillane has said. "The last chapter sells the *next* book."

Very true. But there's even more to it than that. The last chapter sells the next book by convincing the reader that the book he's just finished was terrific. That doesn't just make him a customer for your next effort, but it makes him a powerful salesman for what he's just finished reading. The stronger your ending, the more likely he'll be to recommend the book to his friends. It is word-of-mouth ultimately that creates bestsellers. Nothing else, no amount of advertising and publicity, can sustain a book that does not get touted by those who read it. And a book with an unsatisfying ending just cannot generate strong word-of-mouth on a broad scale.

The End?

"First you've got to get them on board. Then you've got to keep them on the boat for the duration of the voyage. And, finally, you've got to kill them at the end."

That, as those of you without chronic short-term memory problems will recall, has been our premise in this space for the past three months. If, as we're always being told, a work of fiction has a beginning, a middle, and an ending, it seems reasonable to suppose that a writer is variously challenged by each of these three components. His job in the beginning is to hook the reader into the story, while in the middle it is his task simply to keep the person reading.

At the end, he has to pay off all the book's promises. He has to give the reader everything he signed on for—and more. A weak ending can kill a good book, and a really powerful ending can save a book with not that much else going for it.

During the past year I've read a pair of unusually well-written first novels, both of them suspense yarns, one set in Michigan, the other in the Florida Keys. Both books have generated a lot of favorable comment among mystery pros, no doubt because of the genuine excellence of their writing. Neither did as well with the public at large, and I think I know why. The ending of one was improbable, almost silly, while the other ended very inconclusively. I enjoyed both immensely while I was reading them, but ended feeling somehow cheated and unsatisfied.

I know I've hurt my own sales in the same fashion in at least one book. *Ariel,* a novel I published ten years or so ago, was a story of psychological suspense featuring a 12-year-old girl who may or may not be evil, and who may or may not have murdered her baby brother in his crib. And the ending is inconclusive. You don't find out for sure what the girl is and what she did. A few reviewers liked the enigmatic ending, but more than a few did not, and I don't blame them. It was vague because I was vague—I didn't know what had happened. I would have greatly preferred a less uncertain ending if I could only have come up with one.

But Would It Make It on MTV?

What makes an ending work?

Maybe the best way to answer that is to listen to a Beethoven symphony. By the time the last note of the coda has sounded at the end of the fourth movement, you damn well know it's over. When that last ringing chord hits you, every musical question has been answered, every emotional issue has been resolved, and you don't have to wait for the folks around you to start applauding in order to be certain the piece is done. If Ludwig van B. had set *Ariel* to music, there wouldn't have been anything enigmatic about the ending, believe me.

Setting Sights

It's generally a good deal easier to write an ending with impact if you have that ending in mind from the onset. The more clearly you are able to perceive it as you go along, the more you can shape the various elements of the story so that the ending will resolve them in a satisfying fashion.

Does this mean that you have to have the whole book outlined, in your mind or on paper, before you write it? As one who almost never uses an outline, I'm hardly inclined to advance such an argument. It is possible, however, to know your ending without knowing just how you're going to reach it.

Several novelists, most recently E.L. Doctorow, have likened the writing of a novel to driving at night. You can see only as far as your headlight beams reach, but you can drive clear across country that way.

Very true, and I've written any number of books in just that fashion. But I've been most successful when, while I could not see past the range of my headlights, I nevertheless knew my ultimate destination in advance. If I just hop in the car with no goal in mind, I may have an enjoyable journey, but I run the risk of not getting anywhere, or not even really knowing when the trip is over. (In point of fact I travel that way all the time in real life, but it doesn't work as well in fiction.)

Dorothy Salisbury Davis, who does very well indeed with beginnings and middles as well as endings, has said that she can't comfortably write a mystery novel unless she knows from the onset who did it. She may change her mind in the course of the book, she may wind up hanging the murder on someone other than her initial choice, but she always has a solution in mind even as she constructs the problem.

I haven't always done this, but I certainly have an easier time when I do. It seems to me, too, that a substantial portion of the books I've abandoned over the years have been ones for which I did not have a strong ending in mind from the beginning. I ran out of gas on those books not specifically because I wound up painting myself into a corner or wandering in an insoluble maze but simply because each book sort of wobbled to a halt. I think it may have been the lack of a concrete destination in the form of a foreseen ending that brought this about.

Final Leg of the Journey

The most satisfactory endings resolve everything. Like that Beethoven coda we just heard, they answer questions we never even thought to ask.

Most of my books are mystery novels, concerned with a crime and its solution. Find the murderer and you've found the ending. Mysteries, however, are frequently concerned with more than crime and punishment, and sometimes an ending has to do more than name a perpetrator and clap the cuffs on him.

Eight Million Ways to Die is a good case in point. The book begins with the murder of a call girl, and my detective, Matthew Scudder, is hired by her pimp to find out who killed her. The stakes are raised when two other prostitutes die, one an apparent suicide. And, finally, Scudder brings the killer to justice. He does so by making himself a stalking horse, a move that almost fails when the killer waits in Scudder's hotel room with a machete. But Scudder and justice prevail, and the bad guy gets what's coming to him, and the ending is dramatically satisfying.

But the string of murders is not all that the book is about. It's also about life and death in New York, and it's very much about Scudder's attempt to come to terms with his alcoholism. He struggles to stay sober as he chases the killer through the city's terrible streets, and the book follows him in and out of ginmills and detox wards and AA meetings. After the book has seemingly ended, after the killer has been found out and dealt with and the solution explained to his client, there is a final chapter in which Scudder is brought face to face with his own illness and has to confront himself or back down.

The first ending, the unmasking and apprehension of the killer, is dramatically effective but not everything it might be. Because of the story itself, the killer is not someone we have met before. (Hollywood can't bear this sort of thing, and in the film version the killer is the sneering villain we've met early on.) But the second ending more than makes up for it. A considerable number of people have told me, in person or through the mails, how much impact the ending had for them. Many of them have assured me that they cried, that they were moved to tears.

And that is what an ending ought to do. It ought to move a reader. It need not move him to tears—although that doesn't hurt. But it ought to leave him knowing that he's been in a fight and that the fight is over. You don't have to leave him feeling happy—although a downbeat ending is usually hard to bring off effectively. But you do have to leave him feeling complete. He may finish wondering what will happen to the characters afterward, and that's all right, as long as you leave him feeling that the issues raised in this part of their story are resolved.

Not every successful book has an ending that works in this sense. Some people break the rules and seem to get away with it. The example that comes first to mind for me is John Le Carré, who has made an occasional habit of endings that I can only assume are intentionally obscure. Both *The Spy Who Came In from the Cold* and *A Small Town in Germany* have ambiguous last pages; you have to read them over a second or third time in order to be certain just what is taking place. The author's writing is so clear elsewhere that it is puzzling that his ending should be so murky. I can't seriously argue that this weakness, if that's what it is, has hurt Le Carré with readers or critics. He's doing just fine, and for all I know maybe I'm the only person who finds his endings opaque.

Any questions? Yes, Rachel?

Why "kill them at the end," sir? Why such a violent image?

I don't know, Rachel. I've asked myself the same question, and originally looked around for a way to paraphrase Donald Westlake's original observation that triggered this series of columns. But I can't find an alternative that works as well.

Comedians, and performers in general, use that metaphor. "I killed them in Keokuk," the vaudevillian would say. "I knocked them dead. I beat their brains in. I slaughtered them."

I guess the implication is that the audience—and in our case the reader—is overpowered by the material. It overwhelms him, and killing is the ultimate way of being overwhelmed because it is undeniably final. What you may be objecting to, Rachel, is the implication of hostility between the comic and his audience, the writer and his reader. If you're trying to kill your readers, doesn't that mean that you hate them?

No, not in this case, not when they pick up the book hoping to be killed in just this fashion. Even if you continue to dislike the metaphor, I'd urge you to strive for fictional endings that seem to fit it. Because this kind of metaphoric death is anything but final. Unless you kill them at the end, they won't keep coming back for more.

26

Joywriting

October 1989

KEEPING THE FUN IN WRITING.

This past spring I spent an hour that will, I trust, pay off handsomely in terms of my spiritual growth and development. My wife and I were guests at Mohonk Mountain House a couple of hours north of New York, where Don and Abby Westlake were conducting their annual mystery weekend. A year earlier Lynne and I had attended as suspects, playing roles in the emerging mystery plot and submitting to grilling by the relentless guests. This year we were back in an even more exalted capacity, that of Freeloader. We toiled not, neither did we spin, but boy did we eat.

The crew of suspects and hangers-on at a Mohonk Mystery Weekend always includes a generous handful of writers, most of them notables in the mystery-suspense field. In the course of the weekend, three or four of these worthies are called upon to give hour-long talks to the assembled guests. Then, on Saturday afternoon, all of the celebrated writers make themselves available in the lounge, where guests can bring books for autographing. A generous selection of books by all the guest authors is on display throughout the weekend in the hotel's gift shop, so books to be autographed are by no means hard to come by.

At the appointed hour, we all of us assembled in the lodge and seated ourselves at separate tables, waiting for book-bearing guests to descend on us. We were, I must say, a reasonably distinguished crew. The

Westlakes were on hand, of course. So were Christopher Newman, author of several well-received New York police novels, including *Sixth Precinct;* Mary Higgins Clark, author of *A Stranger Is Watching* and other bestselling thrillers; William Bayer, author of *Peregrine* and *Pattern Crimes;* and, borne all the way on wings of glasnost and perestroika, Julian Semyonov, the Soviet Union's Robert Ludlum, author of *Tass Is Authorized to Announce.*

There was also a chap from Maine who has made something of a name for himself writing horror novels.

Well, let me tell you. I've had humbling experiences in my time. Indeed, it sometimes seems as though my life has been specifically designed as a whole series of humbling experiences. But this one copped the biscuit.

In the course of the hour, perhaps half a dozen good people came up to me with books for me to sign. About the same number more or less presented themselves to Bill Bayer and Chris Newman. Mary and the Westlakes drew a few more, and there may have been two dozen people in all queueing up for Julian.

I'm not sure of these numbers. I wasn't counting. What I was mostly doing was staring open-mouthed at the line the fellow from Maine had drawn.

It ran all around the room and down the hall and, I wouldn't be surprised to learn, out the building. It moved quickly, because the fellow doing the signing was pretty quick with a pen, but even so the line seemed inexhaustible. The hour for autographing ended at 5 o'clock, but the lad from Bangor stayed where he was, signing hundreds upon hundreds of books, until past 5:30.

I had never seen the like. But others who had were quick to assure me that what I had witnessed was nothing out of the ordinary. It's always like this, they said, when Stephen King does a signing.

Droves of Fans

Of course Stephen King is an enormously popular writer, and deservedly so. He has essentially created modern horror fiction as a commercial category. All of his books sell in the millions. He is enormously productive, and his fans wish he wrote twice as fast as he does.

Even so, this somehow fails to explain that endless line of autograph seekers. Mary Higgins Clark is also immensely popular, with her every novel an immediate entrant onto the bestseller list, but she doesn't have King's astonishing crowd appeal, which seems to me to extend beyond the books themselves. The people in that line wanted the books, but they wanted something more. They wanted to carry a piece of the author home with them.

I know of one other writer who elicits a similar response among book buyers. When he is available to sign books, people turn out in droves; other writers, witnessing the phenomenon, grind their teeth down to nubbins.

The author in question is Isaac Asimov.

What do these two gentlemen have in common? They're both successful, to be sure, and hugely popular. Both are extremely personable fellows, although I don't know that most of the folks seeking their autographs would know this, or not until they got to the front of the line.

I can think of one unusual quality the two writers share. Both of them absolutely love to write. They are pure fools for writing. It's a source of pure joy to them, and they'd rather do it than anything else.

Sticking to It

Can it be that simple?

I do not want for a moment to suggest that that is all there is to it, that if you enjoy your work others will enjoy it, and vice versa. That's simply not true. There are quite a few writers I could name who find writing a painful chore, who have to force themselves to their desks each morning, and who liken the whole creative process metaphorically to the sweating of blood. And many of them do very well, and the books that provide them with so little pleasure are a source of considerable enjoyment for a legion of loyal readers.

Conversely, there are at least as many writers who take unremitting delight in the hours they spend at their desks, getting no end of pleasure and satisfaction from the pastime of putting words on paper, whose work is unfortunately pleasurable to no one but themselves. There are those of us who hate writing but who nevertheless write like angels, and there are those of us who love it but who haven't the talent to write our names in the dirt with a stick. It doesn't seem fair, but then what does?

All that notwithstanding, I must say that I don't think it coincidental that Stephen King and Isaac Asimov love to write. I suspect that their delight and enthusiasm is somehow instilled in what they write and somehow communicates itself to their readers, touching off a corresponding delight and enthusiasm not only for the books but also for their authors.

I don't want to belabor this point. I don't even want to argue that the first step in getting other people to enjoy your work is to enjoy it yourself. Let me merely suggest that experiencing the act of writing as pleasurable rather than painful would probably do us no harm in the marketplace, and might even do us some good.

Reading and Reeding

Even if it didn't, you'd think we'd already have every incentive to enjoy it. We seem to be stuck with it anyway, sentenced to spend the rest of our lives making up stories and jotting them down. If writing is inevitable, why not sit up and enjoy it?

In other arts, such an argument would probably not be necessary. Painters love to paint. Musicians love to make music. Why should scribbling or tapping a keyboard be more agonizing and less pleasurable than rinsing out a brush or blowing through a reed?

I think the answer, or a good part of it, lies in our propensity to get fixated upon the ultimate result of our work and to regard the actual process of writing as a means to an end, an arduous and time-consuming business that must be endured if we are to wind up with a finished book in our hands. With our eyes so firmly fixed upon the far horizon, how can we possibly take delight in the journey itself?

For an actor or a musician, the process is really all there is. When it is finished, nothing remains other than what lingers in the mind and memory of the audience. The sonata and the soliloquy echo for an instant and are gone. (This is not altogether true if the performance has been filmed or recorded, which may help explain why many performers find less pure joy in film than in stage work, in recording sessions than in live performance.)

For a painter, the canvas is transformed bit by bit from a blank expanse into a finished work. Throughout, the artist can look upon the emerging whole even as he concentrates on the particular. The work on a given day may go well or poorly, but in any event the artist is involved with the process.

There's something different about a book. The process is a lot less demonstrably fascinating. A painter in a public place invariably draws a crowd, but it's hard to imagine anyone getting much satisfaction out of observing a writer at work. The writer himself can't really see how he's doing, or get a real look at the emerging work. All I can really tell is that I'm making progress, and I can determine this by watching the stack of finished pages to the left of my typewriter mount ever higher. (Folks with word processors don't even have this for reassurance; they have to take it on faith that an ever-increasing number of words is stored somewhere in the mysterious recesses of their machines. Some writers have taken to printing out each day's work at the day's end, not so much because they have any real use for words on paper at that stage but because they need tangible evidence of their progress on a daily basis.)

Whether or not we print out as we go along, the fact remains that a book is not a book until it's finished, and for many of us it isn't really a book until it's printed and bound and somebody's actually reading it. Our pleasure is thus postponed until long after the work itself has been completed, and even then we can't find much enjoyment in it, because by the time one book is out, it's out of mind as well; we're busy working on a new one, and hating it.

Is there a way out of this?

I think there is. The trick consists of becoming as completely involved as possible in the process of writing and correspondingly less concerned with the future. In a sense, this may be as simple (and as tricky) as staying focused in the present and taking the book one day at a time.

For my own part, I can say that I've enjoyed writing more during the past couple of years, and that this seems to be the result of allowing myself to enjoy the process.

This is not to say that I have grown less eager to complete what I've started. I'm writing my books as rapidly as ever, and I begin each writing day with a goal in mind, a specific number of pages I intend to complete before calling it quits for the day. I don't really know that I *do* anything differently these days. Whatever change there is seems to be largely attitudinal. More and more, I find I'm able to enjoy the act of writing. Not just the magical creative bursts, when whole pages compose themselves at the speed of light and all I have to do is type them out. But also the more tedious times, when the brain seems to be composed of Jell-O and words flow like sludge. And, sometimes, I can even experience something close to pleasure when one false start follows another, and I rewrite the same damned scene time and time again, until the wastebasket overflows while the stack of finished pages stays the same.

All of this is part of the process. All of this is writing. And all of this leads, eventually, to the moment when someone plucks the finished book from the shelf and carts it off to the cash register.

All of it, too, is something that can involve me totally, something that can take me magically out of the prison of self and let me fly away on wings of thought, on gossamer strands of words. My God, if I can't enjoy that, what *can* I enjoy?

Between the Lines

I'm writing these lines in a friend's house in the Poconos. I've been here for almost a week. It's spring, and the weather's gorgeous, and in the late afternoon a herd of deer comes within 20 yards or so of our windows. I finished a book two months ago, and I'll be starting the next one in August, so all I really have to do is enjoy the weather and the deer and the fresh air.

I've been going nuts. Everything's fine in my life, and I've been anxious or depressed for the past ten days or so. Sometimes both at once.

I don't know why, and I'm not sure it matters. Part of it very likely derives from the fact that I've been agonizing over the book I want to start in August. I know a little about the book, and I spent a few weeks in New York scouting locations and doing background research, but I don't know anything yet about the plot or the characters. And of course I'm afraid that, come August, I'll be holed up in a writers' colony with a fresh ream of bond paper and a dozen film cartridges for my typewriter and no book to write.

It's happened before. It could happen again.

On the other hand, there's nothing intrinsically alarming about the idea of not knowing in April what I'm going to be writing in August. I don't have that much advance information about other aspects of my life. Why should my writing be different? I have to have faith while I'm writing a book that it will all make sense at the end. Why can't I have similar faith beforehand, when I'm getting ready to write a book?

For the most part, I do. It's when I don't that I have weeks like this.

And maybe they're necessary, maybe they're part of my own particular creative process. Last night, after a couple of days of abject moping, of sleeping all day and reading all night and being such rotten company that even the deer were beginning to avoid me, I Got An Idea. It's just an idea, it's not an entire plot, but it's the kind of idea that feels right, the sort that seems likely to develop to the point where, by the time I'm encased in my studio in August, I'll know what to write.

If I ever really get the hang of this, I'll learn to enjoy all of it. Not just the time I spend at the typewriter. Not just the part when the idea begins to form and the plot and characters take shape. But the whole thing, the whole kit and caboodle. Including the depression and the anxiety and the days when I think I've written my last book and the nights when it all seems hopeless.

Because it's all part of being a writer, and all part of the process of writing. And that's all I really wanted when I first signed on for this voyage, years and years ago, and, when all is said and done, it's still all I really want.

So it looks as though I might as well learn to enjoy it.

27

No Tense Like the Present

November 1989

OUR COLUMNIST DISCUSSES USE OF THE PRESENT TENSE
IN FICTION. OR SHOULD WE SAY HE DISCUSSED?

The man, a purposeful air about him, slips into the bookstore through that establishment's front door. Behind the counter, a salesclerk riffles the pages of a tabloid newspaper, pausing to acknowledge the new customer with a laconic nod.

The man proceeds to the rack where new hardcover fiction is displayed. His eyes scan the rows of brightly colored jackets. One book, no more arresting in appearance than its fellows, catches his eye. He takes it from the shelf, opens it at random. He scans a few paragraphs and his brow darkens in a scowl. He closes the book, reopens it again at random. He reads. Then, with a muffled curse, he slams it shut and returns it to the rack.

"Present tense!" he cries out—to the salesclerk, to the heavens, to the uncaring walls. "The whole damn thing's written in the present tense!" Furious, livid, he turns on his heel and stalks out of the store.

Somewhere a dog is barking . . .

The foregoing, I should assure you, is fanciful. I have never yet shouted out my dismay at encountering a novel written in the present tense. Nor, for that matter, have I ever had a purposeful air about me.

Still, the attitude is my own. I am invariably disheartened when something I'd hoped to read turns out to have been written in the present tense, and more often than not that aspect alone is enough to dissuade me from reading it. Sometimes I'll read such a book anyway, and sometimes I'll enjoy it, but it's always in spite of the tense the author has chosen to employ.

This has been true for years, and it never occurred to me to wonder why. I just accepted the fact that I was put off by present-tense fictional narration and let it go at that, writing it off as a personal quirk, and by no means the only one in my possession.

Then in September of 1988 *The Atlantic* ran a brief essay by Peter Davison in which he inveighs against the dominance of the present tense in contemporary poetry.

"Many casual readers of today's poetry misunderstand their own discomfort and complain only of the absence of rhyme and meter," Mr. Davison states. "What really underlies their dissatisfaction, I think, is that so many contemporary poets lack conviction. They have lost some degree of belief in the validity of poetic utterance."

Nineteenth-century poets, he points out, were sure of what they were saying, and they wrote in the past tense, asserting their message as factual. "The present tense, in contrast, constrains us to hear only the voice of the watcher. The present indicative lets a poet stand a foot away from commitment, three or four feet away from identification, six feet away from declaration . . . . Contemporary poetry tends to cast the poet in the role of witness. Between the poet and the event falls a shadow: 'The apparition of these faces in the crowd: / Petals on a wet, black bough.' Pound's split figure implies externality, irony, remoteness, alienation, impotence. It omits relationship, intimacy, interaction, community, and the passage of time. Poems descended from it and composed in the present indicative encourage us to draw back lest we plunge in . . . . They enable us to avoid recommendation, passion, announcement. Speaking in the present tense says that everything is usual but nothing is special."

I think Mr. Davison is on to something. I wouldn't presume to say what's right or wrong with modern poetry, but it seems to me that his

observations apply as well to fiction. The present tense distances both
the reader and the writer from the events. It takes away both engage-
ment and certainty.

The past tense in fiction states unequivocally that a given thing happened, that it happened in a certain way. The present tense calls upon us
to believe that the thing is happening now, as we read about it, that it is
unfolding in some alternate universe.

Consider the following versions:

> *McGraw came through the door with a length of pipe in his hand. I picked
> up my chair and threw it at him. He ducked, and I came in low and knocked
> his feet out from under him. He got me a good one across the small of the back
> before we both careened into the wall. I was up first, and I kicked his wrist and
> the pipe went flying.*

And:

> *McGraw comes through the door with a length of pipe in his hand. I pick
> up my chair and throw it at him. He ducks, and I come in low and knock his
> feet out from under him. He gets me a good one across the small of the back
> before we both careen into the wall. I am up first, and I kick his wrist and the
> pipe goes flying.*

Here the present tense wouldn't seem to afford the narrator an opportunity for disengagement. After all, how disengaged can you be
when you're in the middle of a barroom brawl? Even so, the second example strikes me as less real, less gripping, less involving than the first.
When, we wonder, is all this happening? If it's happening now, as we're
supposed to believe, how can the narrator be telling us about it even as
he's rolling around on the floor with McGraw? If it happened a while
ago, why is it cast in the present tense?

Reading both examples, I find that the first, the past tense specimen, carries more conviction. I'm more apt to get caught up in something like this, more apt to care what happens next. But, interestingly enough, I find it a little easier to visualize what is taking place in the second example. Because it is in the present tense, it is not so much narrative—telling a story—as it is descriptive. I am not so much asked to believe that this has taken place as I am told to see it taking place. Thus I can see it more vividly in the present tense, even though I am less inclined to give a damn about it.

Much of the fiction being written these days in the present tense is the sort of minimalist work that's very much in vogue now, with critics if not with great numbers of readers. These books, often called experimental for reasons I find elusive, probably work better in the present tense than they would in the past. For the most part they are not books that would greatly interest me whatever tense was employed for their narration, so I would be hard put to argue that they would be more effective in past tense.

What does unsettle me, though, is when an otherwise traditional novel is cast in the present tense for no discernible reason. A recent example of this was *Presumed Innocent,* the hugely successful courtroom novel by Scott Turow. Except for the fact that the book was recounted in first-person present tense, there was nothing experimental or unorthodox about its narrative structure.

Why the present tense? I'm damned if I know. It certainly didn't fit the book, and if it added anything I can't imagine what it might be. The author certainly did not have disengagement and distance as a goal. I can't too effectively argue that Mr. Turow made a horrible mistake, that some editor should have persuaded him to rewrite the entire manuscript in the past tense; after all, the book was enormously successful, and even readers like myself who would have greatly preferred a past-tense narrative stayed with Mr. Turow right through to the end.

I can't argue that the book would have sold a single extra copy in the past tense. But I don't think it'd have sold any fewer, either, and I'd certainly have had a better time reading it.

Easing Tension

Why the present tense?

I think it may be an effect of film and television. Have you ever had anybody tell you a movie? When I was young, some of the kids were particularly good at this. They could recount a film so that you got it almost as effectively as if you saw it for yourself. Sometimes it was better getting it secondhand from them, because they could skip the dull parts, and render comprehensible the parts that might have been confusing.

"Clark Gable's a rancher, see, and he's on a trip buying stock, and there's an Indian raid and they come swooping down on his ranch and kill his wife and burn his cabin. Only when they ride off you see them take off their war paint and feathers, and they're not really Indians! But he doesn't know this, and he comes back, and he goes nuts, and right away he swears to get revenge . . . ."

Outlines are written in the present tense. So are film treatments. The present tense is useful when we want to enable the reader to visualize what a particular piece of fiction will be (if it is as yet unwritten) or what it already was (if we're recounting a movie, or summarizing a novel in a review).

But the work itself is different. It does not exist to tell you about something you haven't read, or something that has not yet been written. It is telling you about something that you are supposed to believe has occurred. You're not just supposed to be able to visualize it. You're supposed to be able to believe it, and it is rendered most believable by being presented in the tense one always uses to describe that which has happened—i.e., the past tense.

In an age that increasingly regards the entire past as something to be shrugged off or disposed of or rewritten, it is perhaps not surprising that we would tend to employ the present tense for fiction. The argument would seem to be that a story will become more immediate for being kept out of the past tense. If it already happened, like, it's history. But if it's happening, wow!

Except it doesn't really work that way. Past-tense fiction doesn't necessarily seem over and done with; all we know is that the action took place before the narrative voice told us about it. Most science fiction is written in the past tense, even though it may be set in the future. You wouldn't write a novel set in the 25th century in the future tense—not if you expected anybody to read it. So why use the present tense for something contemporary?

Days of Future Past

If there are sound arguments against writing an entire work of fiction in the present tense, there are nevertheless times when the tense is useful in small doses. Prologues, and occasionally epilogues, lend themselves to this treatment. In *Out on the Cutting Edge*, I used a prologue in which my hero, Matthew Scudder, imagines a murder scene at which he was never present. He tells you that he is imagining the scene, and then renders it in the present: "They are walking in the woods, and he has his arm around her. She is laughing." The whole tone here is conjectural, we are dealing not with what emphatically was but with what might have been, and the present tense, inviting the reader to picture something rather than stating it as fact, seemed called for.

Hamlin Garland does something similar in *A Son of the Middle Border*, not as prologue but intermittently throughout the text. The book is autobiography rather than fiction, but stylistically it might as well be a novel; Garland did in fact write several autobiographical novels before finding that he could deal more effectively with the same material by presenting it as straight autobiography.

The book is written in past tense, except when the author wants to show you a picture. Here's an example:

> *To most of our harvest hands that year Saturday night meant a visit to town and a drunken spree . . . . After a hard week's work we all felt that a trip to town was only a fair reward.*
>
> *Saturday night in town! How it all comes back to me! I am a timid visitor in the little frontier village. It is sunset. A whiskey-crazed farmhand is walking barefooted up and down the middle of the road defying the world. From a corner of the street I watch with tense interest another lithe, pock-marked bully menacing with cat-like action a cowering young farmer in a long linen coat . . . .*

And so on. Mr. Garland wants you to see it, he wants to see it himself in memory's eye, and that recollection is what's important, not exactly what happened or when. So he has written this section and others like it in the present tense.

It may be that you want to write an entire short story in the present, and it may work out well that way. As a reader, I find myself able to tolerate present-tense narration in short fiction more easily than in novels, and I doubt that I'm alone in this.

Finally, you may take all of this into consideration and find that your novel works in the present tense and just won't work in the past. This happens, and ultimately all a writer can do is honor his intuition and do what seems most effective. Jay McInerney wrote *Bright Lights, Big City* not only in the present tense but also in the second person. He did so not because he figured that sort of unorthodox approach would give him a good shot at the bestseller list, but because he'd been getting nowhere with a story for a while, then started it over in the second person and present tense, and the damn thing flowed like water from a cleft rock. I think the book probably gains from Mr. McInerney's narrative device—the first three fourths of it does anyway—and Lord knows he did well enough with it, but I wouldn't be quick to advise you (or him either) try that sort of thing again.

We Are Finishing

Before someone else does it for me, let me cite Damon Runyon's short fiction as a rule-proving exception. Runyon's Broadway fables were all traditionally plotted narratives, and the reader was told what happened, not invited to picture it for himself. Yet every sentence was invariably in the present tense.

But not really. Runyon's narrator is speaking what we might legitimately call dialect, and that's all the present tense amounts to when it issues from his lips. You'll note that every verb in a Runyon story, including the dialogue of the characters, is in the present tense. "A week ago Friday I am sitting in Mindy's with Harry the Horse . . . ." That's not present tense. That's a kind of dialect, and it worked brilliantly, but it's not what we're talking about here.

Even so, it might be a trial at novel length.

28

A Question of Character

December 1989

THE BEST FICTIONAL CHARACTERS ARE CREATED BY THE
CHARACTERS THEMSELVES.

Back in the mid '70s I had written three books about an ex-cop named
Matthew Scudder and made several attempts at a fourth book. This was
during a period of a couple of years when I had more trouble than usual
finishing what I started, and indeed it wasn't until 1980 that the fourth
Scudder book actually did get written.

One of these false starts, however, was by no means a complete waste
of time. It opened with Scudder contacted by a fellow he'd known
during his years as a policeman. The chap was a professional criminal, a
burglar, and Scudder had arrested him once or twice in years past. The
big oaf had spent more years behind bars than in front of them, and
in the ordinary course of things he didn't much mind getting arrested,
considering it one of the inescapable risks of his profession. He didn't
mind prison that much, either.

But in a burglary, he had broken into an apartment in which someone had been recently murdered, and he'd panicked and fled when the
police came to arrest him for burglary and homicide, and now he wanted Scudder to get him off the hook. He didn't mind going to prison for
the burglaries he committed, but he drew the line at getting sent away
for a murder he'd had nothing to do with.

Well, it was a nice enough premise for a detective novel, but unfortunately I didn't have a plot to go with it, nor did one evolve as I labored

at the thing. I pressed onward for 40 or 50 pages, then gave up and put them in a drawer. (In a briefcase, actually. I was traveling at the time.)

Some months later I was in Los Angeles, still trying to find something to write. My agent suggested that a non-series mystery might be a good thing for me to write, and I thought of what I'd written and realized that the basic situation would work just as well without Scudder, that the burglar could save himself by turning detective and solving the murder on his own. I still didn't have a plot, but I decided to sit down at the typewriter and see what would happen.

On the first page, my burglar, wearing a stylish topcoat and carrying a Bloomingdale's shopping bag for camouflage, breezed past a doorman at a fancy Manhattan apartment building. In a few sentences, Bernie Rhodenbarr was born as a witty, urbane, button-down burglar. I still had my problems with the book—I had to work out the plot as I went along, and I didn't know who did it until I got to the end and had to solve it myself—but I never did have a problem with the character. Somehow or other I knew exactly who he was. He came to life right there on the page, and all I had to do was let him talk.

And I still can't tell you how this came about. Because the Bernie Rhodenbarr who emerged in *Burglars Can't Be Choosers* (and whom I managed to write about in four subsequent volumes as well) was nothing like the lumpen dolt who'd hired Scudder in that earlier fragment. The earlier Bernie had been large and heavyset and plodding and dumb. The new Bernie was quick and clever and lithe. And I hadn't had any of his new character consciously in mind until his lines started appearing on the page before me.

Real Characters

It's an exciting thing when a character comes to life, and the experience is one with which most writers are at least occasionally familiar. We often say that the characters take over, that they write their own dialogue, that they do things we hadn't consciously devised for them. Sometimes we sound too cute by half, talking about our characters the way other people talk about their pets. ("He doesn't think he's a doggie. He thinks he's a people!")

What we're describing, albeit imperfectly, is real enough. I think the same thing happens to actors. The actor becomes a character and the character seems to exist autonomously. Onstage or at the typewriter, it's a wonderful feeling, and that feeling is the least of it. It is the characters who take over, the characters who come to life, who are most likely to be real and compelling for the reader as well as the writer.

How do you make this happen?

It seems to me that it's difficult to *make* it happen, and it may indeed be counterproductive to try. The process would appear to involve channeling a subconscious portion of the mind in some way, so that rather than *making* a character come to life, what we're really doing is stepping aside and *letting* the character emerge. Still, that leaves us in pretty much the same place, doesn't it? How do we do this? How do we get out of our own way, and how do we tap into whatever it is inside ourselves that permits the magic to happen?

There are a number of exercises designed to help in the fashioning of a character. You can jot down random facts about a character, compose a biography for him, write out a scene extraneous to your story in which he plays a key role, or otherwise try to pile up data or impressions of him. These are interesting exercises, and sometimes they may enable you to generate an original character and one with dimension, but that's no guarantee that the character will come to life in the way we've been talking about.

Sometimes, as with Bernie Rhodenbarr, all you really have to do is type. The character is simply there—you open the door for him and he goes into his act. But I've had other characters come to life in a more gradual fashion, and what seems to work best for me is making myself receptive to them, and tuning in to my own inner senses.

Often in my case the trigger is auditory. I hear the character talking, I know how he uses words, what kind of an edge his voice has. There are times when I will find myself copying down a character's dialogue almost as effortlessly as Mozart is said to have transcribed the music he heard in his head, but it is not always thus. Often my own craft has a role to play; I'll hear a line of dialogue, or an exchange, and if it's not right, if it fails to fit the scene or advance the story in the way I want, I'll hear alternatives until I hear the one I want. The character, you might say, is writing his own dialogue, but he's obligingly providing me with choices.

When I can hear a character clearly, when I know (not so much intellectually as intuitively) how he sounds and what sort of things he says, I'm not likely to have much trouble with the character. That auditory point of entry gives me access to the character and lets me know whatever else I need to know about him. If I need to know his past history, I'll let myself hear him running it down to someone else. If I need to know how he thinks or feels about something, I'll tune into a monologue he'll offer on the subject.

Occasionally the trigger is visual. A principal character in the latest Scudder novel, *Out on the Cutting Edge,* is one Mick Ballou, a saloon keeper and professional criminal with whom Scudder develops a curious friendship. I knew things about Ballou—that he was the child of an Irish mother and a French father, that his capacity for violence was legendary, that he had once gone from bar to bar in Hell's Kitchen carrying an enemy's head in a bowling bag, hauling it out by the hair and showing it to people. I knew enough about Ballou so that he probably would have been a very successful character for me even if he hadn't come to life.

But he did. When Scudder walked into his place of business and met him for the first time, I not only got Ballou's voice right away, but I also could see him. Later on I realized that I'd unconsciously chosen a specific physical model for Ballou, that he looked exactly like a fellow who used to own a couple of bars in Greenwich Village. I had never known this particular man. I saw him two or three times, and I'm not sure that I ever heard him speak. I guess he made an impression on me without my realizing it, and his physical appearance was what my subconscious conjured up for Mick Ballou.

True Lies

One time Pablo Picasso and a friend walked through a gallery with a large show of Picasso's paintings. Now and again Picasso would point to a canvas and quietly denounce the painting as a fake. At one point the friend demurred. "Pablo," he said, "I saw you paint that one. How can you say it's a fake?"

Picasso shrugged. "Sometimes I paint fakes," he said.

I think I know what he meant. Sometimes I write fakes, in that sometimes I create characters who are largely or entirely the product of conscious craft, and who have never come to life for me. This does not necessarily mean that there's anything wrong with them as characters. One that has received considerable critical approval and has been a big hit with readers is one I'll always regard as a fake, because I see him as no more than the sum of a whole body of conscious decisions I made about him. His voice did not speak unbidden into my inner ear, nor did his face spontaneously take form behind my closed eyelids. I still don't really know what he looks like, although I may very well have described him.

It may not be right to call him a complete fake, because there are things I've known intuitively about him, but he still feels like a fake to me. As a result, although I know he's an effective character, I'm not as confident of him as I am of those characters who have taken over, who have come fully to life.

A character can be a fake in this sense without being full or predictable or clichéd or ordinary. Conversely, a character can be quite ordinary and unremarkable in his externals while being a real character, a character who has come to life.

Sometimes, especially with minor characters, it's simpler and easier to go for the fake. If you've got a bit player who's onstage for just a couple of minutes, just long enough to say a few words on his way out the door, why bother breathing real air into his lungs? Why not just give him a limp or a loud sports jacket or a habit of sucking his teeth? Have him call the person he's talking to *hoss* or *chum* or *friend*, or let him whip out a comb and run it through his hair in times of stress.

You can do that, certainly, and the resulting character may well appear more like an individualized character than the bit player you take time to discover within your unconscious mind. When you do this, though, you run the risk of selling the character (and yourself) short. Because the real character, the character who comes to life on the page, will resonate for you and for your readers in the way an exclusively conscious creation cannot. Because you don't control him, he may surprise you, and he may give the most trivial scene a dimension it would otherwise lack.

Of Picassos and Pinocchios

There are, it should be noted, shades of gray throughout this continuum. Our Pinocchios are never entirely puppets or entirely real boys. Every fake character has a little life to him, and no character, no matter how completely he takes over, is entirely unformed by craft.

That said, I think there's value in always reaching for the real before the fake, the unconscious creation before the crafted specimen. If you can convince readers that your characters are real, not that they are modeled on real people but that they are themselves real people in their own right, you will probably never have to go out and get a job delivering pizzas. Because real living characters are damn near irresistible. There aren't that many of them around.

29

Stop Making Sense

January 1990

EXAMINING SOME FICTION RULES OF LOGIC.

A couple of years ago, two friends of mine, a man and woman I'd known for most of a decade, made the papers. They did so in a rather spectacular fashion when the husband, a Wall Street stock analyst, murdered the wife, drove around for a while with her in the trunk of the car, dumped her at the side of the road, and was in very short order apprehended and charged with homicide. At the time of his arrest, he was wearing women's underwear.

Eventually the case came to trial, but not before he had been released on bail, married someone else, beat up the new wife, and had his bail revoked. He stood trial, was convicted, and was in jail awaiting sentencing when he rather abruptly died, evidently of AIDS. The new wife attended his funeral service in the company of a woman who'd been in the news a while back when a former Miss America stood trial on a charge of using unlawful influence to get a judge to lower her lover's alimony payments to a former wife. The new wife's companion at the funeral was the daughter of the judge in question, and achieved some local notoriety by testifying against the former Miss America. What she's doing in *this* story is beyond me, but I guess everybody has to be someplace.

After the funeral, the wife and her friend hurried back to the deceased's house and stole everything they could carry.

I just learned of the latest chapters in this saga—the death, the funeral, the guest appearance by the judge's daughter—a few days ago as I write this. Upon returning to New York I ran into an old friend and made the mistake of asking him what was new. He told me all of this, and then he told me some other things that had happened to some other people we both know, and with which I won't burden you. Then we looked at each other, and I shrugged and said something about it all being a lot like a soap opera.

"No," he said. "No, soap opera has a certain internal logic to it. That's how you can distinguish between it and Real Life."

Coming to Your Senses

Fiction has to make sense. Life does not, and I suppose it's just as well, or vast chunks of life would bounce back from the Big Editor in the Sky with form rejection slips attached to them. When we want to praise fiction, we say that it's true to life, but that's not often the case. Life, unlike fiction, gives every indication of operating utterly at random, with no underlying structure, no unifying principles, and no rules of drama. I think it was Chekhov who pointed out that it was dramatically essential that any cannon that appeared onstage in Act I had damn well better be fired before the final curtain. Life doesn't work that way. In life, onstage cannons are forever silent, while others never seen go off in the wings, with spectacular results. Characters play major roles in the opening scenes, then wander off and are never heard from again. Perhaps it all balances out, perhaps there's some sort of cosmic justice visited in another lifetime or another world, but all that is hard to prove and not too satisfying dramatically.

What I'm really getting at, though, is not so much that life is a tale told by an idiot as that fiction had better be otherwise. And, simply because fiction has to make sense, we take for granted certain things that hardly ever happen in real life.

Consider premonitions. Now, everybody has premonitions from time to time—the sudden illogical hunches that lead us to stay off an airplane, bet a number, or cross a street. Every once in a while a premonition actually turns out to be warranted—the number comes up, the plane comes down, whatever.

But in the vast majority of instances the premonition is a bum steer or a false alarm. The warning that came to us in a dream, and that we did or didn't act upon, winds up amounting to nothing at all. The lottery ticket's a loser. The plane lands safely.

Not so in fiction. Every premonition means something, though not necessarily what it seems to mean; in fiction, we ignore omens and hunches at our peril, and to our chagrin.

Some months ago they aired the final episode of *Miami Vice,* after a few weeks of preparatory ballyhoo and hype. Crockett and Tubbs, as portrayed by Don Johnson and Philip Michael Thomas, are up against a couple of arch-villains, and if they win you just know a drug-free America is in the cards for all of us.

Early on, Tubbs looks over at Crockett. "I have a feeling I'm not gonna make it through this one," he says. Or words to that effect.

Watching it, I knew that was the end of Tubbs. Because the poor guy had had a premonition of doom, and we all know what that means. We know what happens in war movies, after the young subaltern gives his buddy a letter home "just in case." We know what happens in westerns, when they're circling the wagons and one character says, "You know, I had a funny dream last night." Why should Tubbs be any different? By the time they rolled the last commercial, the guy was going to be feeding worms.

Except that's not how they did it. When the episode ended, Tubbs was still on his feet, and there were no more references to his earlier intimations of mortality. For the first time ever, as far as I know, a fictional premonition turned out to be what they so often are in real life—i.e., nothing at all. And Tubbs didn't even explain his premonition away with a sheepish grin. Like most of us in that sort of situation, he probably didn't want to think about it, let alone discuss it. The subject very likely embarrassed the man.

I have no idea how the producers managed to put such revolutionary material on the air. I don't think they were trying to break new ground artistically, and suspect one of two things happened. Perhaps they wanted to heighten tension by making you certain Tubbs was going to buy the farm. ("But that's cheating! If he has a premonition, he has to die at the end." "So what are they gonna do, sue us? It's the last episode. If they get mad, let 'em turn the set off.") Or, just as plausibly, Tubbs was destined to die in an earlier draft; after the decision had been made to save him, nobody bothered to excise the premonition. You can decide for yourself whether they were cynical or sloppy.

Writing in the Future Tense

In much the same fashion, fictional fortunetellers are always on the mark. Whatever their mode of divination, tea leaves or tarot cards, astrology or phrenology or foot reflexology, their predictions always come true. There may be a catch, as Macbeth discovered when Birnam Wood came marching to Dunsinane, but such ironic twists of fate don't lay a glove on the basic assumption—i.e., that all predictions are accurate.

Well, I've had my chart done a couple of times, and my palm read, and my psychic temperature taken on various occasions. A friend of mine is a rather brilliant psychic, and some of the things she comes up with are uncanny, but she's nowhere near as accurate as any storefront gypsy palmist ever met with in fiction.

In Life As We Know It, most fortunetellers are wrong most of the time. The more specific they get, the less accurate they seem to be. Whether they're forecasting the end of the world or a romantic interlude with a tall dark stranger, you wouldn't want to bet the rent money on what they tell you.

Just look at the supermarket tabloids. They usually run extensive predictions around the first of the year, with famous psychics telling us what to expect over the next 12 months. Except for the can't-miss shotgun predictions ("I foresee that somewhere in the world there will be a disaster, with great loss of life. Washington will be rocked with charges of political corruption and financial mismanagement. And, on the Hollywood scene, I see a marriage breaking up." No kidding.), the predictors hardly ever get anything right.

In fiction, they almost always get almost everything right, and it never occurs to us to regard this as unrealistic. On the contrary, we'd be annoyed if it happened otherwise, as I was half-annoyed when Philip Michael Thomas survived on *Miami Vice*. We'd feel that we had prepared ourselves for a certain eventuality and that our preparations had been wasted. Because we've come to know that all predictions and premonitions come true in fiction, we took them for foreshadowing and braced ourselves for their fulfillment.

"Oh, this is silly," a character says. "I'm not superstitious. I'm going to walk under this ladder." Or break this mirror, or forbear to throw this spilled salt over my shoulder, or whatever. And he does, and we know something's going to happen to him before his story's over. We may not be superstitious ourselves. We may detour around ladders, just on the general principle that it couldn't hurt, but we don't take the whole thing seriously.

Not in real life we don't. In fiction, we know better.

Making Sense of It All

And what does all this mean?

I'm tempted to say that this column must be true to life, in that things aren't going to be all worked out at the end, with everything neat and logical. Because I'm not sure just what it all means, or precisely what implications it has for us as writers of fiction. It could probably be argued that one of the reasons fiction exists, a reason it is written and a reason it is read, is that it is orderly and logical, that it makes sense in a way that life does not. Frustrated with the apparent random nature of the universe, we take refuge in a made-up world in which actions have consequences.

Truth, as we've been told often enough, is stranger than fiction. Of course it is—because it can get away with it. It flat-out happens, and it's undeniable, so it doesn't have to make sense. If my friend's story, replete with uxoricide and transvestism and the remarriage and the beating of the new wife and the trial and the death, if all of that were placed without apology between book covers and presented as fiction, I'm sure I'd have tossed the book aside unfinished; if I made it all the way through, I'd surely be infuriated by the *virus ex machina* ending. The loose ends would annoy me and the inconsistencies would drive me nuts.

But it's fact. It happened. I can't dispute it on dramatic grounds. I can't say it's improbable, or illogical. It happened. It's what is. I may not like it, I may be saddened or horrified by it, but I can't lay the book aside because it's not a book. It's real.

I've seen writers react to criticism that their stories were implausible, that they relied too greatly on coincidence, that they were unresolved dramatically, by arguing that their fiction had been faithful to actual circumstance. "How can you say that?" they demand. "That's how it happened in real life! That's *exactly* how it happened!"

Indeed, and that's the trouble. If real life were fiction, you couldn't get the damn thing published.

30

Why Fiction?

February 1990

WHAT CALLS US TO THIS SPECIAL FORM OF WRITING? AND
SHOULD WE RESIST ITS CALL?

I'd like to tell you about a friend of mine. I'll call him Jack. (And why
not? That's what his parents called him, that's what his friends call him,
so why should I be different?)

As far back as he can remember, Jack has wanted to write fiction. He
has worked on various novels over the years, and has brought a couple
of them to completion, which is to say that he reached a point when
he ceased working on them. Since none of his work was published, it
sometimes struck him that his novels weren't completed so much as
they were abandoned.

Still, he got along, and there was usually a novel that he was at least
thinking about, if not actually working on. And he taught writing with
some success, even though he himself was not a published writer.

(And that seems worth a digression. Many of us who do publish
regularly are frequently amused by the great number of people in this
country who teach creative writing in schools and universities despite
having had precious little success with it themselves. Where do people get off teaching what they can scarcely do? As unassailable as this
argument seems on the face of it, it strikes me as every bit as illogical
to assume that the ability to write publishable material in and of itself
qualifies one to teach others to do the same. I could carry this further
but I won't. It is, after all, but a digression.)

Back to Jack. Somewhere in the course of his fifth decade, a need to be published made itself known to him. He realized that he'd reached a point in life where getting work into print was of more importance than the nature of the work involved. He wanted to see his byline in some sort of publication, and he wanted there to be words under that byline. Furthermore, he wanted to get money for it. Not to get rich, but to get paid for his efforts.

So he started doing travel pieces. He found a magazine that would take brief travel articles from him, and he began writing regularly for it. He got very little money for his work, fifteen or twenty dollars for each brief article, but it was money he'd earned at his typewriter and he got a kick out of it. Furthermore, he was amassing credits as a travel writer, and in very little time he began getting invited on press trips. He got to travel to some of the more interesting parts of the globe, and to do so free of charge, with his comfort seen to by people who had every reason to hope he was having an excellent time. The trips led to opportunities to publish more ambitious travel articles with more prestigious and lucrative markets, and this opened new vistas to him for future travel.

It was a cinch for him to write the articles. When he was facing a deadline he just sat down and turned out acceptable copy. And he loved to travel, he'd always loved to travel, and here he was traveling for free and making money from it. And he was seeing his name in print all over the place.

I'll tell you, I envied him. I travel all the time, but I generally wind up staying at some equivalent of the Bates Motel and damn well pay for it myself, too. I'd thought about doing travel pieces in order to get on the list for press trips, but I knew I'd have a horrible time writing the articles, that I'd agonize over each one and not do a very good job with them.

Last time I ran into Jack, I asked him where he was going next. He told me about a trip he had lined up for the following month, an excursion to South America that sounded sensational. "But I'm cutting way back on travel," he said. "I've been turning down press trips left and right. They're fun, but, well, I never set out with the goal of making my mark as a travel writer. This was a means to an end. I wanted to get published so that I could validate myself as a published writer. Because what I really want to do, what I've always wanted to do, is write fiction. And the damn press trips are taking so much time I can't get a novel written."

Shoes of the Fictionman

In an early cartoon of Jules Feiffer's, a man explains that from early childhood on he always knew he was destined to be a shoe salesman, that he felt this powerful longing to be a shoe salesman, but that he'd felt he had no choice but to bow to the wishes of his parents and the realities of the job market and make a living as an abstract expressionist painter. He hated it, it ate away at his soul, but he had a family to support so that was what he did. "The world," he says in the last frame, "should make a place for shoe salesmen."

The cartoon resonates for us because it is a switch on the way the world works. We long to be artists, and various pressures make shoe salesmen of us. Merely switching things around is enough to make us smile.

I wonder, though. Maybe we're so prepared to believe that our longing ought to be for the artist's life that we're loath to recognize it when we're geared the other way.

Let's get away from painters and shoe salesmen and bring it back to writing, shall we? Why is it, I wonder, that such a high proportion of us have our hearts set on writing fiction? Why is that always the hope, the dream, the goal?

My friend Arno Karlen, who has had some deserved success with both fiction and nonfiction, likes to confound audiences by maintaining that nonfiction is harder to write. Since his listeners generally include a good number of writers who have published nonfiction with some regularity while having the devil's own time getting their fiction accepted, his argument would seem to fly in the face of their experience. But Arno generally qualifies his thesis. Really *good* nonfiction, he explains, is more difficult to produce than really good fiction.

My own sense of things is that genuinely first-rate work of any sort is in short supply; one's individual degree of difficulty in various pursuits probably varies with one's aptitude for each. It is surely more difficult, on balance, to publish fiction than nonfiction. The market for nonfiction is vast, that for fiction virtually microscopic. There are ways to apprentice oneself in nonfiction, starting out in local journalism, writing for church bulletins, whatever. In fiction, those areas we might characterize as entry-level positions—ghosting series westerns, say—are by no means abundant, and are generally available only to the genuinely talented.

Taking Credit, Taking Blame

When I decided (or discovered) that I wanted to be a writer, I assumed almost automatically that I would be a writer of fiction, a novelist. I can think of two sources for this assumption. First, my chief interest as a reader was in realistic American fiction. Since that was what I enjoyed reading, since that was the sort of writing I greatly admired, it seemed reasonable that I would seek to emulate those writers who appeared so heroic to me.

Second, it seemed to me that a novelist was right up there at the top of the writing heap. Being a novelist was clearly worth the effort.

I don't know that this explains why I wound up a novelist, however. I think a large part of the credit (or blame) for that lies in the fact that my talents lay in that direction. I was cut out to be a writer of fiction. It was relatively easy for me to come up with ideas and turn out acceptable stories and books.

I'll tell you something. If this hadn't been the case, I don't know that I would have stayed with it.

I'd be hard put to prove this. But I have a hunch it's true. When I read about someone like Jack Kerouac, who is said to have completed 15 novels before one was accepted for publication, I am awestruck. What on earth made him keep at it? I can't make myself believe for a moment that I'd have had the grit. I'm damn lucky my early efforts met with some measure of success or I might very well have said the hell with it.

I have trouble admitting this, because I've always tried to tell other people of the importance of keeping at it, and especially of having realistic expectations for early work. I've said in this space more than once that we should not consider ourselves to have failed if a first novel turns out to be unpublishable, that a singer would hardly expect to be paid for a first song or a painter to sell a first painting.

But the first novel I wrote did get published, and I'd say it's a good thing it did. I won't argue that I wouldn't have written a second book otherwise, because I did in fact write a second book before that first one sold, but I don't know how long I'd have kept at it. And I might not have been able to write that novel, either, if I hadn't been encouraged by the sale of a dozen or more short stories first.

If my fiction had kept meeting with rejection, and if I'd had an easy and successful time with nonfiction pieces, I don't think it would have taken me too long to rethink a career decision I'd made in the 11th grade. But it worked the other way around, and it has continued to work the other way around for me ever since. I have a hard time writing nonfiction. With the exception of writing about writing, of the sort you are reading at this very moment, nonfiction is difficult for me and I am not terribly good at it. I'm a rotten interviewer and a poor fact-gatherer.

When it comes to the actual writing, I can hammer out an acceptable sentence or paragraph, but even there the dozens of small decisions that I make easily and intuitively in my fiction are arduous in my nonfiction. I agonize over things that someone with rudimentary journalistic ability could toss off in his sleep.

Having discovered this limitation in my ability, I've made it a point not to do much nonfiction, and to limit myself to the sort of occasional piece that is within my grasp. Remember that Dr. Kronkheit vaudeville routine?

"Doctor, it hurts when I do this."

"So don't do that!"

Longing Too Long?

And what about Jack?

Well, really, who am I to say? Perhaps he really does want to write fiction, and perhaps his experience as a travel writer will give him the confidence he needs to turn out a solid novel and see it through to publication. And, even if he never does publish a book, maybe fiction will hold enough internal rewards, will be sufficiently worth doing for its own sake to justify whatever he puts into it.

And maybe not.

Maybe my friend is stuck with a decision *he* made in the 11th grade, for about as much reason as most decisions most of us made way back then. Maybe Jack believes he has a longing to write fiction simply because that belief has been an article of faith for so long. Maybe, if that longing were genuine, he would have written more books and put more into them in the past 30 years. Maybe, if his talent pointed in the same direction as his desire, he would have gotten someplace by now.

Maybe the fact that travel writing comes so easily to him suggests that his talents lie in that area, or one allied to it. I'll tell you a secret. Talent means it's easy. It's never a cinch, it always demands something from you to work at the top of your form, but the possessor of a talent is able to do with relative ease what someone else must labor very hard at, and often cannot do at all. And it's very easy to overlook talent in oneself, because when something comes easy we think there's nothing to it, and that what we've done was probably not worth doing in the first place.

Why do so many of us want so desperately to write fiction? I don't know, and it may not be important to know. If it's important to you, God bless you, and go for it. Even if you don't start out abundantly talented, you may be able to get somewhere, and you may get very far indeed.

But if it's not important to you, if you think it's important only because it ought to be important, if you're locked into an ill-informed decision you made back in the 11th grade, you might want to take a moment to rethink things. Perhaps the world ought to make a place for shoe salesmen. Perhaps you owe it to yourself to find out what you really and truly want to do.

31

Writer to Writer

March 1990

ON THE VALUES AND BENEFITS OF PARTICIPATING IN
WRITERS' GROUPS.

A friend of mine, a talented young writer, just moved from Virginia to
California. She was excited about the move, but told me she expected to
miss the two writing groups of which she had been a member. "One of
them is very incisive," she said. "They criticize everything—they really
tear it apart. And the other is very New Age and do-your-own-thing,
and they love everything. Between the two of them, you get a good
balance."

Writers' groups play an important role in the lives of a great many
writers. For the most part, such groups serve the needs of writers who
are functioning on an amateur or semiprofessional level, publishing in-
frequently if at all. But this is emphatically not to say that a writers'
group is a childish thing to be put away upon reaching professional
maturity. I know a group of a dozen or so successful veteran writers who
meet regularly, not so much to share their work as to discuss common
problems and items of mutual interest. And I know a woman who recently signed a ten-million-dollar contract and who still meets once or
twice a month with the group of which she has been a member for the
past 30 years. She regularly reads her work to her fellow members, and
claims to profit greatly from the feedback she receives.

I can't furnish an inside view of writers' groups because I've never been inside one. While I can understand their appeal, I've always been inclined to privacy in my approach to writing. I've never cared to show work in progress, and over the years I've reached a point where I'd sooner breakfast on road-killed armadillo than let somebody read something before I'd finished writing it.

Nor have I ever much wanted criticism. All I really want is praise, lavish and abundant praise, and if you can't supply that I'd just as soon not hear your views on the subject. I'm not fool enough to think my writing is perfect, but that doesn't mean I want to be told what's wrong with it. All of this very likely amounts to a character defect on my part, but it's one I seem to be prepared to go on living with.

I mention this to advise you of my lack of expertise on the subject, and lest I seem to be beating the drum for something I've avoided in my own life. That said, I'd like to look at some of the things a writers' group can provide.

Perhaps the most obvious benefit is feedback. In a sense every writer is flying blind, piloting his sullen craft through starless skies. This is especially true of the beginner, whose work is not being read regularly by an agent or an editor, and who cannot generally find a qualified person to read it without paying a substantial fee.

The need for feedback is probably less acute with short fiction. You spend a few days or a few weeks writing a short story, tuck it into an envelope, drop it in the mail, and wait. Whatever comes back to you, be it the manuscript itself or a letter of acceptance, constitutes the sincerest form of feedback.

Even so, a rejection slip isn't wildly informative. It won't tell you much beyond the fact that whoever read it didn't like it enough to buy it. It may have just missed and may be chock full of literary merit, or it may be absolutely vile. Either way, the same slip winds up clipped to its corner.

The neophyte novelist, however, not only is working in the dark, but also must remain in the dark for a whole Arctic winter. It is, as we have frequently observed, a great act of faith to write a novel, and that faith is sometimes sorely tried when one has to work for months or years without any way of knowing whether the emerging book is wonderful or hopeless. Who could fail to wonder from time to time how it's going, and if it's any good?

Fellow members of your writers' group will tell you. Whether you're writing short fiction or a novel, they'll show keen interest in your work and let you know what they think of it. They'll assure you that they liked this scene while expressing reservations about that one. They'll praise your dialogue but find your description a little weak. They'll discuss your characters until you believe that they believe that they're real people. They may suggest ways for you to revise what you've written, and tell you where they think you should send it.

But what's their feedback worth? That's an interesting question, and one you may find yourself trying to avoid asking yourself. In order to profit from the group, you may want to banish the thought that all of you are nothing but the blind leading the blind. But suppose it's true? Are you really getting anything useful? Does it really matter what these people think of your work?

I suppose that depends somewhat on the group. And, in any group, some members will be astute readers capable of incisive criticism, while others will not have anything very valuable to say. Over time you will very likely learn whose criticism to heed and whose to ignore.

Two-Way Feedback

It seems to me, though, that a group of writers can provide benefits above and beyond the feedback one receives. The feedback seems to be the justification for the group, it's why the members say they're there, but it may not be the most important element at all.

The first and perhaps most important thing a writers' group provides its members is an audience. Membership in a group virtually guarantees that a certain number of people will be regularly reading your work (or having it read aloud to them, depending upon how you structure things). This may look at first glance like part of the whole business of feedback, but I think it's a thing apart.

One of the chief frustrations of writing is that it so often seems to us who do it to be an incomplete act. Writing is communication, and if we don't get to communicate to someone, what's the point?

That, I think, is why so many of us are so utterly obsessed with getting published. Even if we aren't truly driven to become professionals, even if we'd be perfectly happy functioning as Sunday writers, we can't feel altogether comfortable about being unpublished because our communicative process remains forever incomplete. Why go to great trouble writing something if it's not going to be read?

Belonging to a writers' group assures you of readership. Even if you are years away from writing professionally and reaching an audience through the printed page, you can be read right away by people genuinely interested in finding out what you have to say and how you've set about saying it. They won't be first readers at a publishing house, scanning a couple of pages and then affixing a rejection slip. They'll read every word, and they'll take time to figure out how they feel about what they've read.

Another very real benefit of group membership is that it can help provide a structure for part-time writing. If I know there are half a dozen people expecting to hear my next chapter on Thursday night, I've got a compelling reason to write it now rather than put it off a few days. One of the most difficult things for part-timers to do is prioritize writing, and unless we assign our writing a high priority we simply won't get around to it. There are too many other demands on our time for us to write something nobody wants to read anyway. But when we know there are people waiting to read it, people who will look at us funny if we show up empty-handed, we have that much more reason to sit in front of the typewriter tonight instead of the TV or the sewing machine.

If the feedback we receive is of questionable value, the feedback we supply is clearly worthwhile. Not necessarily for the person who gets it, but for us who give it.

By this I mean that one of the best ways to develop insights into one's own work is by seeing what does and doesn't work in other people's writing. We learn to write by writing, but we also learn by reading. Unfortunately, we usually try to learn by reading the published work of superior writers—and that's not likely to be hugely informative.

We can learn faster by reading the unpublished work of amateur writers. It's not smooth, it's not completely professional, and it's in manuscript rather than a bound book. The critical faculties are less in awe that way, and the flaws are more accessible.

Feeding Oneself

Writing is a lonely business. I don't know that there's any help for that. When all is said and done, the writer has to face a blank sheet of paper and has to do it alone. For all the people who may wind up on the acknowledgments page, all the people without whose help we swear we couldn't have written a word, we still ultimately do it all ourselves, and we do it all alone.

Membership in a group of writers can't make the work itself any less solitary, but it can eliminate some of the isolation that's so much a part of the writer's life. Being regularly in the company of other people who are trying to do essentially the same thing and having the same sort of problems doing it can be enormously helpful. It may even be essential.

In the past several years, much of my writing has been done at a writers' colony. I've written before about the experience, and have told how the privacy and the respite from mundane tasks enables one to concentrate intently upon one's work and get a prodigious amount accomplished. A factor, unquestionably, is that one is surrounded by fellow artists who are similarly engaged. Their presence has a definite energizing effect.

Typically, the writers and painters and composers at the colony don't talk much about what they're doing. An artist may open his studio toward the end of his stay so that his fellows can see what he's done. A composer may give a recital, or a writer a reading. But these are not occasions for feedback. We serve one another as appreciative audience, not as critics.

The company of other writers is important, at a colony or back in the real world. A writers' group can be extremely valuable even if no one ever brings in a manuscript, and even if nobody ever talks about writing. There is something special about being with other writers, whether the subject under discussion is baseball or botany or Byzantium.

In a writers' group, it probably helps if the members are at a similar stage of development; otherwise people can get locked into roles. It may be desirable, too, if everybody's working in the same general area of writing. But the most important thing is simply being in the company of one's fellows. It's one of the reasons we join organizations and attend conferences, one of the reasons we get together in the pages of this magazine. One way or another, we seem to need each other.

32

Writing All the Time
April 1990

CAN YOU BECOME A FULL-TIME FICTION WRITER?

My friend Susan Weinberg is an immensely talented young writer. For several years now she has been publishing short fiction in small literary magazines. Until very recently her writing was a part-time pursuit; she supported herself doing editorial work for a magazine, with her own writing relegated to nights and weekends.

This past fall, however, she moved to Palo Alto, California, where she will spend the next two years writing full-time. She's able to do this because she was awarded a Wallace Stegner fellowship, a prestigious grant that provides four writers a year with a modest annual stipend and participation in a twice-a-week writers' workshop.

In November I was in the San Francisco Bay area for several days in the course of a lengthy promotional tour for *Out on the Cutting Edge,* my latest Matthew Scudder novel. I was able to spend some time with Susan, and over dinner one night I asked her what she wanted from her writing.

She thought for a moment and said that she hoped she could eventually secure a decent teaching job at a good college, one that furnishes her with a satisfactory and secure income as well as time to write.

I asked if teaching was important to her in and of itself.

Well, no, she said, it wasn't. She wasn't particularly drawn to it, but it seemed preferable to other jobs.

Wouldn't she prefer to write full-time, and to support herself with her writing?

That would be ideal, she admitted. But she didn't think it was a realistic aspiration. So far she had been paid only small fees for her stories. And, she pointed out, hardly any of the writers she knows are able to write full-time.

I'm sure that's true. But it's equally true that the great majority of the writers I know *are* able to write full-time, and most of them have been doing just that for years.

The Incredibility Gap

James Michener has said that a writer can make a fortune in America—but can't make a living. I've quoted that remark more than a few times in this space because it seems to me to sum up the enormous gulf between success and failure in writing in America (and indeed in all the arts, and the sports world, and increasingly throughout our society). One either signs a ten-million-dollar contract—"inks an eight-figure deal" in journalese—or one bags groceries at the Safeway and hammers out fiction in the small hours of the morning. You make it big—too big, some might argue—or you just don't make it at all.

There is much truth in this. And yet there are many writers who have consistently made a living without ever making a fortune. Writing is what we do, and we are good enough and diligent enough and, yes, *successful* enough to be able to make a living without doing anything else. Sometimes it is not much of a living. We have, typically, good years and bad years, and some of the bad years are bad enough to make us wonder at the wisdom of our course. But most of us stay with it, and most of us somehow get through the hard times.

Sometimes, curiously, it's harder to survive the good years. One writer I know sold a book to Hollywood every year for three years running. It did not take him long to revise his standard of living accordingly. In the succeeding half dozen years, when nothing he wrote was purchased for filming, he had the more difficult and less enviable task of reducing his lifestyle to fit his circumstances. Since then he's had more good years, but he's learned how to handle them.

The Freelance Life

"Of course I'd prefer to write full-time," Susan said. "Isn't that what everyone wants?"

Well, no, actually. Leaving aside the curious fact that some people don't want to write at all, not even a laundry list or a ransom note, the fact remains that many of our number are happier if they don't have to make it their sole occupation. Many people honestly love to teach—or practice law, or deliver babies, or install floor tile. They may find, too, that a good deal of their creative energy derives from their work, and that it gives them something to write about.

The life of the freelance writer, with its legendary freedom from routine, is hugely attractive to most people; indeed, there is no end of people out there who love everything about the writing life but for the horrible prospect of actually sitting down and writing something. For others, though, the solitude and the absence of routine are positively hellish.

I know one fellow who managed to be self-supporting as a writer but couldn't bear the life that went with it. He hated being in his apartment all the time so he rented an office. He couldn't stand being alone in his office so he rented desk space in a larger office so he'd have people around. Then, because he really yearned to be part of real office routine, he went out and got a job. He's been bitching about the corporate life ever since, and talks endlessly about how he wants to go back to freelancing, but I don't believe a word of it, because he's elected to stay employed ever since.

Finally, not a few people keep their jobs out of a need for financial security. There are no pension plans for freelancers, and no fringe benefits, and no paycheck that comes whether or not the creative juices are flowing. On the contrary, there is the virtual certainty that there will be dry spells and hard times. Steady assignments and multiple-book contracts provide an illusion of security, but they won't always keep the wolf from the door. (On the other hand, when you're your own boss, nobody can fire you. That seems to me to provide a sort of baseline security, but there are times when it's cold comfort.)

Self-Unfulfilling Prophecy

Let's assume, though, that you can live with insecurity. And that you don't have any inner need to work and play with others, and that there's no other occupation with a claim on your soul. You honestly want the life of a full-time freelance writer.

Can you have it? Is the goal a realistic one?

You're a step closer, certainly, if you've allowed yourself to entertain it as a goal in the first place. What I found unsettling about my friend Susan's response was not that she had rejected the idea of writing full-time but that she had not really allowed herself to consider it. If you assume that writing will have to be a sometime thing, a sideline occupation, the assumption will almost invariably turn out to be the truth. It will steer you into a job that you think you have to have, and it will very likely affect what you write, and how you attempt to market your work.

Hardly any of Susan's writer friends write full-time. When I was starting out, almost all of the writers I knew were either writing full-time or doing a little bartending or furniture-moving to make ends meet while they established themselves as full-time freelancers. And hardly anyone I knew intended to teach or write ad copy or have anything resembling a legitimate career while writing on the side.

I'm sure this helped. If you want to support yourself with your writing, I would think it would be worth your while to get to know people

who are doing just that. Not just for the shoptalk and the companion-
ship, both of which are invaluable, but because these people will serve
you as role models. They will show you by their example that what you
want is attainable.

Just Do It

They'll also very likely show you how it is attained. People who write
for a living are a little different from other people. They're also different
from one another, so generalizations are by no means hard and fast, but
there's at least one that seems to hold true most of the time:

They get a lot of work done.

This may mean working every day or it may mean working in fren-
zied spurts. It may involve the discipline of a 9-to-5 workday or it may
consist of shuttling back and forth between the television set and the
typewriter. You find out what works for you—that's part of the life's
appeal, and different things work for different people.

Anyway, nobody pays you for the hours you put in, but for the work
you produce, and successful full-time writers produce a lot. Some of us
enjoy the process while others may liken it to torture—undergoing it,
not inflicting it. But we all seem to get a lot of it done.

Earlier in this promotional tour I was in St. Louis, where I stayed
with John and Barb Lutz. John and I got to talking about short stories.
I had recently had the luxury of spending a month writing short stories.
John's an excellent short story writer—he won an Edgar for "Ride the
Lightning"—and we agreed that we weren't writing as many in recent
years as we'd like to.

One year, John said, he had decided to make a special effort to get a
lot of short stories written. By the time the year was over, he'd turned
out 40 of them.

When I expressed astonishment, he assured me that wasn't so many,
that it was in fact less than one a week. "They weren't all great stories,"

he said, "and they didn't all sell right away. But just about all of them sold sooner or later, and they keep bringing in little checks for foreign sales and anthology use. I ought to write more of them."

Forty short stories sounds like extraordinary productivity for a year, especially when you consider that John Lutz was writing other things as well. Yet it's a walk in the park compared to what some writers have turned out. The late John Creasey wrote 2,500 words before breakfast every day of his life. (Well, not when he was a little kid. You know what I mean.) And another writer I know, who nowadays relaxes and produces a single book a year, had a period of several years during which he turned out two books a month for one paperback house, one book a month for another publisher, and about 50,000 words of magazine fiction a month. And he did all this without working nights or weekends.

I certainly wouldn't want to imply that the more a writer produces the better he is; that's as much of a fallacy as its opposite. But those of us for whom writing works as a full-time pursuit generally do a lot of it. We may write one draft or several. We may find it easy or hard going. But we get it done.

33

The Book Stops Here

May 1990

YOUR NOVEL GRINDS TO AN ABRUPT HALT. WHAT'S THE
DIAGNOSIS?

It's the most mysterious thing. You're working on a book, plugging
away at it like The little Engine That Could, turning out a page a day or
five pages a day or ten pages a day, watching those finished pages pile
up and beginning to see the light at the end of the tunnel. You don't
want to get too cocky, don't want to get the Big Editor in the Sky mad
at you, but, by George, it certainly looks as though you've breezed past
the halfway mark and are closing fast on the three-quarter pole. All you
have to do is keep showing up for work every day, keep putting your
behind on the chair and your fingers on the keys, and it's just a matter
of time, and not too much time at that, before the book will be finished.

Oh, you may still have work to do. Some light revision at the very
least. Maybe a formal second draft. No matter, that's the easy part, what
the military would call a mopping-up operation. When your first draft
is done your book is written, and you can jump up and down and call
people and celebrate and even take that shower you've been promising
yourself for so long. And the first draft's almost done, it'll be done any
minute, all you have to do is keep at it and—

And, all of a sudden, kablooey.

You're stuck. The book's going nowhere. It's dead in the water, finished, kaput.

Now what?

Wisdom of the Pages

The conventional wisdom holds that what I've just described is a disaster, and it's not terribly hard to guess how it became the conventional wisdom. The conventional wisdom goes further to suggest that the thing to do when a book gets stuck is to lower your metaphorical head and charge forward. (It helps, I suppose, if you're wearing a metaphorical helmet.) By pushing on, by damning the torpedoes and going full speed ahead, you can go right through whatever's impeding you and get the book finished as planned. You can turn a deaf ear to the voice that keeps telling you there's something wrong. You can brush all those doubts and anxieties right out of your mind. Casting them as the road and yourself as the chicken, you can Get To The Other Side.

Well, sure. And sometimes that's exactly what you ought to do.

And sometimes it's not.

When a book grinds to a halt, it may have done so for a reason. To avoid looking for the reason is a little like overlooking the trouble lights on a car's dashboard. You can run the car when those lights go on, and you can even do as the previous owner of my car seems to have done, disconnecting a wire so that the lights won't bug you like some sort of mechanical conscience. Maybe you'll wind up all right, but there's a good chance that sooner or later they'll come for you with a tow truck.

A couple of examples. Several years ago, I was writing the fifth volume in a series of mysteries about Bernie Rhodenbarr, a burglar and bookseller by profession, a solver of homicides by circumstance. I was 180 pages into what looked likely to be a 300-page manuscript, when Something Went Wrong. I spent a day staring at the typewriter without getting anything done. I took a day off, and another day off. By the end of the week I realized that I was in trouble. I didn't know what was wrong, but I knew something was wrong.

Now I could have barreled through it and forced the book over the finish line. I knew who the killer was, and how and why the crime had taken place. I had not painted myself into any impossible plot corners. But there was something wrong, and I couldn't see how to fix it, not least of all because I wasn't altogether sure what it was.

I still don't know exactly what was wrong. I think there was something gone off-stroke in the book's timing. I can't tell you how or why I screwed it up in the first place, or just what enabled me to fix it. I know what happened—I moped around for a few weeks, during which time I despaired that the book would join the great body of manuscripts I've abandoned forever over the years. While this was happening, I suspect a portion of my unconscious mind was playing with the problem and looking for a solution. One evening I had a long conversation about the book with a friend of mine. I don't recall what either of us said, or that a specific solution came out of our conversation, but I walked away from it somehow knowing how to proceed. I started the book over from the beginning, using most of the scenes I had written but fitting them together somewhat differently, and running the whole thing through the typewriter again. This time, everything worked. I finished the book without a snag and I think it's the best one in the series.

I probably could have finished the book by just staying with it and forcing myself to write. And it probably would have been publishable. But I'm sure it was better for my having had trouble with it, and for having surrendered to the trouble instead of trying to ride roughshod over it.

More recently, six months ago I settled in and went to work on a new Matthew Scudder novel. I'd spent half a year thinking about the book and felt ready to write it. I had no trouble getting started, worked at a fast clip, and had 200 pages written in a couple of weeks. The writing went well, and I was pleased with the scenes and characters that I had developed.

But, by the time I was a little ways past the halfway mark, I realized that I'd managed a kind of reverse synergy—i.e., the whole of what I'd written was rather less than the sum of its parts. The book was taking too long to get going, and it was wandering off in far too many directions. Some of my best scenes and characters were just marking time, doing nothing to advance the plot. And the plot itself was unwieldy and unworkable. I was going to have to start over. The story I wanted to write was in there somewhere, and I had a feeling I could find it, but all of that would have to wait. I needed time away from the book, and eventually I would have to scrap 90 percent of what I'd written and start over from the beginning.

This didn't mean what I'd written was a waste of time; it was a part of the process, and I evidently had to go through it in order to find the story I'll eventually write. (At least I hope I'll eventually write it, if all of this is to have a happy ending.)

Again, I could have forced myself to keep writing, could have overruled my own doubts and anxieties. And I could have finished the book that way. It wouldn't have been very good, and I'm not sure it would have been publishable, but you never know what is or isn't publishable these days. It certainly wouldn't have emerged as a book I would have been pleased with.

The implication would seem to be clear: If you get stuck on a book, there must be something wrong with it. Set it aside or fix it.

But I could furnish other examples that would seem to prove the opposite. I have had books stall in much the same fashion, have pushed on and seen them through to completion, and have had them turn out just fine. Some years ago, when I was writing a series of paperback suspense novels about a sort of freelance spy named Evan Tanner, I noticed that I always seemed to hit a bad patch somewhere around page 125. (The Tanner books ran around 200 pages in manuscript.) I always stayed with what I was writing, and the books always worked out all right, and when I read them over afterward there was no evident sag or quagmire around page 125.

I suspect what happened was that I tended to have a sort of failure of confidence at around that point. Once I got a chapter or so further along in the work, my confidence returned of its own accord and I felt capable of completing the work. I don't know the source of this, but I have a hunch it had more to do with me than with the work. Years later, during my career as the world's slowest but most determined long-distance runner, I experienced a similar sinking feeling at about the same stage—say, six miles into a ten-mile race. There would be a point at which I felt I really ought to drop out of the race, that to go further would only result in injury, that I couldn't possibly go the distance. I never did quit a race short of the finish (although there were times I probably should have) and once I got a kilometer or so past that crisis point I always knew I would make it. The two processes are vastly different, and none of my runs were the athletic equivalent of publishable, but I don't think it was coincidental that I tended to feel on the verge of failure at the same point in books as in races.

On the other hand, maybe I only noticed crises of this sort when they came at that particular stage, a little past the halfway mark. Maybe I had comparable crises, comparable failures of nerve, at other points along the way—but I didn't recognize them for what they were.

I was packing my office not long ago and I came across two thirty-page chunks of manuscript, one written two years ago, the other a little older. Each was the opening of a novel about Bernie Rhodenbarr, and each had been forever abandoned around the thirtieth page. I had stopped working on them because they just plain weren't working. The writing felt labored, the dialogue seemed flat, and I wisely stopped work on them and said the hell with it.

Well, I read both of those chunks of manuscript, and I was amazed I don't have a clue what I thought was wrong with them at the time I stopped work on them. My writing seemed as spritely as it ever gets, my dialogue was as crisp and lively as I could have wanted it, and all either manuscript lacked to be perfectly publishable was another 270 pages in the same vein. Looking back, it strikes me as highly probable that I would have been incapable of producing those 270 pages back then, and an unconscious recognition of this fact soured me on what I was writing. Not really wanting to go on, I decided that the grapes I'd already reached were sour.

The point, though, is that in neither case did I feel I'd hit a snag. Instead I just figured I'd had a false start, and one that only represented the work of a couple of days. I have tossed off and subsequently tossed out a chapter of a book or a few pages of a short story on more occasions than I can remember, and so have most writers I know, and so what? You can't expect the world to salute every time you run one up the flagpole. Often the only way to find out if something is going to work is to try writing it, and to drop it if it fizzles out.

You can avoid this sort of false start if you never write anything without having it clear in your mind, but you might miss out on a lot of stories that way. Donald Westlake wrote an opening chapter once because he had this image of a guy crossing the George Washington Bridge on foot. He didn't know who the guy was or why he was walking across the bridge, but decided that he (like the guy) could cross that bridge when he came to it. The book turned out to be The Hunter, the first of sixteen books (under the pseudonym of "Richard Stark") about a professional criminal named Parker, who the guy on the bridge turned out to be.

And if it hadn't worked out that way, if Parker, upon crossing the bridge, had turned into a drugstore instead of turning into a terrific series character, well, so what? Don would have wasted a day's work, and we all do that often enough, don't we?

Oh, Sure

You might think that outlining could make a difference, especially in avoiding snags late in the game, where the book is two-thirds written and you can't think of a thing to have happen on the next page. If you've got a detailed outline, all of those problems are presumably worked out in advance. The book can't hit a real snag because you always know what's going to happen next.

Sure you do.

Although I haven't outlined anything in quite a few years now, I used outlines on many occasions over the years, some of them sketchy, others more elaborate. And it's unarguably true that a writer working from an outline always knows what he originally intended to have happen next.

But there's no guarantee it'll work. Sometimes the novel proves to have a will of its own and veers away from the outline. This isn't necessarily a bad thing, but it does mean that you have nothing but your imagination and your vocabulary to help you figure out what happens next.

And, even when the plot hews close to what you've outlined, there's no guarantee that what worked in outline will work in manuscript. Sometimes, indeed, a novel will stall out around the two-thirds or the three-quarters mark because the outlined plot just isn't working and the writer's unable to loosen up and make the necessary departures from it.

What to Do?

So what's the answer?

Beats me. Every book is a case unto itself, and every time we sit down to write one we take a plunge into uncharted waters. It is a hazardous business, this novel-writing dodge, and it doesn't cease to be so after long years in the game. Novelists who have been at it since Everest was a molehill still find themselves leaving a book unfinished, or finishing an unpublishable one. (Sometimes a good writer gets away with a bad book, and publishes it, and sometimes it sells as well as his good books, but only one's accountant is gladdened when that sort of thing happens. The object is not to sneak by with a bad book, it's to write a good one.)

So, when a book hits a snag and the sun goes out and the moon turns black, do you:

1. Keep right on going and finish it? or
2. Figure out where you went wrong and make it right? or
3. Decide that it doesn't say Purina, and bury it in the yard?

The answer, I guess, is:

4. Any or all of the above, depending.

All you have to do is figure out which, and you have to figure it out anew each time it happens.

Look, I never said this was going to be easy.

34

Good News About Bad News
June 1990

THE MORE YOUR MANUSCRIPTS COME BACK TO YOU, THE
BETTER YOU'LL FEEL ABOUT IT. TAKE HIS WORD FOR IT.

During a recent stay in New York City, I had occasion to make two visits to New York University. On my first visit I delivered three pieces of artwork. A week later I returned to retrieve them. My wife, Lynne, had produced the three pieces, and I'd entered them at her request in NYU's annual Small Works show, and they had been rejected.

I had forgotten how painful rejection is.

Know Thy Enemy
Lynne has been making art for a while, but only in the past year or so has she allowed herself to take it seriously. The encouragement of other visual artists and the sale of a few pieces to acquaintances led her to the belief that she might try to do something with her work. The Small Works show was her first real attempt in this direction, and when she didn't get in she was devastated. The rejection seemed to confirm every fear she had about herself as an artist and a human being. She decided she was an untalented dilettante and that her work was superficial and meretricious. If she hadn't been a vegetarian, she would have gone into the garden to eat worms.

From a distance, one could see her reaction as excessive. More than 2,000 artists had entered this particular show, and fewer than 200 made the cut. Accomplished artists, friends of hers, entered every year and *never* got a piece accepted.

So what? She'd taken a chance, had stuck her neck out, and she'd been rejected. And it felt *terrible*.

I felt for her, of course, and it struck me how far removed I was from the sort of thing she was going through. I had certainly had my share of rejections over the years, but that was then and this was now, and I've been an established professional writer for quite a few years now, and I hadn't had any work of mine rejected in ages, had I?

But wait a minute. Of course I had.

During the preceding summer I went on a short story spree and wrote eight of the little darlings. I rejected one of them myself, but the other seven struck me as promising and I sent them off to my agent. He placed three of them almost immediately, two with a top magazine and one with a prestigious anthology. All of that made me very happy indeed, but the other four stories, along with one I'd written in the spring, have been bouncing around ever since, garnering rejections wherever he sends them.

Some of these rejections have been of a kind and gentle sort, resulting from the fact that a couple of the stories are categorically hard to place. One, for example, is a very dark and violent story with a female narrator; it's accordingly not right for the men's magazines, and too stark a proposition for any of the women's magazines that have seen it thus far. "We liked this story very much," I was told more than once, "but it's just not right for us." Well, OK.

On the other hand, another story with which I was very well pleased seemed right on target for another magazine, one that had published a considerable number of my stories over the years. They rejected this one, not because it wasn't their kind of material, but because everybody in the office found it heavy-handed, predictable and offensive. They said just that in a note my agent was kind enough to read to me.

"I guess they didn't like it," I said.

So of course I've had rejections. As I look back over the years, there's never been an extended period of time during which I haven't had efforts rejected, proposals spurned, projects aborted. It's part of the game and comes with the territory.

What's significant, it seems to me, is that it hardly ever seems to bother me much. Sometimes it's disappointing, but it's hardly ever devastating. And often it's not even disappointing.

A few years ago, for example, the British publisher who had brought out my last eight or ten books suddenly rejected my most recent effort. My immediate response was surprise, but close on its heels came a wave of pleased optimism. "Good," I said. "They've been a lousy house all along, and we'll sell it someplace better." This was not a matter of whistling in the dark; they *were* a lousy house, and we did place the book with a better publisher right away. But that's not really the point. More important is my own reaction. I wasn't crushed. I wasn't even dismayed. I'd had a rejection, but I didn't feel rejected.

And that's the good thing about rejection. You get used to it, and eventually it really doesn't hurt all that much.

Removing the Sting

What changes things? What takes the sting out of rejection?

Experience, first of all. The experience of rejection, and the experience of living through it. Only by sending things out, time and time again, and by getting them back, time and time again, can we truly learn what rejection does and doesn't mean. It means that a particular publisher has declined to buy a particular story on a particular occasion. It doesn't necessarily mean that the story's bad. The story may be bad, most stories are, but that doesn't necessarily have anything to do with the fact that it has come back like a well-hurled boomerang. Most fiction markets receive thousands of submissions for every one they buy. Many receive tens of thousands. Sometimes months go by during which they reject everything submitted to them.

You can know all of this intellectually and it's a help, but it's nothing compared to the bone-deep knowledge you acquire gradually and painfully by having your work rejected. With time you begin to understand that all any rejection means is what it says on the rejection slip—the manuscript does not fit the publisher's current needs.

Another big help is acceptance. The more sales you make, the less pain rejection will bring when it comes. Why? Because the acceptance is proof of a tangible sort that your work has merit, and the worst thing about rejection is its capacity to make you believe that your work is worthless and so are you. If one editor supplies validation with an acceptance, it's a lot easier to shrug off the next batch of rejections that come your way.

(And I can see this applying in my own case, incidentally. I might have been a lot less sanguine about the four stories I can't manage to sell were it not for the three that sold right off the bat.)

Acceptance, let it be said, begins at home. To the extent that we accept ourselves, we immunize ourselves against rejection. A writer who accepts himself entirely, who has not the slightest doubt of the worth of his work, is invulnerable to the sting of rejection right from the start. He doesn't need to get used to rejection, doesn't need to be validated from without by having work accepted.

Now I'm not altogether certain someone all that confident has ever existed; if he did, he'd probably go into business or politics instead of choosing our particular path anyway. But, if he did exist, the slings and arrows of rejection couldn't harm him. Publishers might not buy his stories—for that you need talent, too—but failure would not destroy him. Because the pain of rejection owes a lot to one's own suspicion that the person doing the rejecting is right, and that the story and the person who wrote it are awful.

The Good News

Unless you're a masochist, rejection is never fun; unless you're profoundly neurotic, you don't send out your stories actively hoping they'll be returned to you with a form slip attached.

But you learn to live with it. And, if you can't stand the heat, you'll have to get out of the kitchen.

And some people do. Every year many men and women try for careers in sales, and some of them drop out early on because they can't stand being rejected, can't stand having phones hung up on them and doors closed in their faces. The ones who stay learn to shrug off that kind of rejection. They know that the best salespeople in the world get rejected time and time again, and they just plain learn not to take it personally when one prospect after another turns them down.

We have it a little easier than salespeople, a lot easier than actors and models. Our work is rejected at a distance, through the mail. We don't have to come face to face with the people who seem capable of reinforcing our own deepest fears about ourselves.

It still hurts. No question.

But you get over it.

35

Short Story Time

July 1990

OUR COLUMNIST REDISCOVERS THE SHORT STORY . . . AND
SOME LESSONS FOR US ALL.

Last year I settled in at a writers' colony in Virginia. I had a book to
write and a six-week residency to devote to it and nothing else. The
book had been very much on my mind for the preceding six months; I
had a lot of it worked out, including virtually all of the last several chapters, and I knew quite a bit about my characters and the scenes they'd be
starring in. I was keen to buckle down and get on with the job.

My routine was the one I usually follow at the colony. I rose early
each morning and hurried off to my studio, where I worked nonstop
until dinnertime. Occasionally I returned to the studio for a few hours'
more work in the evening.

I kept it up for two weeks, and at the end of that time I had just over
200 pages of manuscript. I sensed that the book would run somewhere
around 350 pages, so I had a nice chunk done, almost certainly more
than half.

There was only one problem.

I didn't like what I'd done.

Let me qualify that. I liked a lot of what I'd written. Most of it, actually. But it seemed to me to be rather less than the sum of its parts. I
felt it was rambling and dilatory, that I was moving in too many directions and not making real progress toward any of them, and that I had

begun work with an insufficient sense of what I wanted to accomplish. Because I did in fact know so very much about the book's ending, I had lost sight of the fact that I didn't know enough about the earlier portions. I had plunged right in, and some of what I'd come up with was very good indeed, but it didn't make a book.

Nor did it make any sense to go on.

But what was I going to do? There I was with four more weeks booked. The place is idyllic, but people go mad hanging around and not working. I had to write something and I didn't have anything to write.

Short stories, I told myself. I'll write some short stories.

I figured short stories would be fun. They always are. I think I probably enjoy them more than novels. When they go well, they provide almost immediate gratification. When they go horribly hopelessly wrong, so what? To discard a failed short story is to throw away the work of a handful of hours, perhaps a couple of days. In a short story I can try new things, play with new styles, and take unaccustomed risks. They're fun.

The Morals of My Stories

I tell you all this, not just because I'm in the habit of keeping you informed in the hope my experience will prove instructive, but because it seems to me that clear lessons can be learned from what followed, and I for one want to make sure I learn them.

The first lesson, I suppose, is that every apparent setback is an opportunity. I was deeply dismayed when the book ground to a halt, and especially annoyed that it had happened with a month of colony time to go. If this hadn't happened, I never would have written the stories I did—and I'm very pleased to have written them.

Another lesson would seem to lie in Woody Allen's observation that 80 or 90% of success owes itself simply to showing up.

Here I was in Virginia, stalled on a book, and thinking that I ought to write some short stories, that I would *like* to write some short stories. Having come to this decision, I awoke the next morning, trudged off to my studio, and wrote almost half of a short story. The next day I went back and wrote the rest of it.

It was a story about an abusive husband, and I had had the idea for it once before—two years ago, at the same writers' colony, at which time I wrote four or five pages of it, didn't at all like what I'd written, and tore it up. I don't think I gave the subject five minutes thought overall during the intervening two years, and when I did think of it I regarded it as a bad idea for a story that wasn't really my kind of story in the first place.

This time I saw how to write it, and I think it's as good a short story as I've ever written.

The day after I finished it I was fresh out of story ideas, but I had an idea for my monthly column and wrote that. The day after that I woke up with no ideas at all, but I had breakfast and went to the studio anyway. I stretched out on the couch and tried to think of something, and an idea came along, and I sat down at my desk and started work on a story. The idea wasn't an absolutely brilliant one, and I was fairly sure that only a limited story could grow out of it.

Well, so what? You don't have to hit a home run every time you step up to the plate, and you'll probably be well advised not to try. I wrote the story. It took two days, and it was easy to write. (The first one had been tricky, and I'd had to work at the top of my form to get it to work. This one was a cinch, and I had fun with it.)

That night I went back after dinner and got an idea for a story set on a mink ranch. I wrote two pages just to feel my way into the character. I decided I needed to know more about mink ranching, so the following morning I went to the library at a nearby college and did several hours' worth of research. It was productive, and I carried my newfound knowledge back to my studio and tried to plot a story about the mink ranch, but it wouldn't come. Later in the day, though, I shoved my notes and photocopies aside and started writing something else. I had a sort of half-baked idea for a story, or at least for the opening of a story, and I wanted to see where it would go.

Sometime the following afternoon it went to the end of the story. Again, it's a somewhat uncharacteristic story. The idea for this one wasn't all that compelling, and it wasn't even all there when I began trying to write my way into it. But I think it works, and I think it will probably get published somewhere, and I enjoyed writing it and enjoy having written it.

Then, the next day, I got up and went to my studio and found myself thinking about the novel. The first chapter functions almost as a sort of curtain-raiser, having precious little to do with the ensuing story. It follows my detective, Matthew Scudder, as he does a day's freelance work for a detective agency, hassling street merchants who are selling articles that infringe his client's copyrights. I thought when I wrote it that it could almost stand as a story by itself, and I went back and read it with that in mind. It needed some trimming and shaping, to be sure, and it needed to make another trip through the typewriter, so I spent the day giving it just that. I don't know if it's a story, really. It doesn't come to a conclusion, doesn't have a plot in the traditional sense of the word, but I'm glad I did what I did with it, and I wouldn't be surprised if it gets published.

What does all of this add up to? Something like four finished stories in something like ten days. And the one thing I did every day was to show up at my studio ready to work. That made me receptive to ideas, and it enabled me to do something with them when they came along.

My third lesson was I realized the inherent weakness of my long-standing policy of writing stories only when I had a compelling idea for one.

From a standpoint of dollars and cents, it's not really reasonable for a writer to concentrate much energy on short fiction. The market is narrow and shallow. There are not many places to sell short fiction, and they don't buy much of it, and they don't pay a whole lot for it.

The economic facts of life have their effect. Some years ago I decided that there was no reason to write a short story unless I happened to get a genuinely good idea for one. And, ever since, I've written a story when such an idea occurred to me. But those ideas didn't come around very often.

They didn't during the time I pursued them in Virginia. The first story was based on an idea I'd managed to ignore for two years. The second was based on an idea that wasn't all that compelling. The third wouldn't have been written if I'd waited for the idea; I pretty much found my way into the idea in the course of writing the story. And the fourth, the salvaged first chapter, is one I never would have bothered to form into a story if I hadn't made short stories my occupation for the month.

Several times over the past decade it's struck me that I'd enjoy writing more short stories, that there's enough unstructured time in my schedule to facilitate their production. While they may not be enormously lucrative, two days spent writing a short story puts more money in my pocket than two days of sitting and staring out the window. If I were to write, say a story every other month, I'd be adding considerably to my overall body of work.

Besides, short stories pay off in surprising ways. They keep turning up in anthologies, bringing me a few dollars each time and keeping my name in front of readers. Two or three times they've been adapted for television; this is neither as glitzy nor as enriching as selling a novel to the movies, but it's not bad, either. One story, written to keep a promise, won me an Edgar award and a Shamus award and, greatly expanded, became what is arguably my best novel. What kind of shortsightedness could lead me to the belief that short stories aren't worth writing?

I think I'm going to have to make a standing appointment with myself. I think I'm going to have to budget time for short stories. If I show up, I suspect the ideas will show up, too. And the stories will get written, and I'll be glad to have written them.

For heaven's sake, I've been writing this column for 14 years now. On more than 150 occasions I've managed to find something to say about writing. It hasn't been a home run every time, as all of you can surely testify, but I'm up there every month anyway, swinging the bat, taking my cuts at the ball. If I didn't have a regular appointment with myself to write a column every month, do you imagine for a moment I would have happened to have 150 ideas about writing worth setting down on paper?

Necessity is the mother of invention, and the wish is father to the thought. If I provide a birdhouse, if I set out wisps of straw and bits of string the bluebird of inspiration will come nest nearby.

I hope I've learned this lesson, and I hope I'll apply it. I don't know whether I'll try to devote a few days every month to short story production or if I'll try to book an annual colony stay for that purpose, but one way or another I want to start budgeting the time and energy for it. Because that seems to be the best way to make it happen.

36

Getting Real

August 1990

WHEN AND WHY TO USE REAL LOCATIONS IN YOUR FICTION.

A while ago a friend of mine named Rita was having dinner at a Chinese restaurant in Greenwich Village. The place was the Hunan Pan, at the corner of Hudson and Perry Streets. As she was tucking into her portion of broccoli with garlic sauce, two of the characters in the book she was reading had dinner at the very same restaurant. She found this coincidence amusing enough to bring it to the attention of the Hunan Pan's proprietor, who became very excited indeed. When Rita admitted that the book's author, Jack Early, was an acquaintance of hers, the restaurateur said that he wanted to buy a copy of the book, and that he wanted Mr. Early to come around and have a meal on the house.

"You know Jack," Rita said. Sure, I said. Fine writer. "And you know the Hunan Pan." Sure, I agreed. Fine restaurant, I eat there all the time. Well, not *all* the time, sometimes I want a plate of pasta or a grilled cheese sandwich or something, but— "And you write books set in the Village," she went on. "And your characters have to eat somewhere, so here's an idea for you. In your next book, have somebody eat at the Hunan Pan. You'll get a free meal out of it." And what, I wondered, would she get. "Well, heck," she said. "You don't want to dine alone, do you?"

Thus far I have somehow resisted the temptation to send any of my characters to the corner of Hudson and Perry for a plate of General Tsao's chicken. But the conversation with Rita caromed off a couple of other things that happened lately, and the sparks that were struck have flared up into something worth considering.

First was a letter from a writer and boxing reporter named Joe Bruno, who had paid a visit to a Tenth Avenue saloon called Jimmy Armstrong's, where a detective character of mine named Matthew Scudder spent much of his time during his drinking days. Joe found the joint awash in classical music and potted plants and (shudder!) yuppies, and complained that it was not at all as he'd visualized it in the novels.

Then, more recently, someone who'd read *Out on the Cutting Edge* wrote to complain that she had been unable to locate either Grogan's Open House or Paris Green, a bar and restaurant respectively in which several of that novel's scenes were set. She had not found them, I advised her, because they did not exist. I had made them up, even as I made up the story.

Real Considerations

How real should the settings of our fiction get? With or without the hope of a free meal, when should we cite a specific restaurant, and refer to it by its real name? What are the advantages of so doing, and what are the drawbacks?

I suppose the first point to address is the legal one, and you might bear in mind that I do so as one who is not versed in the law. It is not necessarily illegal to refer in an uncomplimentary fashion to an actual establishment in a piece of fiction. It may even be arguably within my rights to have a character say something libelous about a particular establishment, the argument being that this is the character's opinion and not my own.

Be that as it may, the idea is not to win lawsuits but to avoid them, so my own rule of thumb is to avoid mentioning a real establishment or institution by name in any derogatory way. This is not to say that every mention of an actual establishment has to be a rave. I can say that

Scudder had breakfast at the Flame and the coffee was weak or the eggs runny. But I wouldn't have him find a cockroach on his plate, or otherwise impugn the establishment's integrity. Whether or not I'd be inviting a lawsuit, I'd be taking a gratuitous swipe at somebody's livelihood, and that's not my job as a fiction writer.

Similarly, I'm more comfortable using invented establishments when people connected therewith are deeply involved in the story I'm telling. In *When the Sacred Ginmill Closes,* for example, several real-life bars and restaurants play a part, including Armstrong's. But the book's principals include the owner of a saloon who hires Scudder to help him regain a set of counterfeit account ledgers and the proprietor of an illegal after-hours joint who commissions Scudder to identify the men who held him up. Both of those establishments were made up out of the whole cloth.

Why use any real names? The best reason—aside from the prospect of a free meal at the Hunan Pan—is that it makes a work of fiction that much more real for some readers. My friend Rita liked happening on a restaurant she knew in the book she read, just as she enjoys reading books set in her own neighborhood. Most of us are like that. For all that we read fiction seeking escape from our own personal reality, we often prefer to escape into a world that mirrors that reality very closely. Westerns sell best in the West.

Another advantage of staying with reality is that it spares you the need to invent, and to keep track of what you've invented. It is one thing to visualize an imaginary setting long enough to write a scene. It is another matter to summon it up days or weeks or months later when your characters pay another visit to the place. Of course you don't have to have precisely the same image in your mind's eye—the reader can't see what you're thinking, only what you've written down. But you don't want to be inconsistent, either specifically or in tone. With a real place, you just describe it as it is, and if memory fails you can go back and look at it.

This is not all that much of a problem in a single book, but let me assure you it can be a pain in the neck when you write an extended series of books over a number of years. I wrote the first book about Scudder, *The Sins of the Fathers*, back in 1973. Since then there has been much water under the bridge or over the dam, as you prefer, and there have been eight more books in the series, with *A Ticket to the Boneyard* due from the publisher around the time this column sees print and another scheduled a year hence.

Over the years and books, certain locations have turned up again and again. One does not want to be inconsistent, to have a restaurant on Barrow Street in one book and move it around the corner to Bedford a few books hence, to describe a bar as having tables to the right of the entrance, then shift the tables to the other side of the room through a lapse of memory. This sort of error, while unfortunate within the confines of a single volume, is somewhat more allowable (and perhaps inescapable) in a series. The only way to avoid it, short of tucking all the data into a computer, is to flip through previous books to see what one has or hasn't mentioned before.

Many series writers display a cavalier attitude, evidently agreeing with Emerson that a foolish inconsistency is the hobgoblin of little minds. Rex Stout didn't always supply a numerical street address for Nero Wolfe's unforgettable brownstone on West 35th Street, but when he did the number changed considerably from book to book. (Literal-minded readers would search in vain for any of the addresses Stout supplies; all of them would be located somewhere in the Hudson River.)

I'd prefer to avoid even this sort of pardonable inconsistency, but it's not easy; one doesn't want to spend all one's time referring to earlier works, and it's not enough to turn up one previous description of a locale. You'd have to check out every mention of the place to be sure you haven't gotten a detail wrong.

But if the place really exists, you don't have this problem. You just describe it as it is. You'll mention one thing one time and another later on, but all your verbal snapshots will be of the same real place, so they won't contradict one another.

It is possible, of course, to manage this without using real locations and names. You do so simply by describing a locale with which you are familiar but calling the place something else, and moving it a few blocks north or south. Because you've given it a fictitious name and address, you can say good or bad things about it, involve the clientele and employees in no end of nefarious schemes, and still know exactly what the place looks like.

Another advantage of so doing—indeed, an advantage of making up your locations as well—is that wholly fictional locations can stay the same. They don't have to change the way their counterparts in reality so often insist on doing.

Back in the early Scudder novels, my hero didn't do all his drinking at Armstrong's. He also dropped in for the occasional quick restorative at Polly's Cage and Joey Farrell's and McGovern's and sometimes had a last drink on the way home at Antares & Spiro's.

Well, I guess it's a good thing Scudder stopped drinking, because he couldn't go back to any of those places. They're all gone. This sort of thing happens everywhere, but in New York it happens at an astonishing pace. Even Armstrong's itself picked up and moved from Ninth to Tenth Avenue a few years ago.

If I had called the joint something else, I wouldn't have had to follow its westward migration. I could keep the place on Ninth, around the corner from Scudder's hotel, and it would exist there forever in that alternate reality that fiction constitutes.

Real Decisions

Some of these problems don't apply unless you're fortunate or unfortunate enough to be involved in a lengthy series. But the choice of reality or artifice confronts every fiction writer all the time, and there are always decisions to be made.

In *Down on the Killing Floor,* the most recently completed Scudder novel, the detective visits a facility for homeless youth in the Times Square area. I of course had Covenant House in mind, but for several reasons decided not to refer to that institution by name. At the time of the writing, some of Covenant House's founder's personal problems were beginning to come to light, and it was impossible to know how that situation would resolve itself. Since my book was in no sense about Covenant House, and since it was to be only the setting for a single scene, I didn't want to load my novel with any controversy that might attach to the institution's name.

However, I'd decided to call it something else even before the place hit the news, because I didn't want to be harnessed to reality. I didn't want to bother discovering the actual practices and rules and policies of the real institution when I could better facilitate the telling of my own story by inventing a parallel institution that would have whatever rules and policies I wanted it to have.

I named the place Testament House, purposely selecting a name that would immediately suggest Covenant House to readers familiar with the actual institution. And, just as purposefully, I changed the locations and architecture of its residential facilities and made its director an Episcopalian. Essentially I created a parallel Covenant House, an alternate Covenant House that would fill the role of that institution without bearing the excess baggage that had no place in my novel.

The Real Reward

Fiction takes place in its own world, and at the same time it reflects the world the writer and his readers inhabit. The extent to which the two worlds correspond is a matter of endless choice on the writer's part. You decide for yourself, sometimes with calculation and sometimes intuitively, how much of the actual landscape you want to transfer to your fiction, and just how you will bring that about. The rewards of getting it right are greater than the occasional free meal.

Still, I've just gone and mentioned Hunan Pan any number of times in the world's leading magazine for writers, and that ought to be worth *something*.

37

Just Spell My Name Right

September 1990

GOOD OR BAD, THE BEST REVIEW IS ANY REVIEW.

A friend of mine had a novel reviewed this past Sunday in *The New York Times Book Review*. The review was prominently featured and took up most of a page.

That's the good news. The bad news? Well, the reviewer hated the book, and said so in a particularly mean-spirited fashion.

It's hard to know how to react to that sort of thing, whether to offer congratulations or sympathy. On the one hand, my friend had just received a lot of ink in a very important medium. On the other hand, the ink had been rather unceremoniously dumped on his head. What's the proper response? Should he rage or rejoice?

My friend was quite philosophical, managing to detach himself from the criticism and regard the review as ultimately beneficial to the book. It was better, he figured, to be reviewed at considerable length, albeit unfavorably, than to receive a scant paragraph of undiluted praise somewhere on a back page. And, he pointed out, there were several passages in the review that would sound laudatory when quoted in advertising or on the paperback edition's cover.

How much do reviews matter? What real difference do they make?

If you ask people in publishing, you get a wide variety of responses, but I don't know that they have much in the way of solid underpinning. The narrator in Donald E. Westlake's *A Likely Story* observes that people in publishing are almost boastful in proclaiming that they don't know how the business works, and many people have told me they don't know how reviews influence sales.

One fellow who seemed to have some real data on the subject was a reviewer for a newspaper in Grand Rapids, Michigan. In the course of an interview several years ago he confided that he'd done his own research to determine what effect his own reviews had on book sales locally. He went to bookstores and inquired.

It turned out that any book he reviewed experienced a slight increase in sales irrespective of whether he liked it or not. And he also learned that, whenever a photograph of the author ran with the review, the review's impact was substantially increased. It didn't seem to matter whether his review was a rave or a pan, or what the author looked like; if a photo ran, the review sold books.

I thought that was interesting, and set about trying to figure out why it should be so. Did a look at the author's face create a bond between writer and reader, so that the reader wound up trooping off to the bookstore to pick up the work of an old friend? Did the photo simply increase the readership of the review by drawing attention to it? Or was there something about the book that subliminally influenced the newspaper editor to run a photo with it but not with some other review?

I wouldn't want to invest too much time in fabricating a theory to explain data that might not amount to anything. Maybe it only works that way in Grand Rapids. Be that as it may, ever since then I've taken care to see that my publisher sends out photos with review copies. What could it hurt?

No News Isn't Good News

Reviewers have more power in certain other areas than they do in the book biz. A Broadway show will often succeed or fail on the strength of the review it gets in the *Times*. The right article in the right medium can have a monumental effect on the career of a visual artist.

Book reviewers are less influential. There have been instances where a review, or a group of reviews, propelled a writer into instant bestseller status but this hasn't happened often. (A favorite example is the case of Ross Macdonald, author of a series of private detective novels featuring Lew Archer. Macdonald had a strong and loyal following, and a fine critical reputation for years, but he had never come anywhere near the bestseller list. Three journalists compared notes, found that he was a favorite author of each of them, and decided on the spot to make a star of him. Three well-placed raves—along with a sort of "Why I Live at the P.O. and read Ross Macdonald" essay by Eudora Welty—somehow did the trick. Thousands of readers read Macdonald for the first time and from then on, everything he wrote was equally successful.)

Booksellers have told me that a good review in an important newspaper or magazine translates instantly into heightened sales for the book in question. A good notice in the *Times Book Review* will increase sales throughout the country; a review in the daily *Times* will move more books in New York but fewer elsewhere. My own book, *Out on the Cutting Edge,* received a good shot in the arm when I was lucky enough to get a favorable review in *The Wall Street Journal;* the manager of a mystery bookstore told me that the book's sales leaped immediately in response, and that sales of all my paperbacks were elevated for several weeks, almost certainly as a result of the *Journal* review.

While a great review can do a lot to make a book, a bad review won't break one. A quick glance at the bestseller list will almost always reveal the names of authors who get rotten reviews all the time, and who hit the list with everything they write. All the negative ink ever spilled won't keep a reader from continuing to read someone he likes. And why should it? If I've had a good time with Paige Turner's last five books, why should somebody else's opinion dissuade me from picking up her new one? The louder the reviewer screams and the more space his review covers, the more he'll succeed in making me aware that Turner's latest epic is waiting for me.

And this is at least as true with a book by a new writer. Don Marquis, the author of *archy and mehitabel,* once likened publishing a volume of poetry to dropping a rose petal into the Grand Canyon and waiting for the echo. Now, 60 or 70 years later, that's as true of fiction as it is of poetry. There are so very many books published every year and so very many other things people have to do beside sit around and read that most books, and certainly most first novels, are universally ignored.

The great likelihood is not that one will be treated shabbily by a reviewer but that one will be overlooked altogether.

This being the case, a bad review is a great deal better than no review at all. A bad review calls to the attention of the reader a book he might otherwise know nothing about. A few days later when he stands in front of a whole wall of books he may recognize yours swimming in a sea of unfamiliar titles. More often than not he will remember only that he read something about it, not what that something was. This brief flicker of recognition may be enough to make him reach out and pluck the book from the shelf.

From there on in, you're on your own. Either the book will engage his interest or he'll put it back on the shelf where he found it. The title, the jacket, the blurb copy, the quotes on the jacket, the opening paragraphs, the page he happens to flip the book open to—these factors will determine whether or not you can mark the book *sold.*

But none of those elements has a chance to work their subtle magic if you can't get him to pick up the damn thing in the first place, and a bad review, even a lowdown, in-your-face *rotten* review, might do that much. And that's true even if the reader *remembers* that the review was negative, because he'll pick the book up to see what the fuss was about and feel free to make up his own mind. It's not like a play, after all, where you have to part with 50 bucks to find out if something's as lousy as Frank Rich says it is. You can preview a book free of charge by flipping its pages, and buy it or not on the basis of your own impression.

At least one author has attempted to capitalize on his bad reviews. Norman Mailer's first novel, *The Naked and the Dead,* was both a critical and a popular success. His second, *Barbary Shore,* had rather less impact with both groups. His third, *The Deer Park,* was positively savaged by the critics. Mailer responded by taking the worst phrase he could find from each of a slew of reviews and composing an ad that he published in *The Village Voice.* It unquestionably brought him more attention than a comparable ad filled with praise, and I can only assume it sold books.

It Happened to Me

In my own case, I've been treated very decently by reviewers over the years. I don't have much in the way of horror stories. And, when I have borne the brunt of a bad review, I can't really say that it's bothered me all that much.

The manner of my entry into the business may have something to do with this. I wrote paperback originals for quite a few years before my first hardcover novel was published, and my paperbacks almost never got reviewed. When they did get a mention in a paperback column of some minor newspaper or other, I knew it was not going to have any discernible effect on sales.

Consequently, the handful of reviews I got over the years pleased me when they were favorable and didn't bother me much when they weren't, because I found them easy to shrug off.

By the time I was being published in hardcover, I had developed a reasonably thick skin where reviews were concerned. In most instances I've been able to get my own ego out of the way and be pleased or displeased about the review depending upon the effect it's likely to have on sales.

I had this equanimity tested some when *Random Walk* was published in the fall of '88. The advance notices, the trade reviews in *Publishers Weekly* and *Kirkus,* were both extremely bad. This was not a great surprise in *Kirkus,* familiarly known as the Mikey of reviewing media ("Give it to Mikey. He hates everything!"), but *PW* reviews books favorably more often than not, and had always given me good notices in the past. They hated *Random Walk,* and said so.

Then the book came out, receiving a tepid notice in the *Times Book Review,* a thoughtful and enthusiastic review in Fort Lauderdale, and a blanket of silence everywhere else. For years everything I've written has been reviewed for good or ill all over the country, and *Random Walk* wasn't getting noticed anywhere.

I'm not sure what happened. It may have been that a great many reviewers received the book, read it (or as much of it as they could stomach) and decided they'd be doing me a kindness by saying no more about it. It may be that they never got the book in the first place. My publisher swore that 200 review copies went out, and maybe they did, but maybe they didn't.

Oh well. I'm not sure reviews would have made much difference. They'd have merely sent readers rushing to buy a book that didn't get on many store shelves to begin with, and that had a lousy cover and stupid blurbs, and that—let's face it—they might not have liked no matter what, because it was a problematic book that never did fit into any convenient publishing categories and that not every reader is going to be nuts about.

You have to be able to shrug these things off. If you let yourself be reached on a personal level by what reviewers say about your books, you are giving faceless strangers power over your life, to which they have no earthly right.

A couple of weeks ago another writer I know was agonizing over a bad review. It appeared in *Entertainment Weekly,* and what possible adverse effect she thought a review in that publication could have on sales is beyond me. While I'm willing to believe that some of that magazine's readers also read books, I doubt that they make their book selections on the basis of the reviews in *EW*.

No, it seemed fairly clear that my friend was responding emotionally rather than rationally. She was letting a reviewer's negative reaction activate all the secret doubts and anxieties she had about her books' real worth, and about her own merit as a writer.

You can let bad reviews throw you, but why? A reviewer is just a person, and more often than not just another writer like yourself. His reaction to your book is the product of many factors, including his own personal taste and the mood he was in when your book came into his hands. It's fair to say that a bad review is a rejection slip for a book that's been published. If you're being published, you've probably been at this long enough not to let rejections spoil your day. Now you can learn to shrug off reviews in the same fashion.

Every writer has horror stories. Reviews where there was clear evidence indicating that the reviewer never read the book. Reviewers who seemed to like the book, but who never managed to say so in a quotable way. Reviewers who missed the point in any of a dozen ways.

Never mind. Experience soon shows that there are two kinds of reviewers in the world. There are the intelligent, perceptive, influential ones, the ones whose opinions count for something. And there are the no-account useless dimwitted hacks who don't know anything and to whom no one ever pays any attention.

It's easy to tell them apart, too. The first class consists of all reviewers who praise you. The second class consists of everybody else. So the hell with it. Enjoy the good reviews, leave the bad reviews unread, and go back to work on the next book.

That's what you should be doing anyway.

38

Are You Sure Chandler Started This Way?

1991 Yearbook

ACTUALLY, HE DIDN'T. BUT PROMOTIONAL APPEARANCES OFFER YOU A CHANCE TO BUILD PROFITABLE RELATIONSHIPS WITH THE PEOPLE WHO SELL AND READ YOUR BOOKS.

There we were, milling around on the second floor of the Broward County Library in Fort Lauderdale. We were, by all reckoning, a distinguished lot. There was M. Scott Berg, the distinguished biographer of Maxwell Perkins and Samuel Goldwyn, and Edna Buchanan, distinguished crime reporter and author of *The Corpse Had a Familiar Face*. There was the distinguished novelist Anne Bernays and her husband, distinguished biographer Justin Kaplan. There was John Katzenbach, the distinguished novelist, and the distinguished playwright-turned-novelist Henry Denker. There was Kitty Carlyle Hart, the distinguished actress-turned-autobiographer. And there was me—feeling, I have to tell you, rather more distinguished than usual.

Earlier in the day we had each had a turn in front of an audience, rattling off some presumably amusing or instructive remarks somehow related to our writing. (I talked about driving around the country in pursuit of towns named Buffalo, and can only hope it was amusing; it could hardly have been instructive, or related to my writing.) After that we had been briefly available to sign copies of our books.

Now, this evening, we were to be presented to a select group of Lauderdalers who had paid a distinguishing price (all in aid of the library's fund-raising effort) for the pleasure of our company, first at a cocktail party on the first floor of the library, then at eight small dinner parties scattered around town. Each of us would lend our presence to one of the dinner parties, playing Literary Lion and occasionally letting out a roar.

Our company awaited us now a floor below. And now a gentleman was calling us one by one and recounting our accomplishments at some length, whereupon we were to descend the great escalator in solitary splendor while Broward County's *haut monde* greeted us with polite applause.

While we waited for our names to be called, I turned to John Katzenbach. "I don't know about this," I said. "Are you sure Raymond Chandler started this way?"

"No question about it," he assured me. "But watch your step. Chandler fell down the escalator."

Lest I (or Mr. Katzenbach) be accused of impugning his memory, please understand that Raymond Chandler never plunged down that escalator. He could hardly have done so, having died years before the library was built. More to the point, he did not start that way, or continue that way; Chandler was more than a little reluctant to give autographs, and would have shunned public signings. Consequently, autographed copies of his works are in very short supply, and command a high price.

Few of us these days seem to share Chandler's reticence. At a bookstore in Los Angeles a while back a young woman handed me a copy of *Out on the Cutting Edge*; while I inscribed it, she said something about the likelihood of its being valuable someday.

"Don't count on it," I told her. "The unsigned copies are the rare ones."

Sometimes it seems that way. Twenty years ago in-store autographing sessions were relatively uncommon occasions. An author might make an appearance at a bookstore in his home town, with his friends and relatives turning out to buy his book in a show of support. And a few stores would have celebrity signings with some frequency. But relatively few authors played the circuit, and there wasn't much of a circuit for them to play.

Now, indeed, the unsigned copies are increasingly the rare ones. Some stores have signings almost weekly, often featuring several writers at a time. Sometimes the writer is expected to read something or give a little talk, while other stores require only that he be prepared to be charming and write his name a lot.

In addition to formal autographing sessions, writers find no end of other opportunities to scribble their names on fly leaves and title pages. On a recent visit to a mid-Manhattan chain bookstore, I noticed an even dozen new titles equipped with bands announcing that the book had been "personally inscribed for you by the author." Each of these authors had recently made a hit-and-run assault on the store, autographing the store's stock of his books in a furious assault, then rushing on to the next store for more of the same.

You get the point. A good many writers are scurrying around signing a good many books. How do you manage to do so yourself? And does it do any good?

Them that's got shall get, Billie Holliday told us a long time ago. Well, it's still the truth. The more successful you already are, the easier it is to set up a heavy schedule of signings.

This stands to reason. If you were a store owner, who do you figure you'd rather have show up at your shop, Stephen King or some earnest chap whose first novel has just been launched with an initial run of 5,000 copies? If you were a publisher, and if that first novelist and, say,

Mary Higgins Clark were both on your fall list whose touring expenses would you be prepared to underwrite? For that matter, if you were a newspaper reporter and both writers turned up in your town, which one would you rush to interview? If you were the *Today* show, which would you book?

Precisely.

Accordingly, if you're not Mr. King or Ms. Clark, you will probably have to hustle a bit in order to set up signing sessions for yourself. Your publisher's publicity department will very likely be concentrating on booking their top authors and will not have time for you. (This is not the hardship it might appear; most publishers' publicity departments are of such legendary incompetence that getting along without them is like getting along without psoriasis.)

Early in your career, you will receive a warmer welcome in stores and in cities where they know you. If you live in a town now, or if you used to live there, or if you have kin there, or if your book is set there, you have some local connection. A store has reason to expect some people to turn out to meet you. The store will have an easier time obtaining publicity for you, because local reporters will have a reason to interview you.

In my own case, the type of bookstore I approach is of more importance than its location. What recognition I have achieved has been primarily in the field of mystery and suspense, so when I booked myself on a 25-store tour last fall, I had the wit to call booksellers who specialize in mysteries, along with a couple of general bookstores that have a reputation for being mystery-friendly.

Note that I called the stores. You can't expect to handle this sort of thing through the mails. When you call, explain who you are and what you've written (unless they happen to recognize your name) and be prepared to offer a choice of dates. Find out, too, if they would prefer you to give a talk or reading, or if they'd rather you just come prepared to write your name. Some stores will be considerably more eager to book you if you'll read or speak, because you're more of a draw that way; a reading or a lecture is viewed as a cultural event, while a signing is just a crass attempt to peddle books.

As you and the store manager work out the details, you may be offered the opportunity to share the spotlight with another writer. Your ego will interpret this as a way to cheat you out of a full share of riches and fame. Tell your ego thanks for sharing, and go for it. When two or more authors make a joint appearance, more customers are drawn to the store and both writers sell more books than either would sell separately.

Remember, don't listen to your ego. If you are asked to share a signing with a more successful writer, you'll fear that your little book will get lost in the shuffle. If you're the prominent one, sharing a table with a first novelist, you'll feel you're not getting the special attention you deserve. Nonsense, all of it. Two pens are better than one, and you'll both profit from the joint appearance.

And you may get a friendship out of the deal, or at least an acquaintance. And, if it turns out to be one of those signings where nobody shows up, you'll have somebody to talk to.

How much good does it do?

Well, that's a hard one to answer. If you are hoping to see your time and expenses offset by the royalties for the books you sell, forget it. It's not going to happen.

Suppose your book is a hardcover edition with a list price of $20. Suppose you sell 50 copies, which would make the day a great triumph. Your royalty at 10% of list would make your earnings for the day around $100. If you traveled any distance to get there, if you put up overnight in a hotel, and if you figure your time as having any value, you have obviously run at a loss.

Well, suppose you're really hot stuff, a writer for whom they'll line up around the block. Suppose you unload not 50 but 500 copies of the work. In that case your earnings would be more like $1,000—but if you can draw that many folks to a signing, you have reached a level of success at which you can earn a whole lot more than $1,000 by staying home and writing something.

And let's face facts. If this is a first book—or a second or third—and if you're not packing the house with friends and relations, you're not going to sell 50 books, let alone 500. You may have to work to sell five. Even if you didn't have to travel, even if you came by subway, you can hardly manage to get comfortably drunk on the proceeds.

So why bother?

Well, some people will argue that you shouldn't bother, that it really is a waste of time and energy. Others will hold that there are benefits to autographing sessions that don't show up in immediate sales.

The most valuable thing a signing does, in my opinion, is build relationships. The most important relationship you build is with the store and the people who work in it. The same signing that means $100 in royalties to you puts $1,000 into the store's cash register, and they haven't had to travel to do it. Even more important a signing brings new customers into a store, customers who have never patronized that store before but have been drawn there to meet you. Some of them will return to buy other books by other writers.

The store is grateful to you for this. More to the point, the store personnel are aware of you not just as a name on a title page but as a human being. They will be more likely to keep your backlist paperbacks in stock, more likely to display your new books prominently, more likely to recommend your titles to customers who ask them what's good. (This all presupposes that you have been a personable and amiable sort during your sojourn there. If you're an obnoxious clod, personal appearances will do you more harm than good.)

Similarly, every time you sign a book for a reader you are creating a relationship with that person. Say you sign five books during a two-hour stint at a store, exchanging a few words with each of those five customers. Each will leave the store with an almost proprietary interest in you. For the next several weeks he will start a good many of his conversations with the words, "Guess who I met the other day." There's no guarantee that he'll buy your next book, but he's likely to—and likely to show up again at future signings.

In any number of ways, your efforts and the store's will combine to get your name around and make the readers that much more aware of you. Notices in the press, displays in the store, all get you attention you wouldn't get otherwise. My own seat-of-the-pants research convinces me that this sort of promotional effort has more of an effect on future sales than on those of the book you're promoting, but I think that's true of most book advertising and promotion.

There are any number of ways you can keep the costs down and make optimal use of your time and energy. While it may not be worthwhile to travel in order to do a signing, it can pay you to schedule signings to coincide with travel you're going to be doing anyway. And, for stores where a signing is not in the cards for one reason or another, it's always appropriate to drop in unannounced, make yourself known to the store manager, and sign whatever copies of your book he happens to have in stock. (If you can call a few days in advance, he'll be more likely to have books in stock.)

Chandler didn't start this way, and he seems to have done fine without it. Thomas Pynchon doesn't sign books or give interviews or even allow the reading public to know what he looks like or where he lives, yet his books seem to find their way into readers' hands.

Do you have to go through all this yourself? No, you don't, and if you hate it you're better off staying home writing the next book. Even if you like it, you have to learn to live with the afternoons when nobody shows up, the bookstore owners who never heard of you and haven't ordered your book, the readers who ask you things like "Have you written anything I've read?" But if you enjoy it, and if you're reasonably good at it, you can probably do yourself some good.

One thing, though. Someone may have told you, or you may have figured out for yourself, that any book you autograph is a book the store cannot return to the publisher, that a book signed is a book sold.

Don't count on it.

My Newsletter: I get out an email newsletter at unpredictable intervals, but rarely more often than every other week. I'll be happy to add you to the distribution list. A blank email to lawbloc@gmail.com with "newsletter" in the subject line will get you on the list, and a click of the "Unsubscribe" link will get you off it, should you ultimately decide you're happier without it.

Lawrence Block has been writing award-winning mystery and suspense fiction for half a century. His newest book is *In Sunlight or in Shadow*, an anthology with 17 new stories, each inspired by an Edward Hopper painting; contributors include Stephen King, Joyce Carol Oates, Lee Child, Megan Abbott, Michael Connelly, Jeffery Deaver, and Joe Lansdale. His most recent novel, pitched by his Hollywood agent as "James M. Cain on Viagra," is *The Girl with the Deep Blue Eyes*. Other recent works of fiction include *The Burglar Who Counted The Spoons*, featuring Bernie Rhodenbarr; *Keller's Fedora*, featuring philatelist and assassin Keller; and *A Drop Of The Hard Stuff*, featuring Matthew Scudder, brilliantly embodied by Liam Neeson in the new film, *A Walk Among The Tombstones*. Several of his other books have also been filmed, although not terribly well. He's well known for his books for writers, including the classic *Telling Lies For Fun & Profit* and *Write For Your Life*, and has recently published a collection of his writings about the mystery genre and its practitioners, *The Crime Of Our Lives*. In addition to prose works, he has written episodic television (*Tilt!*) and the Wong Kar-wai film, *My Blueberry Nights*. He is a modest and humble fellow, although you would never guess as much from this biographical note.

Email: lawbloc@gmail.com
Twitter: @LawrenceBlock
Facebook: lawrence.block
Website: lawrenceblock.com

Manufactured by Amazon.ca
Bolton, ON

14537873R00162